U. S. REFORM SCHOOL

BROOKLAND

LANGDON

MONTELLO

BENNING

MT. OLIVET CEMETERY

COLUMBIA INST. FOR DEAF AND DUMB

TRINIDAD

ANACOSTIA RIVER

U.S. JAIL

ALMS HOUSE

WORKHOUSES

CONGRESSIONAL CEMETERY

LINCOLN SQUARE

MASS

PENN

TWINING CITY

ANACOSTIA

THE CAPITOL

CANAL ST.

GARFIELD

U. S. NAVY YARD

ANACOSTIA RIVER

POPLAR POINT

MONUMENT GROUNDS

BARRY FARM

WASHINGTON CHANNEL

WAR COLLEGE & ENGINEER SCHOOL

BUZZARD POINT

U. S. INSANE ASYLUM

TIDAL RESERVOIR

PARK

POTOMAC RIVER

GIESBORO POINT

THE FIRTH STERLING STEEL CO.

CAPITAL HOUSES

Historic Residences *of* Washington, D.C.

AND ITS ENVIRONS

1735–1965

CAPITAL HOUSES

Historic Residences *of* Washington, D.C.

AND ITS ENVIRONS

———————————————

1735–1965

JAMES M. GOODE

Photography by
BRUCE M. WHITE

ACANTHUS PRESS
NEW YORK : 2015

ACANTHUS PRESS LLC

48 West 22nd Street

New York, New York 10010

www.acanthuspress.com

212-414-0108

Library of Congress Cataloging-in-Publication Data

Goode, James M., author.

Capital houses : historic residences of Washington, D.C. and its environs, 1740–1960

James M. Goode ; Bruce M. White, Photographer.

pages cm

Includes index.

ISBN 978-0-926494-91-6 (hardcover : alk. paper)

1. Architecture, Domestic—Washington (D.C.)   2. Architecture, Domestic—Washington Region.

3. Historic buildings—Washington (D.C.)   4. Historic buildings—Washington Region.

5. Washington (D.C.)—Buildings, structures, etc.   6. Washington Region—History.

I. White, Bruce, 1962— illustrator.   II. Title.

NA7238.W3G66 2015

728.09753—dc23

2015004243

FRONTISPIECE: TUDOR PLACE, INTERIOR VIEW OF THE CIRCULAR TEMPLE PORCH

Printed in China

CONTENTS

GREEK REVIVAL HOUSES
1818–1849

VICTORIAN HOUSES
1850–1892

ARTS AND CRAFTS HOUSES
1897–1911

BEAUX-ARTS HOUSES
1901–1931

GEORGIAN REVIVAL HOUSES
1908–1928

TUDOR REVIVAL HOUSES
1910–1927

ART DECO HOUSES
1935–1949

MODERN HOUSES
1952–1966

PREFACE

CAPITAL HOUSES IS A WIDE-RANGING SURVEY of historic houses in the Washington, D.C., metropolitan area. This study traces their stylistic development, from the first Georgian example—Mount Vernon (1735) in Fairfax County, Virginia—to one of the city's best midcentury Moderns, the Kreeger House (1966) on Foxhall Road in Washington. Each chapter represents an architectural period: Georgian, Federal, Greek Revival, Victorian, Arts and Crafts, Beaux Arts, Georgian Revival, Tudor Revival, Art Deco, and Modern. Of the 56 houses in this volume, 44 are in the District of Columbia and a dozen in the Maryland and Virginia suburbs. Publishing constraints did not allow inclusion here of the many other important historic houses in Washington, D.C., and the greater outlying area.

This project was well under way when, in 2010, I was fortunate enough to form a partnership with the distinguished photographer, Bruce M. White, whose pictures have been published by the Metropolitan Museum of Art, Princeton University, the White House Historical Association, and many others. Over a four-year period Bruce and I walked through the houses you see here to decide which rooms or details to photograph. The result is an outstanding collection of original color photographs, modestly enhanced by period images and custom-drawn plans that help the reader further appreciate these fine architectural achievements.

I used two criteria in selecting the houses: First, each had to be a good representative of its style. Second, the house needed an interesting cultural, historical, or political association. Half the houses are concentrated in three adjacent historic districts—Georgetown, Dupont Circle, and Sheridan-Kalorama. For this reason, I devoted much of the Introduction to describing the cultural history of these neighborhoods and tracing through them the preservation movement in Washington. Maps included here further clarify the whereabouts of the landmarks in these three districts. It is my hope that this work paints a picture of private life, taste, and change in Washington from the first chimneys that rose in colonial forests to the urban scene today.

CARLYLE HOUSE DURING DEMOLITION OF MANSION HOUSE HOTEL, EARLY 1970S.

INTRODUCTION

PRESERVATIONISTS HAVE STRUGGLED TO save Washington's hundreds of outstanding historic houses since the 1930s, beginning with the preservation of Georgetown. The city lost a substantial number of its finest residences twice in its history, due largely to the expansion of downtown business districts into residential areas. The first time was in the second half of the 19th century, between 1865 and 1895, when the business center concentrated on the 7th Street N.W., corridor, between Pennsylvania Avenue and K Street, shifted westward along F Street N.W., from 7th to 15th Streets. During this period the once-fashionable antebellum Greek Revival houses on F Street were replaced with stores, office buildings, apartment houses, and hotels.

Another shift began in the 1920s, when the financial district at 15th Street and New York Avenue next to the Treasury Building started to move north on 15th Street to K Street. As a result many of the large Victorian houses around McPherson Square, were demolished for office buildings including the Warder House by Henry H. Richardson at 15th and K Streets in 1922–23. This second major move of the business center to K Street was accelerated after World War II. It was spearheaded mainly by developer Morris Cafritz who built an empire of modern glass office buildings in the new downtown in the two decades between 1945 and 1965. By the late 1940s preservationists in Washington were growing alarmed by the rapid destruction of the city's architectural heritage. They began to organize and lobby.

This northern and northwestern migration of commercial development also affected Dupont Circle. Many houses on Massachusetts Avenue and the south side of the circle were torn down between the 1950s and the early 1970s. Mundane new office buildings and apartment houses replaced many outstanding Victorian landmarks, such as the Patten House, next to the Anderson House on the southeast corner of Massachusetts and Florida Avenues N.W. One of the greatest losses was on Dupont Circle itself: In 1971 a mediocre and out-of-scale office building replaced the Hitt house, a Beaux-Arts masterpiece on New Hampshire Avenue, designed by John Russell Pope in 1910.

Government Expansion into Lafayette Park

The recommendations of the U.S. Senate's McMillan Plan of 1901–02 had a profound impact on the city. The plan proposed returning the city to Peter Charles L'Enfant's original design by clearing the Mall of buildings and trees and returning it to a 2-mile-long open green space. The plan also advocated the execution of all future public buildings in the classical style to complement the Capitol and White House. The McMillan Plan unfortunately recommended razing all the historic houses around Lafayette Park for future government office buildings, for which architect Cass Gilbert had drawn the neoclassical plans in 1917. Consequently a number of historic houses were razed in 1919 to build the massive U.S. Treasury Annex Building at Pennsylvania Avenue and Madison Place, while the Veterans Administration Building was constructed on the opposite corner of Vermont Avenue and H Street. The razing of another four historic houses on the north side of Lafayette Park followed, in the 1920s—the Corcoran, Slidell, Adams, and Hay houses. Cass Gilbert's U.S. Chamber of Commerce Building, 1924, and Mihran Mesrobian's Hay-Adams Hotel, 1927, replaced them. President Franklin D. Roosevelt, at the urging of the Blair family, preserved their historic residence in 1942; the government purchased Blair House for the president's guesthouse (see Chapter 2). The rest of the remaining historic houses were preserved in 1961 through the efforts of Jacqueline Kennedy. John Carl Warnecke designed the new government office buildings, setting them back behind the surviving historic row houses. President Lyndon Johnson saved the historic 1859 Corcoran Gallery building next to Blair House from the wrecker's ball in 1968 by transferring it to the Smithsonian American Art Museum. It is now the Renwick Gallery, named for its New York architect, James Renwick Jr., and houses a collection of American craft and decorative arts.

The Threat of Highways

Fortunately, a number of other proposed plans for the federal government's physical expansion before World War II, as well as those for construction of superhighways within the city after the war, never materialized. The National Capital Planning Commission (NCPC) was established in 1926. At the same time, Congress established a massive triangular set of seven large blocks for the consolidation of major federal office buildings in the heart of Washington. This Federal Triangle, bounded by Pennsylvania Avenue, the Mall, and 15th Street, was begun in 1928 and finished a decade later. The NCPC also established a plan in 1928 for future expansion of federal government buildings along East Capitol Street between the Capitol and the Anacostia River. This two-block-wide enclave of office buildings would have extended between Constitution and Independence Avenues. In the proposed plan, some 5,000 Victorian houses would have been razed. Luckily, only two of these government buildings came to be, both at the east end of East Capitol Street—the D.C. Armory

and a sports arena. The plan was finally scrapped in 1958 during the Cold War. Because of the threat of an atomic attack, it was decided to build future government office buildings in the suburbs, away from the center of the city.

After World War II the automobile became king and threatened to reconfigure the city: In 1955 the NCPC recommended construction of two beltways to relieve traffic congestion. The outer circular highway around the city, located about 10 miles from the White House, was begun in the late 1950s and opened in 1964. The second beltway was an inner-city system of connecting freeways, located only 1 or 2 miles from the White House. The drive for this proposed system was spearheaded by Congressman William H. Natcher (D-Ky.), chairman of the powerful House Appropriations Committee, who tried to force it on the District of Columbia to ease suburban workers' commute. Despite a majority of the Washington population's opposing the freeways, Thomas F. Airis, head of the D.C. Department of Highways and Traffic from 1964 to 1974, strongly supported them. Airis liked the plan because 90 percent of the funding for it came from Congress. After the Whitehurst Freeway opened in 1951, Natcher pushed through the Southeast and Southwest Freeways in the mid-1960s; the massive urban renewal to which their construction was linked resulted in the destruction of almost the entire southwest quadrant of Washington, more than 18,000 Victorian row houses, according to newspaper accounts. These two unattractive elevated freeways slashed through the city's southwest and southeast and connected to Virginia Avenue on the east side of Capitol Hill, wiping out more houses there. A part of this same freeway was proposed to plow through the upper portion of the historic districts of Dupont Circle and 16th Street, entailing the destruction of more than 4,000 historic houses. Outraged citizens arrested the potential nightmare; their groups—including the Committee of 100 on the Federal City and the D.C. Federation of Civic Associations—filed lawsuits in opposition. Ranging over a five-year period, the suits were conducted by attorney Roberts

HAY-ADAMS HOUSES, 1884, DESIGNED BY HENRY H. RICHARDSON, WERE RAZED IN 1927.

Owen, working pro bono, under the auspices of Covington & Burling. He ultimately won in the U.S. Court of Appeals. Assistance also came from Peter S. Craig, a Cleveland Park advocate, who had worked for the same firm. Their long legal battle in the 1960s and early-1970s saved Washington from a fate similar to that of Boston. Congressman Natcher retaliated by withholding for three years the federal funds to build the Washington Metro, the subway system providing the area's public transportation. Some stretches of Natcher's unfinished freeway system survive, including the ramp near the intersection of Rock Creek Parkway and Virginia Avenue N.W., and the stretch running north–south at the intersection of New York Avenue N.W. near 3rd Street.

Georgetown's Development

At the same time that the government was trying to tear the city apart with express highways, Congress in 1950 established Georgetown as the city's first historic district. The oldest neighborhood in the nation's capital, Georgetown was originally an independent town in Maryland that predates Washington by 50 years.

The boundaries of the Georgetown neighborhood are clearly defined by Rock Creek on the east, the Potomac River on the south, Georgetown University on the west, and Dumbarton Oaks Park on the north. The town got its start in 1745 when the Colonial Maryland Assembly passed a law requiring the

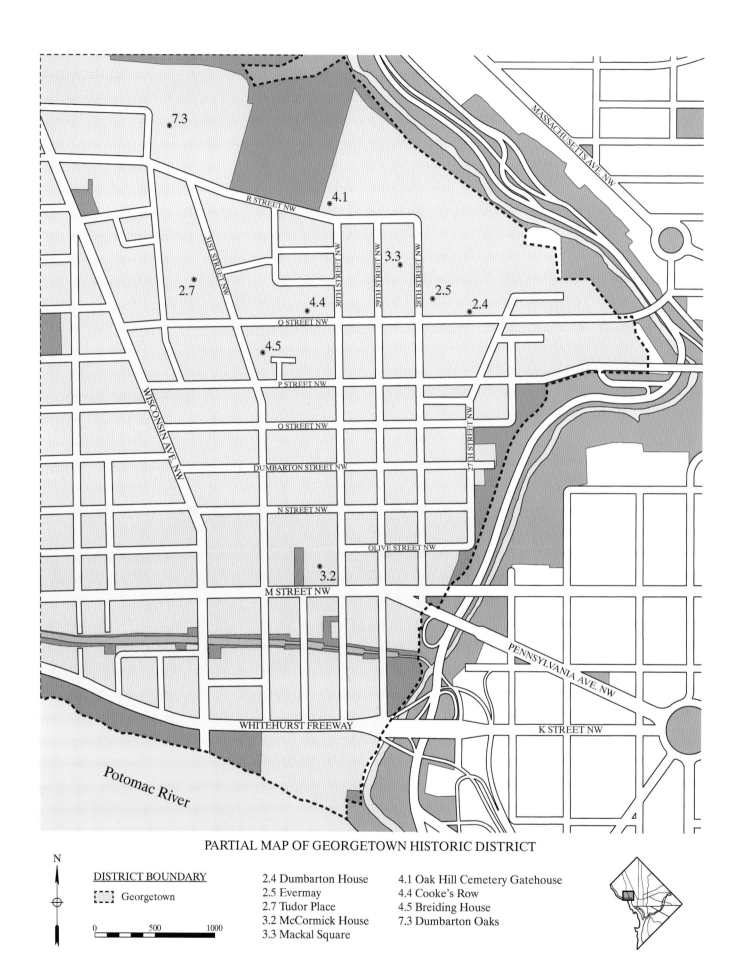

PARTIAL MAP OF GEORGETOWN HISTORIC DISTRICT

N

2.4 Dumbarton House
2.5 Evermay
2.7 Tudor Place
3.2 McCormick House
3.3 Mackal Square

4.1 Oak Hill Cemetery Gatehouse
4.4 Cooke's Row
4.5 Breiding House
7.3 Dumbarton Oaks

THE KEY HOUSE, LOCATED AT 3518 M STREET, N.W. IN GEORGETOWN,
WAS BUILT ABOUT 1802 AND RAZED IN 1948 FOR THE WHITEHURST FREEWAY.

establishment of official inspection stations for shipping tobacco from Maryland to Britain. A warehouse owned by merchant George Gordon, who bought and shipped Maryland tobacco to Glasgow, Scotland, was already in operation on the Potomac River near the present location of Wisconsin Avenue and K Street, N.W. His warehouse was appointed the official inspection station on the upper Potomac River. By 1751 a number of other merchants had built their warehouses next to Gordon's. That year the Maryland legislature approved their petition to lay out a town at this location. It was named not for King George II, but for the two principal landowners in the area— George Beale and George Gordon. The new town was small, covering 60 acres, extending from the Potomac River north only to present-day N Street.

Another Glasgow shipper, Robert Peter, became a prominent early Georgian merchant and the first mayor of Georgetown when it was incorporated in 1789 by the Maryland legislature. His son, Thomas, married Martha Parke Custis, the granddaughter of Martha Dandridge Custis Washington, and the step-granddaughter of George Washington; the Peters lived in style in the early-19th century on Georgetown Heights, on their newly built estate, Tudor Place (see Chapter 2). Another luminary of the era was Benjamin Stoddert, a tobacco merchant who became President John Adams' first secretary of the navy; his noteworthy residence, Halcyon House, at 3400 Prospect Street, has recently been restored.

Much of Georgetown's 19th-century prosperity came from the Chesapeake & Ohio Canal, which was established in 1826 at the foot of Georgetown and coursed 184 miles west to Cumberland, Maryland. Sailing ships at the Georgetown harbor carried chiefly coal. Horse-drawn barges also brought wheat to Georgetown mills for processing into flour.

Part of Georgetown's identity was lost in 1871 when Congress dissolved the separate, locally elected governments of Georgetown and Washington City, replacing them with a combined territorial form of government in which the governor was appointed by the president and the legislature had an appointed upper house and an elected lower house. Congress in turn abolished that system in 1874 after the second governor, Alexander R. Shepherd, instituted a massive program to modernize the city's infrastructure that engendered a $20 million city debt. The new government consisted of three commissioners appointed by the president, one of whom had to be a member of the U.S. Army Corps of Engineers. Georgetown further lost part of its identity in the 1890s, when most of its colorful Colonial street names were changed to conform to those in use in Washington, namely numbered and lettered streets.

The economic life of Georgetown was severely damaged by the massive flood of 1889, the same storm that killed 2,000 residents of Johnstown, Pennsylvania, when that city's dam burst. The flood broke through the walls of the Chesapeake & Ohio Canal and put several hundred canal boatmen and their families out of work. Many of the flour mills on the Georgetown waterfront were also ruined. The canal went bankrupt and ownership passed to its rival, the Baltimore & Ohio Railroad. The poverty that ensued in the town and the resulting slow growth helped preserve its historic houses. It was not until the 1920s that a number of wealthy individuals discovered the charm of the Georgetown neighborhood and began to restore the large estates on Georgetown Heights. Two prominent examples include the remodeling and enlargement of Dumbarton Oaks by Robert and Mildred Bliss and the restoration of Evermay by Ferdinand Lammot Belin—both of which are surveyed in the following pages.

Although Georgetown experienced a 30-year period of economic decline between 1890 and 1920, many of the old families remained, entertaining in gracious style, giving dinner parties in houses full of Colonial furniture, attending dances at the Georgetown Assembly and performances at the Georgetown opera house. The presence of Georgetown College, the first Catholic institution of higher learning in the United States, established in 1789, also culturally enriched the neighborhood.

Beginning in the late-1930s, the Progressive Citizens Association spearheaded the movement to make Georgetown a historic district. They were influenced by the 1931 creation of a historic district with a board of architectural review in Charleston, South Carolina—the first of its kind in the country. An influx of new residents to Georgetown in the 1930s swelled the ranks of the Progressive Citizens Association. They were leading figures in President Franklin D. Roosevelt's many New Deal agencies and carried influence with members of Congress. The neighborhood's picturesque tree-lined streets and old brick houses with intimate courtyards and patios charmed the new residents, and they were much better represented in the Social Register as well: 688 in 1933 as opposed to 117 in 1919.

A further effort to preserve Georgetown as a historic district came in 1948, when a group of local citizens led by Eva Hinton and Harriet Hubbard were successful in getting the residential area above M Street rezoned to restrict building heights. Bolstering Congress's determination to establish the Georgetown historic district was the fate of the Francis Scott Key house. When construction of the Whitehurst Freeway began in 1947, the plan included a connecting ramp from the Key Bridge to the highway heading to downtown Washington that necessitated relocating the Key house. It was dismantled and stored near the Key Bridge, to be reassembled at a nearby site when funds became available. The house's components—brick, woodwork, mantels—were stored in the open, and thieves helped themselves to the materials. The house disappeared completely by

1949. It was clear that the Key house would not have been lost had a Georgetown historic district existed with a board of architectural review. Accordingly, Congress passed the Old Georgetown Act in 1950, requiring property owners in Georgetown to seek approval from the U.S. Commission of Fine Arts for any exterior additions or alterations to their houses or commercial buildings.

Beginning in the early-1980s the blighted Georgetown waterfront began to experience a revival. Its abandoned mills, warehouses, and factories were replaced with upscale office buildings, hotels, and apartment houses. This culminated in 2011 in the National Park Service's converting extensive surface parking lots that covered much of the Georgetown shore along the Potomac River into Georgetown Waterfront Park. The project had been planned a number of years before by the NCPC. The National Park Service had also restored the C & O Canal after a 1954 attempt by the Interior Department to pave over the entire 184-mile canal for an express highway. Concerned citizens, led by Supreme Court Justice William O. Douglas, blocked the scheme.

The Establishment of Historic Districts

In 1964 the Commission of Fine Arts and the National Capital Planning Commission established the Joint Committee on Landmarks to identify and list important historic buildings worthy of preservation. Two years later Congress passed the National Historic Preservation Act (1966) and created the National Register of Historic Places to list such buildings nationwide. Many of Washington's houses soon appeared in the National Register of Historic Places. The threat of the federal government's demolishing the historic Old Post Office Pavilion on the Federal Triangle provoked establishment in 1971 of Don't Tear It Down, an activist lobbying group that successfully petitioned Congress to preserve the landmark. More change for the better came soon after Congress granted the city

of Washington limited home rule in 1974. Don't Tear It Down, in partnership with the D.C. Preservation Office, was able to persuade the city council to establish a rule in 1975 to delay the proposed demolition of a threatened historic building to provide time to negotiate saving it. Although a weak law, it was a step in the right direction. Because of the rapid destruction of historic houses by developers for office buildings in various neighborhoods—especially in Dupont Circle, Massachusetts Avenue, and the lower section of 16th Street, N.W.—the city council established, in 1978, its own preservation law, the Historic Landmark and Historic District Protection Act. Don't Tear It Down, renamed the D.C. Preservation League in 1984, was a major influence in the law's creation. It established the current Historic Preservation Review Board, which reviews and approves demolition, new construction, and exterior additions and alterations to historic landmarks and to buildings in historic districts. Several historic districts were created in 1979, and others soon followed. The D.C. Historic Preservation Office also has the authority to nominate local landmarks to the National Register of Historic Places.

Dupont Circle Historic District

One of the richest neighborhoods today for historic houses is Dupont Circle. Six examples in this volume are included in the Dupont Circle Historic District and the bordering districts of 16th Street and Massachusetts Avenue. This area was rural, with open fields before 1871. In that year, Alexander R. Shepherd, head of the Board of Public Works and later governor of the District of Columbia, began a massive four-year program to improve the city's streets: gas, water, and sewage lines; and landscaping of public parks. A group of wealthy Western mine owners, headed by Nevada Senator William Morris Stewart, was privy to Shepherd's plans and in 1870 bought, for a fraction of its future value, much of the land around what would develop as Dupont Circle. The circle was graded, fenced, and landscaped in 1871. To prove his

WASHINGTON, D.C. RESIDENTIAL HISTORIC DISTRICTS

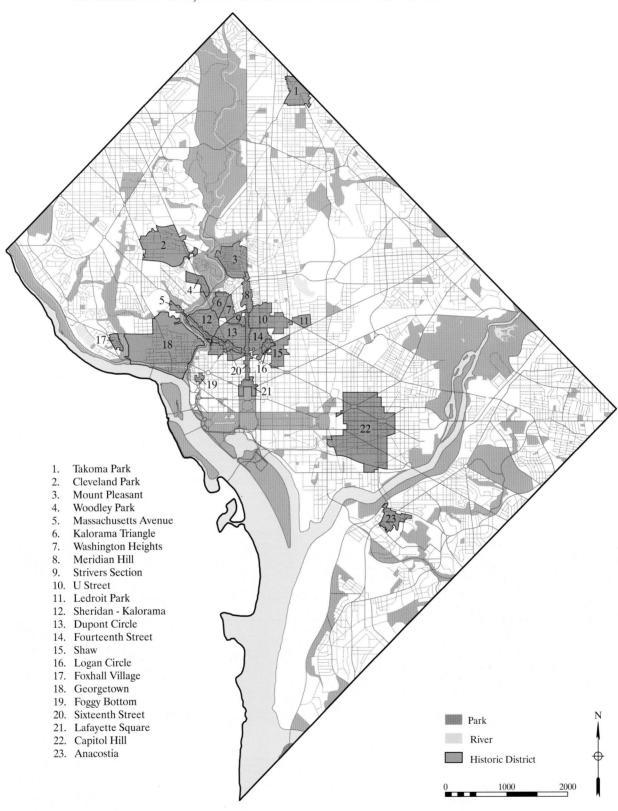

1. Takoma Park
2. Cleveland Park
3. Mount Pleasant
4. Woodley Park
5. Massachusetts Avenue
6. Kalorama Triangle
7. Washington Heights
8. Meridian Hill
9. Strivers Section
10. U Street
11. Ledroit Park
12. Sheridan - Kalorama
13. Dupont Circle
14. Fourteenth Street
15. Shaw
16. Logan Circle
17. Foxhall Village
18. Georgetown
19. Foggy Bottom
20. Sixteenth Street
21. Lafayette Square
22. Capitol Hill
23. Anacostia

Park

River

Historic District

N

0   1000   2000

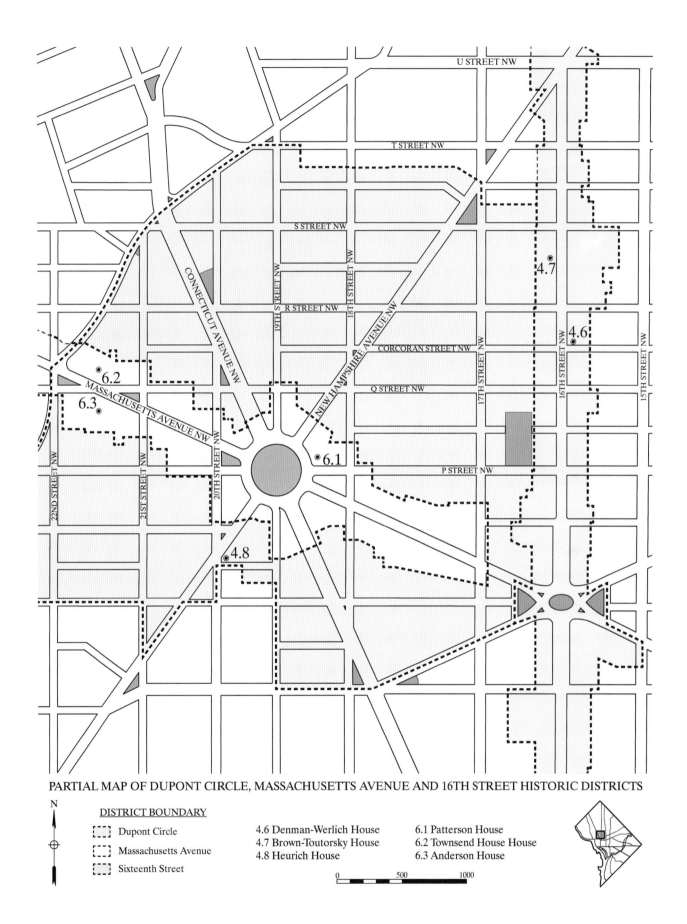

PARTIAL MAP OF DUPONT CIRCLE, MASSACHUSETTS AVENUE AND 16TH STREET HISTORIC DISTRICTS

N

<u>DISTRICT BOUNDARY</u>

Dupont Circle

Massachusetts Avenue

Sixteenth Street

4.6 Denman-Werlich House
4.7 Brown-Toutorsky House
4.8 Heurich House

6.1 Patterson House
6.2 Townsend House House
6.3 Anderson House

0   500   1000

SHEPHERD'S ROW, 1873, OPPOSITE MCPHERSON SQUARE ON THE
NORTHEAST CORNER OF CONNECTICUT AVENUE AND K STREET, N.W.,
WAS RAZED IN 1952 FOR AN OFFICE BUILDING

faith in the future of the area Stewart erected the first mansion, his own, the next year on Pacific Circle—named after its Western developers. The circle soon became the intersection of three fashionable residential avenues—Massachusetts, Connecticut, and New Hampshire. The race to build opulent houses really took off in 1874, when the British government built its grand Second Empire–style legation south of the circle at Connecticut Avenue and N Street, N.W. The name of the circle was changed in 1884 to Dupont Circle, when a bronze portrait statue of Rear Admiral Samuel Francis Dupont (1807–1865) was erected there to honor his service in the Civil War. (To prevent confusion during his military career he changed his name from du Pont to Dupont.) In 1921 the du Pont family of Delaware replaced the bronze statue, which was moved to a park in Wilmington, with a more fashionable marble fountain, designed by Daniel Chester French, featuring three classical allegorical figures.

After the Civil War the nouveaux riches, with fortunes inherited or made elsewhere, had the means to build palatial second residences. Approximately 200 of them built their mansions in the nation's capital, often occupying their properties only during the fashionable winter season that began in December and ended in late spring. Washington quickly became the winter Newport of America. The earliest of these mansions, beginning in 1872 with the Hillyer house (remodeled as the Townsend house in 1899 and now the Cosmos Club), were built of red brick in many eclectic Victorian modes (see Chapter 4). The city had become an attractive place for the wealthy (and everyone else) to live in the early 1870s, when Gov. Shepherd

STEWART'S CASTLE, 1873, BY WASHINGTON ARCHITECT ADOLPH CLUSS
AND BUILT ON THE NORTH SIDE OF DUPONT CIRCLE,
WAS RAZED IN 1901 FOR A BANK BUILDING.

transformed it into a model city. Most of these grand redbrick Victorian houses on Massachusetts Avenue have been demolished. Still standing are the massive 1881 Blaine mansion at 20th Street, N.W. and the impressive red-sandstone-and-brick Heurich house, along with their more numerous Beaux-Arts companions on New Hampshire Avenue as well as 16th Street, N.W.

The second set of grand houses—limestone-clad Beaux-Arts examples—were designed by architects from Washington, Philadelphia, New York, and Boston who had studied architecture in Paris. They were built mostly during the "Imperial Season" between 1890 and 1920. Outstanding local architects of these turn-of-the-century palaces include Jules Henri de Sibour, Hornblower & Marshall, Harvey L. Page, George Oakley Totten Jr., Glenn Brown and his son

Ward Brown, Waddy B. Wood, and Nathan Wyeth. Others, often called society architects, were nationally known: McKim, Mead & White, Carrère & Hastings, William Lawrence Bottomley, Little & Browne, Horace Trumbauer, Delano & Aldrich, Warren & Wetmore, and John Russell Pope.

More than 30 of Washington's Beaux-Arts mansions contained ballrooms. Many of the large red brick Victorian mansions in the neighborhood—built in eclectic revival styles—were pulled down between 1900 and 1915 and replaced with even larger limestone-clad Beaux-Arts palaces. The new style was made popular by the neoclassical buildings erected at the Chicago World's Fair of 1893, orchestrated by the architect Richard Morris Hunt. Many of these remain on the north side of Dupont Circle, such as the Patterson house designed by McKim, Mead &

THE SCHNEIDER HOUSE, 1890, BY WASHINGTON ARCHITECT T. FRANKLIN SCHNEIDER.
LOCATED ON THE SOUTHEAST CORNER OF 18TH AND Q STREETS, N.W.,
THE LANDMARK WAS RAZED IN 1957 FOR AN APARTMENT HOUSE.

White and the Perry Belmont house, by Horace Trumbauer.

In addition to the historic houses, Dupont Circle is also noted for its many early luxury apartment houses—17 were built between 1890 and 1910; 20, between 1910 and 1920; and 32, between 1920 and 1930. The Queen Anne–style Analostan Flats by George S. Cooper (1893) at 1718 Corcoran Street is the oldest, while The Cairo by Thomas F. Schneider (1894) at 1615 Q Street, N.W., is the tallest, at 160 feet. The Northumberland (1910), at New Hampshire Avenue and V Street, is the best preserved, with spectacular interior detailing, including a massive iron double-branched central staircase that sweeps up seven stories, and even private safes in the outer walls of each apartment. The Cairo caused Congress to pass a height law for Washington, limiting apartment houses to 90 feet and office buildings to 110; the law remains in effect today. Because of its fashionable location, five private schools were founded here in the early-20th century: Miss Madeira's School for Girls; Holton-Arms School; Maret School; Landon School; and the Emerson Institute. A resident of Dupont Circle, Phoebe Apperson Hearst, a teacher who married California mining millionaire George Hearst, also helped found the Cathedral School for Girls, the Parent-Teacher Association (PTA), and in the 1880s, the first kindergartens in the United States.

Beginning in 1900 the first floor of many of the elegant row houses fronting Connecticut Avenue were converted to luxury specialty shops, giving the street in the Dupont Circle area the impression of Fifth Avenue in New York or the Rue de la Paix in Paris. Between 1920 and 1930, Connecticut Avenue also became a center for showrooms of luxury automobiles—for example, the first floor at 1636 Connecticut Avenue was remodeled to provide space for the Rolls-Royce Company in 1924. At this time the Stewart house on the north side of Dupont Circle was demolished and replaced by the Semmes Motor Company showroom.

Dupont Circle changed rapidly after 1930. The Great Depression took a toll on many of the families residing in their limestone palaces there; they could no longer maintain a staff of a dozen full-time domestics. Five of the great mansions became clubs—the Townsend house became the Cosmos Club; the Patterson house, the Washington Club; the Wadsworth house, the Sulgrave Club; the Whittemore house, the Woman's National Democratic Club; and the Perry Belmont house, the home of the Eastern Star, the women's branch of the Masonic order. Automobile traffic congestion prompted many families in the 1930s to move to newer residential neighborhoods such as Wesley Heights and Chevy Chase, which offered spacious lawns and quieter living.

Some of these palaces became embassies. An early example is the Thomas Gaff house, on the southwest corner of 20th and Q Streets, N.W., with its elegant ballroom, designed in the Châteauesque style in 1904 by architect Jules Henri de Sibour, which became the Colombian embassy in 1938. The luxurious apartment house on the northeast corner of 18th Street and Massachusetts Avenue, N.W., built in 1915 as a rental investment for the family of millionaire Cyrus McCormick of Chicago, held six apartments, each with 25 rooms; its residential use ended forever when the government appropriated it for offices in World War II. It had been famous as the long-term residence of industrialist and banker Andrew Mellon while he served as secretary of the treasury under Presidents Harding, Coolidge, and Hoover. It was here that Mellon developed his plan to found the National Gallery of Art. After the war it was also well-known for many decades as the headquarters of the National Trust for Historic Preservation.

The 16th Street and Massachusetts Avenue Historic Districts

Two additional long, narrow historic districts border the Dupont Circle Historic District—the 16th Street Historic District on the east and the Massachusetts Avenue Historic District on the south. One of the best-known numbered streets in Washington is 16th Street, N.W., bounded by Lafayette Park on the south and Columbia Road on the north. Many palatial houses were built here between 1880 and 1930. Most of the great houses built on 16th Street south of Scott Circle, such as the Guggenheim mansion, were razed for office buildings and hotels between 1940 and 1970, before the historic districts were created. One of the few surviving in that stretch of the street is the Pullman house, now part of the Russian embassy. Two houses in the 16th Street Historic District are included in this volume. The first is the Denman-Werlich house, designed by distinguished architects Fuller & Wheeler, of Albany, New York. It has the finest detailed Romanesque Revival elements of its type in the city, including chimneys, dormer windows, wrought-iron window guards, and stone work. Nothing could be more picturesque than the Flemish Revival stepped facade of the Brown-Toutorsky house, the work of William Henry Miller, the leading architect of Ithaca, New York, during the post–Civil War years, who designed several of the early buildings at Cornell University. The interior is noted for its spacious entrance hall with a diagonally set fireplace, intricately carved staircase, and paneled walls and ceilings; the house has one of the few surviving high-style Victorian carriage houses.

Moving north one finds the sleek Art Deco–style 1937 Hightowers apartment house, John Russell

Pope's elegant Beaux-Arts 1911 Scottish Rite Temple, and the once-fashionable Roosevelt Hotel, now apartments, designed by Appleton P. Clarke Jr., in 1919. Diagonally across the street from the Roosevelt, at the northwest corner of 16th Street and Florida Avenue, was once the red Seneca sandstone castle built on a 6-acre site in 1888 by Sen. John B. Henderson of Missouri and his wife, Mary Foote Henderson, who spent 43 years promoting 16th Street. She began buying land in the area, known as Meridian Hill, in 1890 and had her favorite Washington architect, George Oakley Totten Jr., design nine mansions in the Beaux-Arts style; they were built nearby between 1906 and 1927. She then rented or sold them as embassies, establishing the city's first diplomatic center, or embassy row, along 16th Street and Meridian Hill Park.

Totten was a great admirer of Boston architect Henry Hobson Richardson, who made his version of the Romanesque Revival style popular in the United States in the 1880s. As a result, when Richardson's Warder house, one of four houses he designed in Washington, was slated for demolition in 1923 for an office building on K Street, Totten purchased and dismantled it. He had it rebuilt at 2633 16th Street in front of his own house on property that he owned on Meridian Hill. The Warder house and other Beaux-Arts mansions on upper 16th Street, between Florida Avenue and Columbia Road, became part of the new Meridian Hill Historic District at the end of 2014.

Mary Foote Henderson had even grander plans for 16th Street. When the White House was inspected and found to be in poor condition in 1898, she hired Paul J. Pelz (architect of the Library of Congress's Thomas Jefferson Building) to design a new White House for Meridian Hill, opposite her house. That plan fell through when the government commissioned Charles F. McKim to remodel the White House in 1902. She next attempted to get John Russell Pope's design for the Lincoln Memorial to be built on the same location on Meridian Hill rather than the west end of the Mall. She finally succeeded in having the federal government build the spectacular 12-acre Meridian Hill Park, designed by Horace W.

Peaslee and John Joseph Earley, across from her house. Its construction spanned two decades, beginning in 1914. One of the park's highlights is a cascading fountain, surrounded by a number of sculptures. The extensive use here of exposed-aggregate concrete is one of the best examples in the country. The park was a center for drug activity during the 1970s and 1980s, and the public avoided it. Fortunately, owing to the herculean efforts of the Friends of Meridian Hill Park, it has experienced a renaissance in popularity since 2000. Another of Mrs. Henderson's concerted projects—to have Congress rename 16th Street with the grand title "Avenue of the Presidents"—did not succeed. She was successful, however, in lobbying to prevent commercial development along the full length of 16th Street and so codifying it in the city's first zoning regulations, established in 1920.

Like 16th Street, Massachusetts Avenue is a lengthy major boulevard that encompasses a separate historic district, beginning at 17th Street and extending westward to Observatory Circle. The part of Massachusetts Avenue that runs through the Dupont Circle Historic District has three mansions that are included here—the Patterson, Anderson, and Townsend houses. The outstanding architectural firms of McKim, Mead & White of New York, Little & Browne of Boston, and Carrère & Hastings of New York, respectively, designed them. The construction of the British embassy in 1927 on Massachusetts Avenue had a profound effect on the city. It was designed to be the largest embassy in Washington by celebrated British architect, Sir Edwin Lutyens, in the Georgian Revival style, and built by developer Harry Wardman (see Chapter 7). Its construction prompted the migration of Embassy Row from 16th Street to Massachusetts Avenue.

The Sheridan-Kalorama Historic District

The Sheridan-Kalorama Historic District, which borders Dupont Circle on the west, contains eight

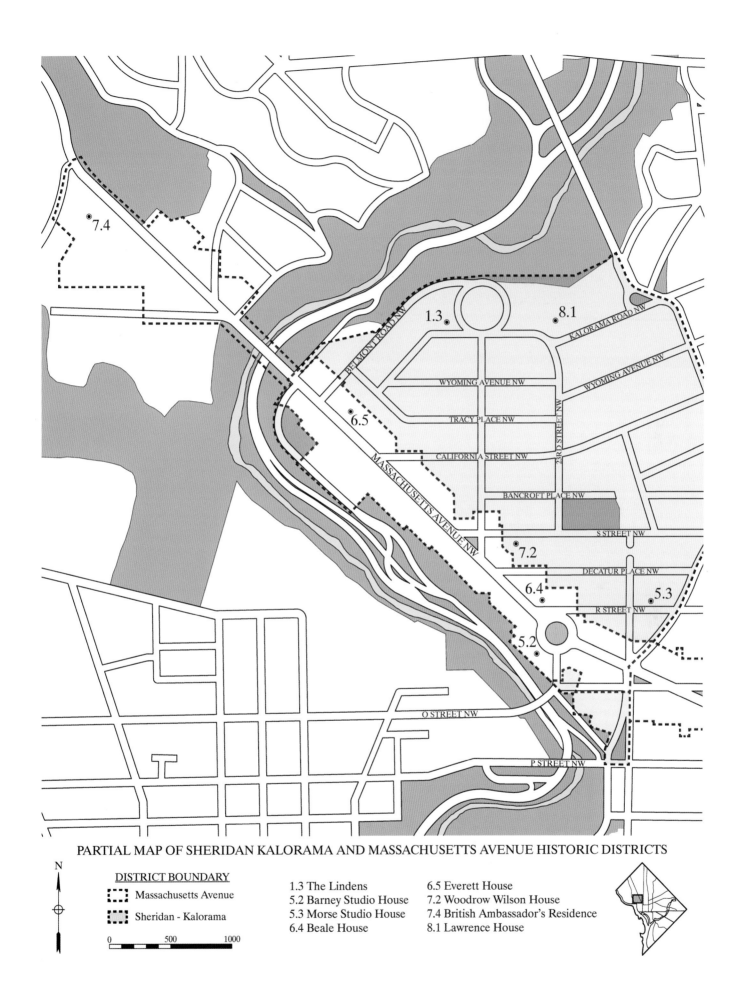

PARTIAL MAP OF SHERIDAN KALORAMA AND MASSACHUSETTS AVENUE HISTORIC DISTRICTS

N

DISTRICT BOUNDARY
Massachusetts Avenue

Sheridan - Kalorama

0   500   1000

1.3 The Lindens
5.2 Barney Studio House
5.3 Morse Studio House
6.4 Beale House

6.5 Everett House
7.2 Woodrow Wilson House
7.4 British Ambassador's Residence
8.1 Lawrence House

houses that are surveyed in this book. Sheridan-Kalorama is a large area enclosed by Florida Avenue on the south, Connecticut Avenue on the east, and Rock Creek on the north and west. It takes its name from Sheridan Circle, which contains an equestrian statue of Civil War hero General Philip H. Sheridan, and Kalorama, the name of a large estate that occupied much of the area in the late-18th century. This district, composed of 610 historic houses and apartment buildings, was established in 1989. A group of neighborhood residents organized the Sheridan-Kalorama Neighborhood Council to oppose the encroachment of commercial buildings into their residential neighborhood. The Sheridan-Kalorama Historical Association was formed from this organization to study the history of the area.

The first residence here was a large classically styled house, Belair, built in 1795 by Gustavus Scott, a large landowner and a commissioner of the District of Columbia. The estate, with its main house located at 23rd and S Streets, N.W., was bought in 1807 by Joel Barlow, a wealthy author and diplomat, who renamed it Kalorama after the Greek word for "beautiful view." Barlow entertained many prominent people here—frequent guests in the early 1800s included President Thomas Jefferson and inventor and painter Robert Fulton. During the Civil War, the federal government appropriated Kalorama for use as a military hospital. The house burned in 1864, and after the war, the estate was slowly divided and streets cut through the property. The former governor of Ohio, William Bebb, built the first house here in 1865. His large octagonal house at the current address of 1830 Phelps Place, N.W. soon became a tourist attraction. The area quickly began to develop in 1886 when Massachusetts Avenue was extended over Rock Creek. Soon after, Connecticut Avenue was extended and crossed Rock Creek, when the Taft Bridge was built in 1906. The new streetcar line along Connecticut Avenue greatly spurred development. Kalorama Circle, a choice location, was created at the end of 24th Street in the late-19th century. The houses here are a mixture of Beaux-Arts, and Georgian and Mediterranean

Revival. The one surviving Queen Anne mansion, designed by Franklin F. Schneider in 1892, was built for furniture merchant William H. Moses, at 2129 Wyoming Avenue.

By 1910 the area had become an exclusive residential neighborhood. Five U.S. presidents lived in houses in the Sheridan-Kalorama neighborhood: William Howard Taft, from 1921 to 1930; Woodrow Wilson, from 1921 to 1924; Warren G. Harding, from 1917 to 1921; Herbert Hoover, from 1921 to 1929 and 1933 to 1944; and Franklin D. Roosevelt, from 1917 to 1920. In addition to the Wilson house, three other Sheridan-Kalorama houses are discussed in the following pages: the Lawrence house, now the French embassy; the Everett house, now the Turkish embassy; and Beale house, the current Egyptian embassy.

A number of luxury apartment houses were constructed in the Kalorama area in the early-20th century, especially along California Street and Connecticut Avenue. Among them are the Highland, 1902 (now the Churchill Hotel), Wendell Mansions, 1906, and the Dresden, 1910. Other notable buildings in this district include St. Margaret's Episcopal Church at Connecticut Avenue and Bancroft Place and the Friends meeting house at 2111 Florida Avenue, whose members included President and Mrs. Herbert Hoover.

The Meridian Hill Park neighborhood, facing 16th Street and extending on the south from Florida Avenue northward to Columbia Road, N.W., became a historic district in 2014. This makes 56 historic districts in Washington, protecting more than 26,000 buildings, mostly houses. Of these 56 districts, half are residential historic districts and the other half represent parks, institutional campuses, and military bases or compounds. For historic preservation, these districts make Washington, one of the best-protected cities in the country. It is a tremendous improvement over the conditions that existed 35 years ago.

JAMES M. GOODE
JANUARY 28, 2015

CAPITAL HOUSES

Historic Residences *of* Washington, D.C.

AND ITS ENVIRONS

1735–1965

GEORGIAN HOUSES

Mount Vernon

Darnall's Chance

Carlyle House

The Lindens

Gunston Hall

Hayes Manor

MOUNT VERNON

3200 MOUNT VERNON MEMORIAL HIGHWAY
MOUNT VERNON, VIRGINIA

————————

1735; 1757-59; 1774-1787

Designers: Augustine Washington, Lawrence Washington, George Washington
Status: Historic House Museum

THE LAND FACADE

THE DILAPIDATED PIAZZA, 1860

GEORGE WASHINGTON'S ACQUISITION AND expansion of Mount Vernon are two of the most interesting aspects of the house's rich history. The land where the main house stands had been in the Washington family for three generations before George Washington leased it in 1754; he inherited it in 1761. His great-grandfather, John Washington, immigrated to Virginia in 1657 and, during his lifetime, acquired more than 5,000 acres along the Potomac River, mainly through "head rights"—paying the passage of indentured servants to Virginia. The Fairfax family owned the Northern Neck of Virginia, a vast 5,000,000 acres between the Potomac and Rappahannock rivers. Lord Fairfax granted land to anyone who paid the cost of shipping an Englishmen to the colony, believing that their increased numbers in the sparsely settled outpost would add to its productivity and benefit the public good.

One of the tracts of land that John Washington acquired circa 1674 was Little Hunting Creek, the present site of Mount Vernon. He left that parcel to his son Lawrence (the first), George Washington's grandfather. Research indicates that he erected a small dwelling there around 1690, probably for tenants. When the son died at the age of 38, he left his extensive lands in a number of locations to his three children: John, Augustine (George Washington's father), and Mildred.

In 1726 Augustine Washington bought Little Hunting Creek from his sister, Mildred, and in 1735 built a house that is today the core of Mount Vernon. Augustine's eldest son, Lawrence (the second), half-brother of George Washington, inherited this property in 1743. Lawrence named it Mount Vernon after his former British naval commander, Admiral Edward Vernon.

George Washington was very close to Lawrence and often left his mother's farm at Fredericksburg, Virginia, to visit his brother at Mount Vernon. Lawrence married Ann Fairfax of Belvoir, who lived on an adjoining plantation to the south. Ann's father, William Fairfax, was the cousin and agent of Thomas, Sixth Lord Fairfax, who owned most of the Northern Neck of Virginia. Upon his marriage in 1743, Lawrence slightly altered the one-and-one-half-story cottage at Mount Vernon, which had four rooms on each

floor—a substantial Virginia planter's house at that time. Lawrence used the side of the house near the river as the main entrance and installed elaborate paneling in the parlor near it.

When Lawrence died of tuberculosis in 1752, his wife, Ann, and their daughter, Sarah, inherited Mount Vernon. In 1753 Ann married into the Lee family and moved to Westmoreland County. When Sarah died in 1754, George Washington leased Mount Vernon from Ann Fairfax Washington Lee and moved in at the age of 22.

In 1757, before George Washington resigned as colonel of the Virginia Regiment toward the end of the French and Indian War, he began to rebuild and enlarge Mount Vernon. Washington moved the main entrance to the land side because he used it more often. That year he married Martha Dandridge Custis, a wealthy widow who owned some 29,000 acres of Tidewater land. Full ownership of Mount Vernon came to George Washington when Anne Fairfax Washington Lee died without surviving children in 1761.

THE RIVER FRONT

Bolstered with additional funds from his marriage, George Washington systematically increased his landholdings at Mount Vernon, which grew from 2,126 acres in 1759 to 6,500 acres by 1772. He also doubled his ownership in slaves to 95. Washington improved his finances at Mount Vernon in the 1760s and 1770s when he switched from growing tobacco to wheat and began to market large quantities of salted fish and flour from his own mill. In the 1790s he started another profitable endeavor, distilling and selling his own whiskey.

The second building enlargement took more than 10 years, between 1774 and 1787, during which time Washington was mostly away commanding the Continental Army. The death of Martha's daughter, Patsy, in 1773 precipitated Mount Vernon's aggrandizement:

Following Pages: BIRDS-EYE VIEW OF MOUNT VERNON, LITHOGRAPH BY T. SINCLAIR, 1859

WEST PARLOR

Patsy's inheritance from her father totaled 8,000 pounds, an enormous sum at the time. It was transferred to Martha, whose husband, George, legally controlled it. He promptly paid his sizable debt to his British purchasing agent, Cary, in London, and began enlarging Mount Vernon.

Major changes during the second expansion included the addition of a pediment on the west facade, which gave the illusion of a symmetrical window arrangement; a cupola on the roof to raise the profile of the house; and a piazza on the east side facing the Potomac River. This highly unusual and impressive portico, with eight pillars spanning the length of the house, provided shelter from the sun during the hot summer months. The house was doubled in size, in part by the addition of the grand New Room on the north side for receptions and dining, and George Washington's study and master bedroom suite on the south. Washington also created a courtyard on the west side, now the main entrance, by building open, curved arcades to connect two new outbuildings to the main house. The kitchen is on the south, and the servants' hall, which provided meals and shelter for the white servants of visiting guests, is on the north. The 12 original outbuildings at Mount Vernon constitute the most extensive surviving assemblage of 18th-century service buildings of any estate in the South.

GEORGE WASHINGTON'S STUDY

Washington consulted English architectural pattern books, including those of Batty Langley, for the construction and design, resulting in the large Palladian window in the New Room to the north. Although he never visited England or the Continent, Washington saw the latest architectural fashions during his travels to Philadelphia, New York, and the New England colonies. He may have gotten the idea to use rusticated boards at Mount Vernon from inspecting the Redwood Library in Newport, Rhode Island, and Roxby, the home of the governor of Massachusetts, while on a trip in 1758. To simulate a stone facade, the edges of wooden boards were beveled and painted white, with sand added to the wet surface.

Washington relied on the service of both farm managers and overseers to raise crops, supervise slaves,

THE LARGE RECEPTION ROOM, OR "NEW ROOM," AT THE NORTH END OF THE FIRST FLOOR

direct work on the house, and look after visitors. Their skilled management was vital to the operation of the estate, since Washington was absent for long periods—during the French and Indian War, the first and second Continental Congresses, commanding the Continental Army during the Revolutionary War, and serving two terms as president of the United States. His first manager was his favorite brother, John Augustine Washington, who supervised the estate while he was in the French and Indian War. Other managers who were relatives included his nephew, George Augustine Washington, the son of his brother Charles, and his cousin, Lund Washington. Washington wrote to them weekly, usually on Sundays, giving directions for erecting the many outbuildings at Mount Vernon, including the brick greenhouse, flower gardens, new

serpentine driveway on the west, and planting hundreds of young trees to create views of interest.

Washington hired John Patterson and Going Lanphier to manage the construction and renovation of the west parlor and dining room off the central passage. A skilled wood carver, William Bernard Sears, was hired to work on the fireplace paneling for the new reception room. He had been indentured by George Mason to work on Gunston Hall. During the six-year period that Washington was at Mount Vernon, between 1768 and 1774, a staff of butlers and slaves cared for more than 2,000 guests, who were often entertained at dinner and usually stayed overnight.

After the deaths of George Washington, in 1799, and Martha, in 1802, the house and land deteriorated

Right: DETAIL OF THE "NEW ROOM"

TOURISTS IN FRONT OF WASHINGTON'S TOMB IN 1855

rapidly. Washington left Mount Vernon to his favorite nephew, Bushrod Washington, a lawyer and early member of the United States Supreme Court. Bushrod lived at Mount Vernon in the summer months and in Washington City the remainder of the year. He added the balustrade on top of the piazza and a porch at the south end of the house, both since removed. Mount Vernon passed to Bushrod's nephew, John Augustine Washington Sr. in 1829. The last owner, John Augustine Washington, Jr., failed to get the Commonwealth of Virginia or the U.S. government to purchase and restore Mount Vernon.

The estate was then rescued by a group of women headed by Ann Pamela Cunningham, who organized the Mount Vernon Ladies' Association of the Union. They raised the funds, with the help of orator Edward Everett, to buy the estate and open it to the public in 1860. The fate of John Augustine Washington Jr. was not as happy. He moved his family to a house in Fauquier County, Virginia, where his wife died shortly afterward. At the outbreak of the Civil War, he became an aide-de-camp to General Robert E. Lee. In late 1861 Washington was killed in combat. His family invested part of the $200,000 they received in payment for Mount Vernon from the Mount Vernon Ladies' Association of the Union in Confederate bonds, which ultimately proved to be worthless.

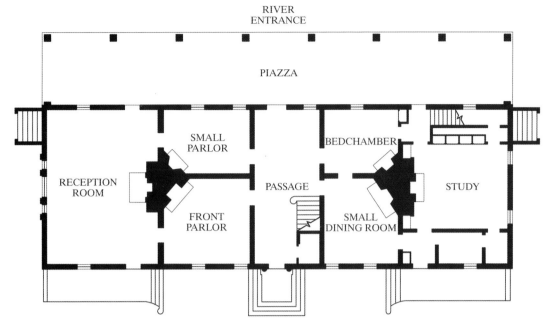

RIVER
ENTRANCE

PIAZZA

SMALL
PARLOR

BEDCHAMBER

STUDY

RECEPTION
ROOM

PASSAGE

FRONT
PARLOR

SMALL
DINING ROOM

FIRST-FLOOR PLAN

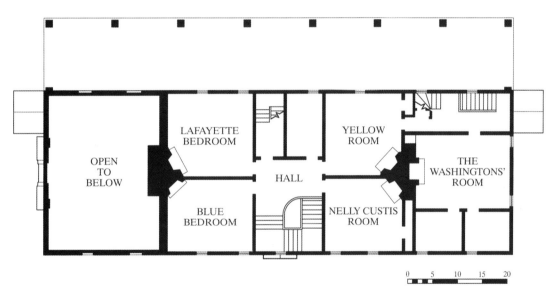

LAFAYETTE
BEDROOM

YELLOW
ROOM

OPEN
TO
BELOW

HALL

THE
WASHINGTONS'
ROOM

BLUE
BEDROOM

NELLY CUSTIS
ROOM

0   5   10   15   20

SECOND-FLOOR PLAN

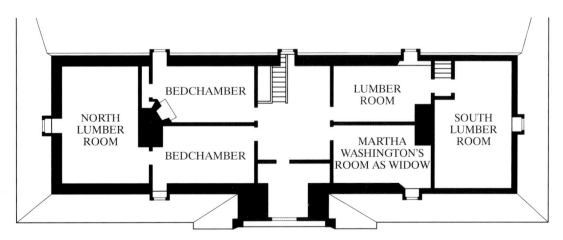

BEDCHAMBER

LUMBER
ROOM

NORTH
LUMBER
ROOM

SOUTH
LUMBER
ROOM

BEDCHAMBER

MARTHA
WASHINGTON'S
ROOM AS WIDOW

THIRD-FLOOR PLAN

DARNALL'S CHANCE

14800 GOVERNOR ODEN BOWIE DRIVE
UPPER MARLBORO, MARYLAND

1741–42

Architect: Unknown
Restoration Architect: James T. Woolen
Status: Historic House Museum

FACADE

A VERY SUCCESSFUL SCOTTISH MERCHANT, James Wardrop, built Darnall's Chance in 1741–42. When the house was extensively remodeled in 1858, its 18th-century heritage was disregarded and disguised. In 1986 the house was peeled back to its 1742 appearance.

This early Georgian house is particularly interesting because of its jerkinhead roof, which combines a gable roof on the lower half with a hipped roof with clipped corners on the upper half. This type of roof design was used during the 1740s for houses in several of the American colonies, especially in Maryland. The Historic American Buildings Survey of the 1930s recorded more than a dozen in Maryland.

The history of Darnall's Chance and its fortunate survival is almost a miracle. In 1704 Charles Calvert, third Lord Baltimore, granted a large tract of land to his wife's cousin, Col. Henry Darnall I, who optimistically named it Darnall's Chance. During Maryland's colonial period, Col. Darnall became one of the three largest landowners in Maryland. The three tracts he owned—comprising 30,000 acres—were named Darnall's Delight (his primary or home plantation), Darnall's Chance, and Darnall's Grove.

A Roman Catholic, Darnall came to Maryland in the late-17th century and quickly became a member of the General Assembly and the governor's council. The Glorious Revolution in England in 1688/1689 replaced the Catholic King James II with Protestant monarchs William and Mary. As a result, Maryland's government changed from a proprietary colony under the control of the Catholic Lord Baltimore to a crown colony. The Calverts lost their authority to directly govern Maryland and appoint officials. The new royal Protestant governor, Lionel Copley, arrived in Saint Mary's City, the colony's first capital, in Saint Mary's County, in 1692 to reform the government. The Church of England became the state church, supported by public taxation. In 1694 the capital was moved from the primarily Catholic Saint Mary's County to the new Protestant town of Annapolis. In 1696 the boundaries of Maryland's old Calvert and Charles counties were redrawn, and the new county

of Prince George's was created and named for the Danish husband of Princess Anne, heir to the English throne. After the Revolution of 1688, Lord Baltimore in England made Darnall his representative in Maryland for the supervision of his land holdings and other interests there. Darnall died in 1711 and was buried on his home plantation, Darnall's Delight, in southern Prince George's County.

Those receiving grants of land in colonial Maryland from either the crown or the sole proprietor (e.g., Lord Baltimore) often gave the property a very quaint name—seemingly more so here than in any other American colony. In Prince George's County, along the lines of Darnall's Chance, such names as Widow's Mite, Friendship, Knave's Disappointment, Plain Dealing, Fortune, Clean Drinking, Pretty Betty, His Lordship's Kindness, and Girl's Portion were popular.

The government of Maryland changed again in the early-18th century. Charles Calvert, third Lord Baltimore, died in 1715. The title passed to his son, Benedict Leonard Calvert, who became the fourth Lord Baltimore. When Benedict converted to the Anglican Church, the crown restored Calvert to power, and Maryland reverted once again to a proprietary colony.

Upper Marlboro, originally named Marlborough, was one of six new municipalities established by the Maryland General Assembly in 1706. The land for the town was purchased from Henry Darnall I and Ninian Beall. It was named for John Churchill (1650–1722), the first Duke of Marlborough, one of England's greatest generals. In 1721 the word Upper was added to its name to distinguish it from the much smaller Lower Marlborough in Calvert County. The town grew rapidly in the 18th century: Being rich tobacco country close to official shipping points on the Patuxent River, it became both the county seat and an important commercial and cultural center. Both towns changed the spelling of their names to Marlboro in 1893.

The Darnall family sold a seven-acre tract on the edge of Upper Marlboro to James Wardrop, a young Scottish merchant. Keeping the estate's original name

CENTRAL PASSAGE LOOKING TOWARD THE FRONT DOOR

Wardrop built his main house on the property in 1741, along with a number of outbuildings—an office, summer kitchen, smokehouse, dairy, slave quarters, stable, even an underground brick burial vault. His primary business involved purchasing tobacco from local farmers, shipping it to England and Scotland on vessels he either owned or rented, and importing luxury English goods. Wardrop amassed a fortune; at his death he was the wealthiest merchant in Prince George's County.

In 1748 Wardrop married Lettice Lee of the Lee family of Virginia. Her father was Philip Lee, a prominent tobacco planter from nearby Westmoreland County, Virginia. Lettice was known for her skillful management of the household and its 32 slaves, and enjoyed entertaining on a grand scale. The

Wardrops counted George Washington, George Mason, and John Carlyle among their many friends.

The facade of Darnall's Chance has a slightly projecting central pavilion with an arched entrance crowned by a simple triangular pediment, a treatment that is rare on such an early house in Maryland. The restoration architect mistakenly believed that casement windows were originally used in the house, so it was these that were installed during the restoration; they will eventually be replaced with sash windows. Heat radiating from chimneys at each end warmed the 15-room house. The floor plan is typical of a Georgian house, with a wide central passage and two rooms in the front and two in the rear. The Wardrops entertained guests at cards or offered tea in the parlor, located immediately to the left of the entrance hall. The

PANELED DINING ROOM WALL, WITH BEAUFAT ON THE RIGHT

master bedroom was directly to the rear of the parlor. The right front room was used as a study, and the right rear room as the dining room. Meals were cooked in the kitchen below the dining room during winter and in the outside kitchen in the summer. Traditionally in 18th-century Maryland, breakfast was served at 8 a.m., the midday meal, called dinner, at 2 p.m., and a light supper at 8 p.m. The dinner would last two hours, after which the men would remain at the table and the women would withdraw for tea in an adjacent room.

The paneled wall of the dining room contains a central fireplace framed by a closet on the left and a beaufat on the right. The latter is a locked closet with scalloped shelves designed to store and display the family's silver and better porcelain. According to an inventory made after James Wardrop's death in

1760, the dining room was furnished with two mahogany dining tables, 14 matching chairs, two marble-top side tables, a mirror and sconces, a clock, a folding screen, and two framed prints.

The basement houses one of the property's two kitchens. Eighteenth-century records indicate that the winter kitchen of Darnall's Chance was managed in 1760 by two cooks who were sisters: Nell and Margaret Bentley. The household included 32 slaves, 15 of whom worked "about the house," while the others worked in the stable, the gardens, the store, the three warehouses, and the dock. Adjacent to the basement kitchen is an enormous wine cellar used to store beverages and perishable foodstuffs.

Wardrop's widow continued to live at Darnall's Chance and married twice more. After her children sold the house in 1788, all the subsequent owners were merchants. Edward Grafton Hall purchased the house in 1857 and remodeled it the following year in the then-fashionable Italianate mode. He raised the house to two full stories, lengthened the front windows to the floor, moved the main staircase, added a cupola to the roof, and stuccoed the exterior. It was soon forgotten that an 18th-century house lay within the new one. The Buck family, also merchants, bought the property in 1907 and lived there the longest of any owner.

In 1975 the Bucks sold a very dilapidated Darnall's Chance to the town of Upper Marlboro for the site of a public parking garage. It happened that funds were not available for the construction, so the house sat abandoned for 10 years. During this time large sections of the plaster on the outer walls fell off, revealing 18th-century brickwork. As a result the case was made for preserving the house.

By 1986 parts of Darnall's Chance had been so far altered that it required dismantling. Much of the brickwork was stacked on the ground awaiting reconstruction. The restoration architect, James T. Woolen, who had previously worked on the restoration of Riversdale, the Calvert plantation house near Bladensburg, rebuilt Darnall's Chance in 1986–88 in an approximation of its original appearance. Today the house is open as a museum and is owned and managed by the Maryland National Capital Park and Planning Commission.

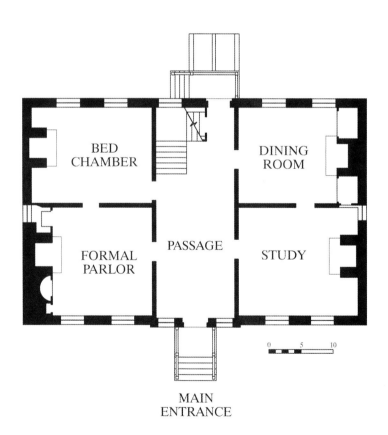

FIRST-FLOOR PLAN

CARLYLE HOUSE

121 NORTH FAIRFAX STREET
ALEXANDRIA, VIRGINIA

1751–53

Designer: John Carlyle
Restoration Architect: J. Everette Fauber Jr.
Status: Historic House Museum

FACADE

FRONT PARLOR

JOHN CARLYLE (1720–1780), THE SON OF A SCOT-
tish apothecary and surgeon, grew to manhood in
England, where he served as a merchant's apprentice.
In 1741, at the age of 21, he was sent to northern
Virginia as a factor, or purchasing agent, of the English tobacco merchant William Hicks. With the income from this job the young man shrewdly invested
in Virginia land and, by 1745, had built his first house
on a 350-acre plantation on Hunting Creek in Fairfax
County. At that time Carlyle started his own business,
exporting wheat, flour, tobacco, and iron, and importing such goods as rum, sugar, and also slaves.

By the early 1740s, it was obvious to both planters
and merchants in northern Virginia that a new Potomac River port, much farther to the northwest near
Hunting Creek, was urgently needed. The Virginia

House of Burgesses approved the creation of the port
of Alexandria in 1749. Eleven trustees were appointed
to manage the town, including nearby landowners
John Carlyle and Lawrence Washington, older half-
brother of the future president. Carlyle purchased two
adjoining half-acre lots, on North Fairfax Street between King and Cameron Streets, in the center of the
town. A choice location, the east side of Carlyle's land
stood on a bluff overlooking the Potomac, while the
west side faced the market square. The town quickly
grew in importance, and in 1752, Alexandria became
the county seat.

Carlyle enjoyed a rapid rise to wealth, partly due
to his marriage in 1748 to Sarah Fairfax, the daughter
of William Fairfax, one of the wealthiest planters in
northern Virginia. Through his wife, Carlyle came

CENTRAL PASSAGE LOOKING TOWARD THE REAR DOOR

into possession of 10,000 acres of land and a number of slaves. Construction of his mansion on the Alexandria site began in 1751 and was completed in August 1753. The stately house, set back 75 feet from North Fairfax Street, was unusual for colonial Virginia in that it was built of sandstone, quarried 30 miles south near the Potomac. This was a reminder of the favorite building material for houses of the wealthy along the border between England and Scotland, where Carlyle was raised.

The design of Carlyle House was influenced by Craigiehall, a house in West Lothian, Scotland, designed by architect William Adam, and is similar in details. The facade of the Virginia house is five bays wide, with a slightly projecting central pavilion that contains the main entrance. The house has a molded water table and a hipped roof with an unusually wide flair at the eaves. The water table consists of a projecting shallow band of bricks near the base of the exterior walls, which directs rainwater away. Massive quoins, or projecting stones, define the corners of the main building, central pavilion, and entrance. The hipped roof on the two-and-a-half-story house has two interior chimneys and dormer windows. The facade is sheathed in finely dressed stone. The other three elevations consist of rubble stone with rough tool marks, coated with plaster for a more polished look.

The floor plan is typical of Georgian houses in colonial Virginia. A spacious central passage extends from the entrance to the back of the house. This wide space was used for daily living, as a reception area for business rather than social visitors, and for parties

and dances. A decorative floor cloth runs the length of the passage, providing visual interest, and protection from basement drafts. The main staircase rises to a wide landing lit by an impressive Palladian window. The small room immediately to the left of the entrance hall is the parlor, hung with green wallpaper. As shown on the accompanying floor plan, it opens to a spacious dining room. These are the only two rooms in the house that retain their original architectural details.

The dining room exhibits the most elaborate original woodwork in the house, including broken pediments over the doors, the cornice, and the paneling over the fireplace. The broad wooden cornice contains alternating carved rosettes and pineapples. The operable interior window shutters in these two rooms fold into recesses in the walls. Carlyle used the carpenters who built his ships to produce the carvings in the dining room.

On the right side of the central passage is a small hallway that separates the master bedchamber from the study, and also leads to a small door to the exterior. The four bedrooms on the second floor open onto corridors connected to the spacious upstairs passage, with the grand Palladian window affording a prospect of the Potomac River in the distance. The large attic, lighted by the two dormer windows, accommodated household slaves and storage.

The summer kitchen and the office were grouped around the spacious front courtyard of Carlyle House. Other outbuildings on the site included the laundry, dairy, stable, and coach house. A blacksmith's shop and Carlyle's tobacco warehouse, convenient to his wharf, stood at the foot of the bluff behind the house.

Carlyle House was an important setting for key figures and events leading to the French and Indian War. General Edward Braddock established his headquarters here, and five royal governors met at the house in April 1755 to plan the British campaign against the

DINING ROOM WITH
PORTRAIT OF JOHN CARLYLE

French. During the conference all five governors declined to help fund the British military expedition. Carlyle himself was promoted to colonel in the Virginia militia and remained in Alexandria, where he served as quartermaster for the disastrous Braddock expedition, dispatching food, supplies, and weapons for the 400-mile march. Although Britain ultimately won the lengthy war, this conflict was a direct cause of the Revolutionary War, because Britain began in 1765 to tax the colonies, without representation, to help pay the enormous costs incurred in the war.

After Carlyle's death in 1780 his young grandson, John Carlyle Herbert, inherited his considerable estate, including the house. The boy's parents, Sarah Carlyle Herbert and William Herbert, administered the estate until he reached adulthood. In 1807 William Herbert completed an impressive Federal-style building for the new Bank of Alexandria on part of the house's front yard. In 1831 the Herberts sold the bank building and Carlyle House to Alexandria businessman John Lloyd, who in turn sold both properties in 1848 to James Green, a prosperous British-born Alexandria cabinetmaker.

During the 1840s and 1850s Green expanded his business interests to real estate, coal, lumber, and cotton. He became one of the largest property owners in the city. Before the Civil War, Green converted the old bank building into a hotel, named the Mansion House, by virtue of its adjacency to Carlyle House. At the same time, he moved his family into Carlyle House. Although Green preserved the original configuration of the small parlor and the "Braddock conference" dining room, he greatly altered the rest of the landmark, removing walls, chair railings, and window seats, and adding rooms, porches, and a terrace, as well as redesigning the staircases and dramatically altering the front entrance.

With a booming hotel business, Green expanded Mansion House in 1855 by building a long three-story addition to the right of the old bank building. The new 70-room hotel, with an octagonal cupola and a prominent Greek Revival iron balcony supported by large brackets, was considered one of the best in Virginia. Unfortunately the extension completely obscured Carlyle House, requiring the Green family to enter through the hotel lobby.

The day after Virginia seceded on May 24, 1861, Alexandria was occupied by the Union Army and remained under military rule for four years, until General Robert E. Lee surrendered at Appomattox in April 1865. Early in the war the Union army seized both the Mansion House and Green's furniture factory and turned them into hospitals. Although Green took the loyalty oath to the United States government at the end of the war in May 1865, he never received the $37,000 rent promised him for the two buildings.

James Green recovered after the war by reopening Mansion House in late 1865, and the furniture factory in 1870. Several years after his death in 1880, Green's family sold Carlyle House and the Mansion House hotel. Without Green's leadership, the furniture company went bankrupt and closed in 1887. Once again Carlyle House suffered disarray and neglect. In 1906 the hotel building was converted into an apartment house known as Braddock Mansion—people were more likely to know about the Braddock conference than John Carlyle, whose importance had faded over time. Lloyd Schaeffer, the last private owner of the properties, opened Carlyle House to the public as a historic house museum and renamed the old hotel-apartment building, now considerably run-down, Carlyle Apartments. Schaeffer finally closed them in 1969.

In 1970 the Northern Virginia Regional Park Authority purchased the property from Schaeffer. NVRPA commissioned local architect J. Everette Fauber Jr. to research the house's history and restore it to its original design. Fauber restored the parlor and dining room and rebuilt the other rooms to their approximate dimensions. The front entrance porch, which was not original to the house, was removed, and the window seats and chair rails were reconstructed throughout the house. The 1807 Bank of Alexandria building, believed gone, turned up in demolition and was saved. The remaining two-thirds of the Mansion House hotel was leveled—in spite of vociferous local opposition—in order to open the view of the Carlyle House from North Fairfax Street for the first time in 118 years.

By coincidence, a direct descendant of John Carlyle's brother in Scotland, Sir Fritzroy Maclean, visited Alexandria shortly after the house was opened to the public in 1976. He owned portraits of both John Carlyle and his brother George, as well as dozens of letters written by John from Carlyle House to his brother in Scotland during the third quarter of the 18th century. This wealth of new information shed light on how Carlyle House was used and confirmed the important events that took place there. Today a copy of Sir Fritzroy Maclean's oil portrait of John Carlyle hangs over the mantel of the original dining room fireplace.

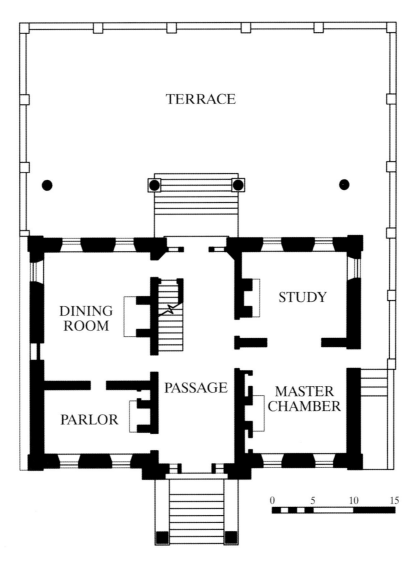

FIRST-FLOOR PLAN

THE LINDENS

2401 KALORAMA ROAD, N.W.
WASHINGTON, D.C.

1754

Architect: Attributed to Peter Harrison.
Reconstruction Architect: Walter M. Macomber, 1935–37
Neighborhood: Sheridan-Kalorama
Status: Private Residence

FACADE, BASED ON A DESIGN BY THE ENGLISH ARCHITECT JAMES GIBBS

THE LINDENS DIFFERS FROM OTHER HOUSES in this study because its original site is 600 miles away. Between 1935 and 1937 it was dismantled and the parts shipped to Washington, D.C., where it was carefully reassembled. Robert "King" Hooper (1709–1790) built the landmark in Danvers, Massachusetts, as his country house in 1754. Hooper owned and maintained a fleet of more than a dozen ships and amassed a considerable fortune in the 18th century by exporting dried cod to Europe.

Hooper's principal residence was 8 miles away from Danvers in the port city of Marblehead. The Marblehead Art Association bought the in-town mansion, at 8 Hooper Street, in 1938 to preserve it; today it is open to the public. Robert Hooper was one of the two wealthiest fish merchants in New England. The other was Col. Jeremiah Lee, who built an even larger mansion in Marblehead across the street from Hooper's. Since 1909 the Marblehead Historical Society has preserved the Lee mansion, considered the finest colonial house in Massachusetts, as a historic house museum. All three historical houses—Lee's mansion, Hooper's Marblehead house, and Hooper's Danvers country house (The Lindens) were built with faux-rusticated facades—wooden boards beveled to resemble stone blocks, then overlaid with white paint mixed with sand. While Hooper's two houses were rusticated only on the facade, the more costly Lee mansion was rusticated on all four elevations.

The Lindens became the scene of much activity in the early days of the American Revolution. During the Boston riots of early 1774, the Royal Governor Thomas Gage decided to move to the country for safety, accepting the invitation of Hooper, a loyalist, to use The Lindens. After the Battles of Lexington and Concord in April 1775, patriots passing the house on their way to join the American army stopped to remove the lead from the gateposts to be melted for bullets. When Hooper came to the door, they shot at him, and the bullet remains lodged in the door today.

Because of his loyalist sympathies, Hooper was forced to flee to Canada with his family. Even though he returned to Marblehead after the war, he never

ROBERT "KING" HOOPER, PORTRAIT BY
JOHN SINGLETON COPLEY, C. 1767

regained his confiscated property and died in poverty. After the Revolution his house in Danvers went through seven owners before Francis Peabody of Salem, Massachusetts, purchased it in 1860, to use as his summer home for 54 years, until his death. George Peabody, a prominent American banker and philanthropist who made a fortune in London, visited his cousin here in 1869. Francis Peabody restored the house and named it The Lindens after the two rows of linden trees he planted on the long driveway leading to the house. Peabody collected and installed three sets of early-19th-century French scenic wallpapers in the house. He also laid out formal gardens behind the house. After Francis Peabody's death, his son sold The Lindens in 1914 to Ward Thorn. During the 1920s, the neighborhood around The Lindens evolved into a semi-industrial area, making the house undesirable as a residence.

In 1933 Israel Sack, a noted New York antiques dealer, bought The Lindens for $10,000 and immediately sold the large parlor on the south side of the house to the Nelson-Atkins Museum of Art in Kansas City, where it remains on display today. In

the meantime, events were developing that would bring The Lindens to Washington. During the 1920s George Morris, a prominent Washington lawyer who was also president of the American Bar Association, and his wife Miriam Hubbard Morris, were creating an important collection of 18th-century American furniture. They bought a large lot on Kalorama Circle to build a replica of Westover, a grand 18th-century Virginia plantation house on the James River, to provide a period setting for their furniture. The Morrises eventually decided not to replicate Westover but to find an existing house of the same era and move it to the lot. After visiting many such houses for sale from South Carolina to Massachusetts, they bought The Lindens from Sack for $14,000 in 1934, with the stipulation that Sack recreate the parlor he had sold.

The Morrises commissioned Walter Mayo Macomber, the principal restoration architect of Colonial Williamsburg and later of Mount Vernon, to transport the disassembled parts of The Lindens—60 feet wide by 48 feet deep—to Washington. Having completed most of the restoration work at Williamsburg by 1934, Macomber was free to take his experienced staff with him to work on the Morris project. Over a period of seven weeks, Macomber and his team carefully disassembled the 15-room house, numbered all the parts, and shipped them in six railroad freight cars to Washington. He then reconstructed The Lindens on Kalorama Circle over a two-year-and-nine-month period from 1935 to 1937. Macomber's careful preservation extended to the original nails, which were reused. By expanding the center of the eight-bedroom house by 5 feet he was able to add modern bathrooms without damaging the original design of the front and rear elevations. The Morrises paid $7,000 to move and rebuild the house. Macomber laid a concrete foundation and supported the walls with steel beams to stabilize The Lindens.

STAIRCASE NEWEL POST AND BALUSTERS

The facade is important among Georgian houses built in the American colonies because it was one of the first to be influenced by the designs of well-known British architect James Gibbs. Attenuated, fluted, and engaged Corinthian columns span the two stories and frame the main entrance and support the steep-pitched pediment. The four richly molded dormer windows on the third floor have alternating triangular and arched pediments. The decorative roof balustrade conceals the upper section of the gambrel roof and adds an elegant touch to the overall design. Faux-stone quoins define all four corners and surround the front entrance as well. The Lindens is probably the only house in Washington with a rusticated wooden facade.

Left: A PAIR OF ENGAGED, FLUTED CORINTHIAN COLUMNS FRAMES THE ENTRANCE

Following Pages: THE MAIN STAIRCASE, WITH ITS EARLY-19TH CENTURY HAND-BLOCKED FRENCH WALLPAPER

The interior of The Lindens is noted not only for its abundantly paneled parlor, but also for the elaborate staircase situated on the right side of the wide passage. Originally the floors of the passage had a painted-stencil border of grapes and grape leaves. The staircase has an impressive carved newel post, while each riser has three extraordinary carved balusters—each cut from one piece of wood with two spirals rotating in opposite directions. Marblehead ship carpenters, idle during most of the winter months, produced this fine woodwork.

The Lindens is the only house in the United States that has three complete sets of early-19th-century hand-printed French scenic wallpaper. At the time the Morrises bought the house, the Metropolitan Museum of Art was considering acquiring the wallpaper, along with the paneling and staircase in the passage, for its collection. When Macomber dismantled the house, he carefully steamed the paper off the walls and backed it with linen before reinstallation. The wallpaper scenes display a common theme: *The Passage of Telemachus on the Island of Calypso,* by Dufour (1825); *Pizarro's Conquest of Peru,* by Leroy (1832); and *The Voyages of Antenor,* by Dufour (1814). Although about 3,000 sets of similar wallpaper were imported to the United States between 1800 and 1850, few survive. The handmade paper was costly, often requiring more than 2,000 wood printing blocks and up to 75 paint colors. After 1860, more affordable machine-made wallpaper became common.

When Mrs. Morris died in 1982 at the age of 90, her three children sold the house to Norman and Diane Bernstein, Washington real estate investors, for $1.5 million; they auctioned the entire furniture collection at Christies in New York. Today Kenneth D. Brody, former president of the Export-Import Bank of the United States and currently the owner of a leading New York hedge fund, owns The Lindens.

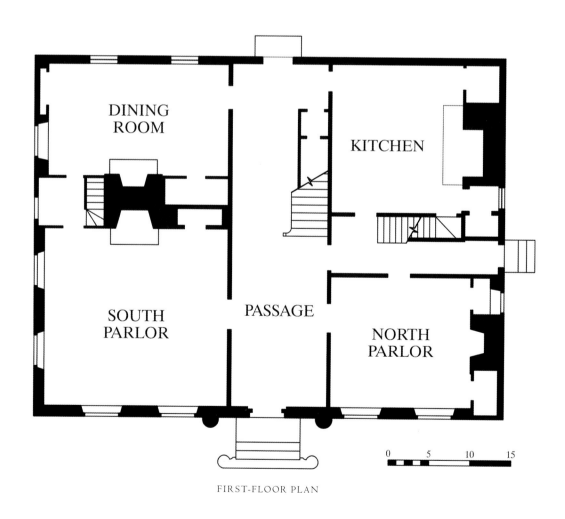

FIRST-FLOOR PLAN

GUNSTON HALL

10709 GUNSTON ROAD
MASON NECK, VIRGINIA

1755–59

Designers: George Mason and William Buckland
Restoration Architects: Glenn Brown and Bedford Brown; Fiske Kimball; Paul Buchanan
Status: Historic House Museum

LAND FACADE

RIVER ELEVATION WITH PORCH IN THE GOTHIC REVIVAL STYLE

GUNSTON HALL, BUILT IN THE MIDDLE OF the 18th century, is located in Mason Neck, Virginia, 20 miles south of Washington. The rather unassuming exterior belies the fact that it contains two of the most beautiful rooms of any colonial house in America. The landmark was the home of George Mason, father of the Virginia Declaration of Rights, forerunner of the Bill of Rights of the United States Constitution.

There were six consecutive generations of George Masons. Gunston Hall was built by George Mason IV (1725–1792), who named it for an ancestral house in Staffordshire, England. His great-grandfather, George Mason I, left England because of his support of Charles I during the English Civil War and settled in Virginia in 1652. At the age of 10, George Mason IV inherited a vast estate edging both the Virginia and Maryland sides of the Potomac River after his father drowned when his boat overturned while crossing the river. His mother, Ann Thomson Mason, skillfully managed the plantation until George Mason IV assumed adulthood in 1746.

George Mason IV (hereafter, George Mason) designed both the exterior and the floor plan of Gunston Hall. After the walls were started, Mason wrote to ask his brother Thomson, then studying law in London, to find someone to assist with the design of the interior detailing. As a result, William Buckland, an Oxford-born carpenter/joiner, was sent to Virginia as an indentured servant to finish the interior spaces. George Mason was like George Washington and many other Virginia planters who educated themselves in architecture through reading pattern books and often designed their own imposing mansions.

Right: CENTRAL PASSAGE LOOKING OUT TO THE BOXWOOD GARDEN AND THE RIVER

THE PALLADIAN DINING ROOM

The very unusual front porch of Gunston Hall opens to a wide passage that terminates at a door at the far end. This leads to an octagonal rear "Gothick" porch that faced a one-acre boxwood garden with the Potomac River in the distance. A deer park once stood between the garden and the river. The two rooms on the west side of the house, reserved for entertaining, feature elegant carvings in the Georgian style by William Buckland: the Chinese drawing room and the connecting Palladian dining room. The passage contains a staircase, 14 fluted pilasters around the walls, and a carved pinecone suspended from the ceiling. Both the passage and the Chinese drawing room are covered in varying handmade papers approximating the originals. The fireplace in the Palladian room features built-in niches or "beaufats" in the sides, with shelves to display silver and china. They are flanked by fluted pilasters and crowned with a broken pediment. Above the fireplace is an elaborate carved panel, a reproduction based on traces of the original. The walls are covered in red fabric.

On the east side of the passage lies the Masons' bedroom, where Mrs. Mason also conducted household business. Across the small corridor was George Mason's study, which also served as the family parlor and dining room. The second floor has seven bedrooms, which were used by the nine Mason children and the governess. A small service stair winds from the basement to the second floor. The second floor also held a "lumber room" or large storage closet. The spacious attic, accessed by a ladder, probably provided additional household storage space.

When George Mason died in 1792, his eldest son, George Mason V, who lived with his family at Lexington, the adjoining plantation, inherited Gunston Hall. In 1866, with the Virginia economy devastated by the Civil War, the Masons sold Gunston Hall and the remaining 1,000 acres for $15,000. From then

DINING ROOM MANTEL, ORIGINALLY CARVED BY WILLIAM BUCKLAND

Following Pages: THE CHINESE PARLOR

until the state of Virginia acquired the estate in 1950, there were four owners, two of whom were unkind to the architectural fabric of the house in removing a number of interior features.

Civil War Union veteran Col. Edward Daniels insensitively made a major change to the house shortly after the war by installing a 20-foot-tall wooden observatory tower in the center of the roof. The last private owner was Louis Hertle, who bought the estate in 1912. A retired executive with Marshall Field & Company of Chicago, Hertle came to Virginia to find a suitable country house. He selected Gunston Hall from among a dozen early estates he inspected near Charlottesville, Berryville, Fredericksburg, and along the James River. Hertle recognized the historic value of the house and in 1913 hired the Washington architectural firm of Glenn Brown and Bedford Brown IV to make plans and oversee the restoration. The unsightly observation tower and other appendages, as well as the gray exterior paint, were removed. The following year Hertle met and married Eleanor Daughaday of St. Louis, who shared his enthusiasm for the restoration.

The Hertles willed Gunston Hall to the state of Virginia to be administered by a Board of Regents appointed by the National Society of Colonial Dames of America. The organization commissioned architect Fiske Kimball to undertake an extensive redecoration in the early 1950s. A second, more thorough, study of the interior by architect Paul Buchanan led to additional changes. Reproductions of missing pilasters were installed in the passage, as well as reproductions of 18th-century wallpaper in the hall and the Chinese parlor. The Palladian dining room received wall coverings and a copy of the missing elaborately carved panel over the fireplace. Few rooms in colonial America could surpass the elegance of Gunston Hall's Chinese parlor and Palladian dining room.

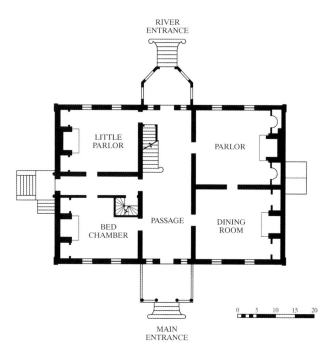

FIRST-FLOOR PLAN

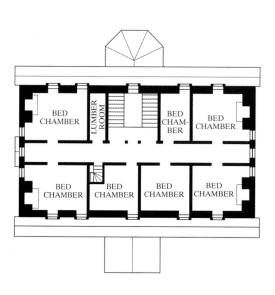

SECOND-FLOOR PLAN

HAYES MANOR

4000 JONES BRIDGE ROAD
CHEVY CHASE, MARYLAND

1767

Additions: East Wing, 1899. West Wing, 1908
Architect: Attributed to John Aris
Architect of wing additions: Walter Peter
Status: Vacant

ALL HEADER BRICK FACADE

DETAIL OF THE ELABORATE
18TH-CENTURY BRICK WORK

HAYES MANOR, LOCATED 2 MILES NORTH OF Chevy Chase Circle and just west of Connecticut Avenue, is today part of the main campus of the Howard Hughes Medical Institute in Chevy Chase, Maryland. The original driveway entrances at the front and rear of the house have pairs of high brick gateposts, in each of which is set a limestone panel inscribed "Hayes Manor, 1762." It is considered the finest surviving 18th-century Georgian house in Montgomery County. The house's builder, Anglican clergyman Alexander Williamson Jr. (1727–1786), purchased the original 700-acre tract in 1762 from John Yates when Yates subdivided his 1,400-acre plantation, named Clean Drinking Manor. Williamson built the house in 1767.

Williamson was the son and namesake of the Rev. Alexander Williamson, who emigrated from Kent, England, to Maryland, where he served as the Anglican rector for Calvert County from 1722 until his retirement in 1761. The father made a fortune as the owner of a tobacco plantation, resulting in each of his children receiving a considerable inheritance. The elder Williamson sent his son to England to study for the Anglican ministry. Soon after his ordination in 1755 he returned to Maryland, where he served briefly at St. Anne's Church in Annapolis before becoming rector of St. Paul's Parish in 1761, in what was Frederick County, Maryland. St. Paul's parish became part of Montgomery County when the county was separated from Frederick County in 1776.

Williamson chose not to live in the modest wooden rector's cottage that stood next to the wooden church and 100-acre glebe, or farm, intended to support the rector. The church and the glebe, now known as Rock Creek Cemetery, became part of the District of Columbia in 1790, when D.C. was created. Instead, he preferred to reside on his own plantation, where he constructed a grand brick residence with his own funds. He named it Hayes, after the country house of William Pitt the Younger, 2nd Earl of Chatham. Williamson greatly admired Pitt, who championed the rights of the American colonists in the British Parliament during the critical period prior to the American Revolution. Williamson became a leading figure in Montgomery County society and was called the "sporting parson" for his love of fox hunting and cockfights.

When the Revolutionary War began in 1775, Rev. Williamson resigned his position at St. Paul's Church and retired to Hayes. Although loyal to the crown, his popular public persona saved him harassment by the Revolutionaries.

Familiar with the latest architectural designs from firsthand observations in England, Williamson built a sophisticated Georgian house and had the good fortune to engage a top-flight brickmason. The original two-story, brick-gabled house, 36 feet by 45 feet, sits on a hill facing south on a gentle slope. Both front and rear elevations have five bays. Plaster quoins, painted white to resemble stone, frame the two central doors on the rear elevation. Vertical brick was used for splayed lintels over the nine-over-nine sash windows. Another refined detail is the raised brick belt course that separates the first and second floors. Molded brick was used on the water table of the facade. The water table on the north elevation is of a simpler, straight design. The principal south and north elevations are

RECEPTION HALL AND MAIN STAIRCASE

laid in all header brick, while the sides of the house consist of common bond with headers every fourth course. The windows have original interior shutters that fold into the walls. Both sides of the house originally had a door to more easily reach the various outbuildings: kitchen, smoke house, slave quarters, stable, and carriage house. The house has a full basement with light wells provided for the basement windows, as well as a large attic lighted by side windows.

The first-floor plan consists of four rooms: a stair hall and a small library in the front and a large dining room and parlor at the rear. A detached kitchen located to the west of the house originally served as the dining room. The second floor contains two large and two small bedrooms, the main stair hall, and a small stair to the attic. All eight rooms in the house have fireplaces with mantelpieces—those in the dining and drawing rooms are the most elaborate.

In 1787, a year after Williamson died, James Dunlop Sr., a good friend of the rector, purchased the furniture from Hayes and then, in 1792, bought the house and the entire 700 acres that comprised the plantation. Dunlop had emigrated to New York City from his native Scotland in 1771 at the age of 16. He moved to Georgetown in 1783 and amassed a fortune as a tobacco merchant. Dunlop was a cousin of Robert Peter, the mayor of Georgetown from 1790–91, who had emigrated earlier from Garnkirk, near Glasgow, the same village as Dunlop. In 1797 James Dunlop Sr. married Robert Peter's eldest daughter, Elizabeth, and for their wedding, Peter gave the couple a new house he had built on High Street in Georgetown (1239 Wisconsin Avenue, now the site of the Aged Women's Home). James and Elizabeth Dunlop and their family used Hayes as their summer home until James's death in 1822.

STAIRCASE DETAIL

Hayes remained a residence to the Dunlop family for six generations. The plantation was divided when Elizabeth Peter Dunlop died in 1837. Her son, Robert Peter Dunlop, who was a partner in Francis Scott Key's Georgetown law firm, purchased the house, along with 350 acres. The remaining 350 acres were sold outside the family. The house continued in the Dunlop family until sold by the last descendant, Alexander McCook Dunlop, in 1961. The name was changed from Hayes to Hayes Manor in the early-20th century to better define that it was a house.

Several architectural changes took place at Hayes Manor at the hands of its various owners. About 1830 a raised Greek Revival porch supported by two sets of paired Ionic columns was installed in front of the main entrance. The porch was removed in 1975 and replaced with the current circular steps. The present east wing, built in 1899, consists of a kitchen and

pantry on the first floor and two bedrooms and a bath above. It was therefore logical to reverse the uses of the two principal rooms on the first floor, moving the old dining room to the east, next to the new kitchen in the east wing. At the same time the original staircase was rebuilt. Four steps and a lower landing were added to make it less steep. The rebuilt, now three-part staircase is more graceful and easier to ascend. This skillful remodel retained the original newel post, balusters, and rail pattern. Walter Peter, a cousin of the Dunlops who had just finished architecture school, designed these changes. Peter's further work, in 1908, included a west wing addition of a sunroom with three sets of French doors. The two new wings were built solely with header brick to match the main house. Peter carefully removed the wall separating the breakfast room and the stair hall, and replaced it with a pair of Ionic columns, greatly enlarging and enhancing the space. Also in 1908, Peter extended the east wing by adding a greenhouse and a garage. With the new wings, the total length of the house is nearly 150 feet.

Since the property left the Dunlop family in 1961, ownership of Hayes Manor has changed several times. The owners following the Dunlops in 1965 were George D. Iverson V, a businessman who worked in the Washington office of Hughes Helicopter Corporation, and his wife Ellen Iverson. After they divorced, Ellen Iverson sold Hayes Manor to the adjacent Columbia Country Club in 1991. The current owner is the Howard Hughes Medical Institute (HHMI), which purchased the house and remaining 9½ acres in 2002 for $4.7 million. The institute bought Hayes Manor for the attached acreage, which was used to build low-rise office buildings. HHMI never wanted the house itself and it has remained empty since the purchase.

Originally located in Miami, Florida, the institute relocated to Chevy Chase, Maryland, in 1986, and then moved to its present location shortly after it acquired Hayes Manor. By purchasing two connecting land parcels, the campus has since been enlarged to approximately 50 acres. Featuring low-scale brick and stone buildings and attractive landscaping, the new campus blends well with the surrounding residential community. This campus houses the institute's administration and space for conferences.

American business magnate Howard R. Hughes Jr. (1905–1976) founded the Howard Hughes Medical Institute in 1953 to undertake original biological and medical research. The institute benefited from the founder's gift of the Hughes Aircraft Corporation, which it sold to General Motors in 1985 for $7.9 billion. This endowment has grown to more than $16 billion, making it the second wealthiest philanthropic organization in the United States. The institute today gives five-year research grants to 330 scientists, totaling about $825 million annually for biomedical research. The researchers enjoy autonomy in their work at some 70 universities and institutions across the nation.

In 2006 the Howard Hughes Medical Institute enlarged its permanent quarters by erecting the Janelia Farm Research Campus, a new facility on 281 acres in Ashburn, Virginia. In addition to a large laboratory building, it provides apartments for visiting researchers.

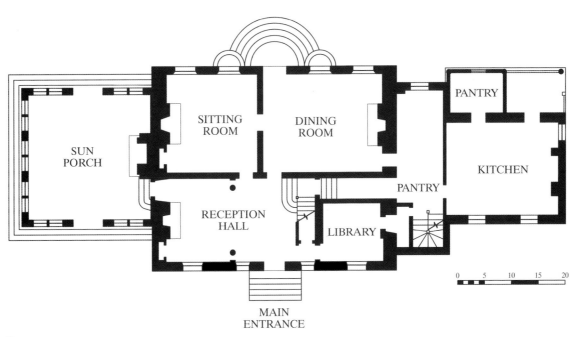

N

FIRST-FLOOR PLAN

FEDERAL HOUSES

Rosedale

White House

The Octagon

Dumbarton House

Evermay

Tudor Place

Woodley

Caldwell House

Riversdale

Blair House

ROSEDALE

3501 NEWARK STREET, N.W.
WASHINGTON, D.C.

MAIN HOUSE   1793
REAR STONE WINGS   1730; 1740

Designer: General Uriah Forrest
Neighborhood: Cleveland Park
Status: Private Residence

THE OLDEST SURVIVING FARMHOUSE IN WASHINGTON

IT IS ALMOST A MIRACLE THAT ROSEDALE, a late-18th-century clapboard farmhouse, has survived intact after two centuries of increasingly dense development around it. Built by General Uriah Forrest (1746–1805) and his wife, Rebecca Plater—natives of St. Mary's County, in tidewater Maryland, who became friends in childhood—this landmark originally sat on a 1,000-acre tract comprising most of today's Cleveland Park neighborhood. Forrest was the son of a successful, middling planter. Rebecca was raised in the much grander setting of Sotterly, a large tobacco plantation established in 1703 and owned by her father, George Plater III, the sixth governor of Maryland. Sotterly remained in the possession of the Plater family for many generations before it was sold in 1826.

Forrest served with distinction during the Revolutionary War as an officer in Maryland's famous Flying Camp, a special unit that served directly under the command of General George Washington. He fought in the battles of Brandywine and Germantown in 1777. In the latter engagement, a large British musket ball severely fractured his leg, which subsequently required amputation.

Following his discharge from the Continental Army, Forrest joined Benjamin Stoddert to form the merchant firm of Forrest-Stoddert Company in 1783. They maintained offices in both London and Georgetown, then part of Maryland. Both men became very successful, shipping tobacco to London in their own fleet. With a fortune made in trade, Forrest received permission from the widow of George Plater to marry her daughter, Rebecca, in 1789. After their wedding at Sotterly, Rebecca remained at her family's plantation until Forrest built their new house in Georgetown, now known as the Forrest-Marbury House, near the corner of present-day M and 34th Streets. Rebecca joined her husband there with their first child, Elizabeth, in 1791.

Forrest became politically active, serving as mayor of Georgetown and in the U.S. House of Representatives from Maryland in 1793. During the 1790s the laws of Maryland and Virginia remained in force in their respective parts of the District of Columbia until the national capital relocated there from Philadelphia in 1800. In 1792 President George Washington and the commissioners of the District of Columbia dined

FRONT STAIRCASE

with the Forrest family at their Georgetown house to finalize plans for the acquisition of federal land from the original proprietors of the new Federal City.

Georgetown boomed due to increased shipping after the Revolutionary War and construction of new government buildings in the adjacent Federal City. Many wives of successful businessmen in Georgetown moved elsewhere to avoid the noise and the crowded and unsanitary conditions. Mrs. Benjamin Stoddert, wife of Forrest's business partner, left their house on Prospect Street to reside in Philadelphia with her children. Rebecca Forrest fled Georgetown in the summer of 1792 for a stone cottage 2 miles north, near the Frederick Town road (now Wisconsin Avenue). The original, crudely built stone cottage, which dates around 1730, according to recent archaeological research, had a later, more refined 1740 stone addition. It was located in the northwest corner of a 1,000-acre tract of land that Uriah Forrest, Benjamin

Stoddert, and William Deakins Jr., had purchased not long before from the Beall family as an investment. The purchase came from a much larger land grant that planter Ninian Beall had bought in Prince George's County in 1703. The Beall family also sold smaller parcels in the 1790s for the sites of large houses on the heights of Georgetown, including Dumbarton Oaks, Tudor Place, Dumbarton House, Evermay, and Mackall Square.

After living in the cottage for a year, Uriah and Rebecca Forrest decided to make the bucolic retreat their permanent home. They erected a large, two-story wooden house in front of the stone cottage in 1793–94. The new house displayed the symmetry typical of Federal houses of the period, with six bays and matching chimneys at each end. The Forrests also added a large, gabled, clapboard wing at the rear. In the early-19th century, they built an addition that connects the stone cottage to the main house. The front of the house has a passage separating a parlor and dining room. In the rear wing, two bedrooms flanked the central hall on each side. On the second floor, there were two large bedrooms in the front, and four small bedrooms in the rear. Once the new wooden house was built the stone cottage in the rear was used as the kitchen and living quarters for the servants. Rosedale was a working farm with a dozen outbuildings, including a barn for livestock, a dairy, granary, corn house, poultry house, smokehouse, stable, carriage house, and a cottage for workmen. While these structures have disappeared over time, part of the impressive stone wall for the front terraced garden remains.

The design of Rosedale was probably influenced by Rebecca Forrest's childhood home, Sotterly, which is located near present-day Hollywood, Maryland. Sotterly, a two-story clapboard house with dormer windows, was begun in 1711 and added to by generations of the Plater family. Now a historic house museum, Sotterly is the best-preserved 18th-century plantation in Maryland, with six surviving outbuildings, including a schoolhouse, gatehouse, privy, tobacco barn, tobacco inspection station, and a slave cabin.

REAR STONE WING INTERIOR

In 1793 Uriah Forrest became sole owner of the Rosedale estate when he bought out, by mutual consent, the interests of Col. Benjamin Stoddert and William Deakins Jr. He thus became one of the largest landowners in the area; he was also a partial owner of the Bank of Columbia and the Georgetown Bridge Company. His reputation grew when he was appointed brigadier general in the local militia. In addition to advising President Washington on the founding of the Federal City, Forrest became a friend of President John Adams and gave a dinner party in his honor at Rosedale in June 1800.

The financial empire carefully built by Uriah Forrest over a 15-year period crumbled with the depression of 1797, perpetuated by the disruption to trade during the Napoleonic wars and the collapse of land values in Washington. The crash also ruined many of Forrest's friends: Benjamin Stoddert, Thomas Law, Thomas Addison, and Thomas Sims Lee. In 1802, as conditions worsened, Forrest mortgaged both the Rosedale estate and its furnishings to his brother-in-law, Philip Barton Key, a prominent attorney, of nearby Woodley Oaks. Fortunately, he was able to survive on the income from his position as first clerk of the U.S. Circuit Court of the District of Columbia. After Forrest's sudden death in 1805 in the parlor at Rosedale, his wife stayed on and managed the farm. Rebecca Forrest's financial situation improved when Key died in 1815 and forgave the mortgage in his will. She then rented Rosedale to tenants and moved to a row house in Georgetown at 30th and P Streets. Her income was boosted in 1838 when Congress passed the first Pension Act for Widows of War Veterans, which provided her an annual allowance of $600, then a substantial sum. When Rebecca Forrest died in 1843, Rosedale became the property of her daughter, Ann Forrest Green. Ann gave her son, George Green, 23 acres just south of Rosedale, where

VIEW FROM THE GARDEN

he built a two-story stone summerhouse about 1865; President Grover Cleveland purchased it in 1886 for his seasonal use. After Cleveland remodeled and enlarged the house, it became known as Red Top for the red tiles on its roof. It was razed by developers in 1926. The Cleveland Park neighborhood derives its name from the president's onetime house there.

After the streetcar line was extended north on Connecticut Avenue in 1892 by the Chevy Chase Land Company, the Forrest-Green heirs sold off most of the remaining acres of the Rosedale estate, and developers laid out streets in Cleveland Park. The first of many charming Queen Anne houses, mostly designed by local architects, appeared on Newark Street, Highland Place, 34th Street, and 34th Place. The Forrest-Green heirs finally rented the neglected landmark, damaged as a result of deferred maintenance, in 1917 to Mr. and Mrs. Avery Coonley. The Coonleys moved from their enormous Frank Lloyd Wright—designed house in the Chicago suburb of Riverside to

Rosedale and installed plumbing and lighting, replaced the roof, and landscaped the remaining 8½-acre grounds. Avery Coonley added a wooden guesthouse, tennis courts, greenhouse, and a gazebo, and improved the stable, which he used for early morning horseback rides in adjacent Rock Creek Park. After Coonley's death in 1920, his widow, Queene Coonley, purchased Rosedale for $80,000. Her daughter married a promising young Washington architect, Waldron Faulkner, at the house in 1921. Some 16 years later, Faulkner built his own distinctive Art Deco house nearby. The Faulkners inherited Rosedale when Queene Coonley died.

Rosedale changed hands again in 1959 when the Faulkners sold the house and land, now 6½ acres, to the Washington National Cathedral for the campus of their school for girls. The neighbors, fearful that the original Rosedale farmhouse might be torn down, formed the Cathedral Rosedale Neighborhood Committee. The Washington Cathedral agreed not to raze the landmark, and the neighbors, in return, agreed not to block the zoning variance needed by the school. The Cathedral School promptly commissioned Faulkner to design three three-story dormitories for boarders, which were located behind and to the sides of Rosedale and connected by glass corridors. By 1977 the school decided to stop accepting boarders and put the property up for sale. When the Bulgarian Socialist Republic attempted to buy it for their embassy and consulate, neighbors organized and blocked the sale.

A happy solution came about in 1979 when an international student exchange organization, Youth for Understanding (YFU), bought Rosedale. Cleveland Park neighbors persuaded the organization to sign a covenant to ensure continued public access to Rosedale's 3-acre front lawn and a provision that if it were sold, the neighbors would have the right during a 90-day period to match the buyer's bid. In 2000 the financially strapped YFU put the property up for sale. The Jewish Primary Day School, with 200 pupils, placed the highest bid on the property, at $12 million. Once again Cleveland Park neighbors rallied and, after much hard work, matched the offer and bought it.

Per the final agreement, the three dormitories and the parking lot were demolished. The major investors in the purchase arrangement, two neighborhood residents Jonathan Abram and his wife, Eleni Constantine, took ownership of the original Rosedale house. They agreed to a two-year restoration of Rosedale, sensitively carried out by architect Stephen Muse. The original 3-acre front lawn was permanently secured as an open park, deeded to the Rosedale Conservancy, and given tax-free status by the D.C. government. To recover the funds invested, the remaining 3 acres were sold to developers, who built five houses, designed in traditional styles, to the side and rear of Rosedale. The old guesthouse built by Avery Coonley was restored and sold as a private residence. Since the Coonley's tennis court had long since disappeared, a tennis court was built at the rear of the old house to be used jointly by all the residents of the new houses on the former Rosedale land. In the end the many problems facing Rosedale were happily resolved.

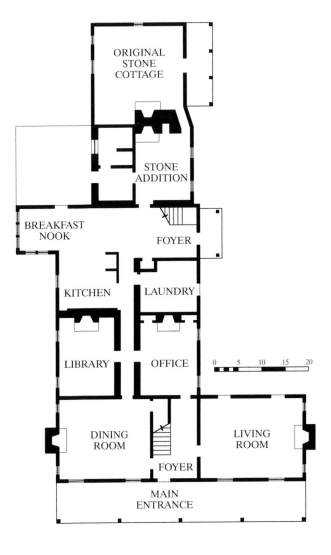

FIRST-FLOOR PLAN

WHITE HOUSE

1600 PENNSYLVANIA AVENUE, N.W.
WASHINGTON, D.C.

1792–1800; 1805–08
REBUILT 1815–18
RENOVATIONS 1902; 1927; 1934; 1947
REBUILT 1948–52

Architect: James Hoban, 1792, and rebuilding 1815–18; Benjamin Henry Latrobe, 1805–08

Renovation: Charles F. McKim, 1902. Renovation: Maj. M.C. Mehaffey, 1927

Renovation: Lorenzo S. Winslow, 1934 and 1937

South Portico balcony: William A. Delano & Lorenzo S. Winslow, 1947

Renovation: Lorenzo S. Winslow, 1948–52

Neighborhood: Lafayette Park

Status: Residence of the President of the United States

NORTH PORTICO, ADDED 1829

SOUTH PORTICO

T HE WHITE HOUSE IS THE BEST-KNOWN residence in the United States and one of the first houses built in Washington City. Its long history includes a series of renovations—undertaken during the administrations of seven presidents: James Madison, James Monroe, Andrew Jackson, Theodore Roosevelt, Calvin Coolidge, Franklin D. Roosevelt, and Harry S. Truman—that have transformed its exterior and interior appearance.

In July 1790, after much debate, Congress passed the Residence Act, which authorized the permanent capital of the United States to be built on the Potomac River. Eight months later, President Washington recommended and Secretary of State Thomas Jefferson appointed Peter Charles L'Enfant to lay out the Federal City and design its government buildings. The Frenchman had strengthened his reputation as an architect and designer when he remodeled Federal Hall in New York City for the first United States Congress. For the new Federal City L'Enfant worked for 11 months to design the street plan and locate sites for the government buildings. He selected the site for the President's House about a mile west of the Capitol, near the present intersection of 14th and F Streets, N.W. L'Enfant envisioned an enormous building, five times the size of what was actually constructed in 1792–1800. On one of President Washington's first trips to the new capital he inspected L'Enfant's site

GATEPOSTS ALONG PENNSYLVANIA AVENUE

for the President's House and had the location changed to higher ground two blocks to the west, where construction soon started.

While L'Enfant was doing the work, he consistently failed to report to the three commissioners appointed to govern the District of Columbia—he reported only to the president. When the commissioners faulted him, L'Enfant quit the job and returned to Philadelphia in February 1792. Although he had laid out the city's streets and parks, he had not designed the government buildings, with the possible exception of a schematic for the President's House.

With L'Enfant no longer on board, President Washington consulted his cabinet and asked Thomas Jefferson to solicit architectural designs in the leading American newspapers. Designs for both the President's House and the Capitol were to be submitted to the commissioners by July 15, 1792. Washington met with them in the Federal City on July 16, and selected James Hoban's design for the President's House from the nine submitted. Hoban was an Irish-born architect who had worked in Dublin, in Philadelphia briefly in 1787, and moved in 1789 to Charleston, South Carolina. President Washington

STONE CARVINGS AT THE NORTH ENTRANCE

had met Hoban in Charleston in May 1791 while on a tour of the Southern states and had liked a neoclassical public building Hoban had built there.

Hoban's schematic, which derives from the design of the Duke of Leinster's neoclassical house in Dublin, shows a rectangular stone building with the main entrance on the north side. His original plan of three stories and a basement was reduced by one story. Even so, Washington had Hoban make two minor changes: enlarging the house by one-fifth both in length and width, and adding carved stone embellishments all around. The architect arranged for two lodges of skilled stonemasons to travel from Scotland to work exclusively on the President's House. Hoban supervised the construction over the eight years it took to complete the residence, and he rebuilt it after it burned in the War of 1812.

Both the President's House and the Capitol were first occupied in November 1800, when the federal government with its 130 employees moved from Philadelphia to Washington. President John Adams and his wife, Abigail, occupied the President's House for only four months near the end of his term of office. They could not wait to return to their residence in Quincy, Massachusetts, because of the unfinished condition of the President's House, including wet plaster, missing staircases, lack of service rooms, and lack of household staff.

Hoban's first-floor plan, which basically remains in place today, consists of a large north square entrance hall that opens through a screen of columns into a long transverse corridor. At one end is the East Room, while a grand staircase, state dining room, and family dining room lie at the west end. On the south side between the East Room and the state dining room extend three parlors. The center one, the Blue Room, is oval-shaped and projects out toward the south garden.

Thomas Jefferson, who succeeded John Adams, designed low wings for the east and west ends of the house to accommodate service areas, and had architect Benjamin H. Latrobe build them (1805 and 1808). The wings discreetly housed the many functions essential to such a house, including a laundry, dairy, smokehouse, stable, root cellar, and accommodations for household staff. Today both wings are still in use. The east wing contains offices and a movie theater; the west wing houses the press room.

Following public indignation over British seizure of American ships on the high seas and subsequent mistreatment of American sailors, President James Madison asked Congress to declare war in June 1812. Having recently defeated Napoleon, the British were able to send 4,000 experienced troops to attack the United States. They reached the Chesapeake Bay, sailed up the Patuxent River, then marched overland, and handily overcame the poorly trained American militia and their inexperienced officers on August 24, 1814, at the Battle of Bladensburg, Maryland, 7 miles from the city. Dolley Madison fled the President's House after having arranged for a supper to be laid for her husband and his cabinet. The unopposed British army reached Capitol Hill by early evening. The British commander, Major General John Ross, at the urging of his cohort, Rear Admiral George Cockburn, burned the two wings of the Capitol (the rotunda and dome had not yet been built). The British troops then marched to the President's House, where the officers enjoyed the waiting banquet and wine before burning the landmark. The following day they returned and burned the executive office buildings next to the President's House, sparing only the Patent Office at 8th and F Streets, N.W.

After the British left the city, the Madisons moved to the nearby Octagon, and Congress voted to borrow the funds to rebuild the destroyed buildings.

The president nominated new commissioners of the District of Columbia, who immediately hired James Hoban to supervise rebuilding the President's House in March 1815. Hoban ultimately found that about 40 percent of the standing stone walls could be stabilized and kept. The new president, James Monroe, then living in Caldwell House at 2017 I Street, N.W., urged Hoban to finish the rebuilding so that he and Mrs. Monroe could hold their New Year's Day reception there in January 1818. To accelerate the process Hoban substituted wooden interior supporting walls for brick walls, a factor that made the interior walls less durable and necessitated their reconstruction 130 years later. In the summer of 1817 more than 190 men, including 60 hired slaves, worked to finish the building. The outer walls were painted for the first time with lead-based white paint; since its completion in 1800, the building had been whitewashed periodically to protect the very porous Aquia sandstone. By Monroe's administration, the President's House was popularly known as the White House. It was not until President Theodore Roosevelt's administration, however, that the name White House became official, and its formal use began on stationery and state documents.

Before leaving office, Madison directed Hoban to prepare drawings for north and south portico additions; Latrobe's designs may have inspired Hoban in this task. The Panic of 1819, the young country's first major peacetime financial crisis, forced delay of the porticoes' construction. Finally, during James Monroe's administration, in 1824, Hoban built the South Portico from his design. Monroe also made changes to the north lawn: He had an iron fence installed on the circular north driveway, flanked by two pairs of tall stone gateposts with iron gates. Feeling the grounds of the President's House were too large, Monroe also had Pennsylvania Avenue cut through the north lawn in 1824. This produced land for the public park named in 1825 after the Marquis de Lafayette's visit to Washington.

Right: THE OVAL BLUE ROOM

When President Andrew Jackson took office, he had Monroe's stone gateposts moved closer to Pennsylvania Avenue. Today they are crowned with iron replicas of the flamboyant gas lamps originally added in 1854. The larger North Portico was finally built at the beginning of President Andrew Jackson's administration, in 1829–30. Hoban died in 1831, well liked and respected, much more so than either Latrobe or L'Enfant. By 1830 the exterior of the White House had been completed as we know it today.

The next White House alteration took place in 1902, when architect Charles F. McKim was given charge of a major renovation. He modernized the interior by replacing all the Victorian elements with elegant Beaux-Arts detailing. McKim enlarged the state dining room on the west end by moving the grand staircase to the east end, added rooms in the attic, and turned the eastern half of the basement into bright, spacious public rooms and offices. The dark and dismal oval furnace room became the elegant Diplomatic Reception Room, and the term *basement* was changed to *ground floor.* McKim reconstructed Jefferson's east wing and added to it a reception room that served as the main public entrance. By removing the large Victorian greenhouse on the west, he was able to relocate Theodore Roosevelt's office staff from the second story of the White House into the new one-story West Wing. During the six-month project, the Roosevelts moved between their Oyster Bay, New York, house and a row house on Jackson Place, on the west side of Lafayette Park. The public raved over the transformation of the once-dreary Victorian spaces into elegant Beaux-Arts public rooms.

During the administration of Calvin Coolidge, in 1927, another White House renovation took place. Coolidge and his wife, Grace, stayed in rented quarters in the Patterson House at 15 Dupont Circle from March to September 1927, while the attic and roof of the White House were replaced. The attic became a full third floor, with a steep pitched roof and steel reinforcing. The space was doubled, providing 14 major new rooms, including guest bedrooms, the housekeeper's bedroom, five household staff bedrooms, and numerous storage rooms.

Shortly after President Franklin D. Roosevelt moved into the White House, he requested construction of a swimming pool, a facility he had consistently used for exercise since he had contracted polio. He had benefited from a pool in his home in Hyde Park as well as the naturally heated pool in his vacation retreat in Warm Springs, Georgia. In March 1933 a number of New York newspapers began a campaign to raise funds for an indoor swimming pool in the White House. Government architects Lorenzo S. Winslow and Maj. D.H. Gillette were commissioned to design the pool, which opened, to Roosevelt's delight, on June 2, 1933. The following year, FDR, an amateur architect, drew the basic floor plans for a new and much larger West Wing, which Winslow implemented. Roosevelt wanted a second story, but the Commission of Fine Arts would not approve it. Nonetheless, Roosevelt ordered the modified project to go forward: Construction began in August 1934 and concluded in December. The new presidential offices even included an oval office, a near duplicate of the one President Taft originally built in 1909 for his one-story west wing.

One of the most controversial renovations took place in late 1947 and early 1948, when President Harry Truman had architects Winslow and William A. Delano design and install a new second-floor balcony on the South Portico. Truman disliked the unsightly canvas awnings and wanted more living space for his family. One of the original windows was lengthened into a door, but otherwise the facade was preserved. Even though the Commission of Fine Arts disapproved and journalists enjoyed attacking Truman for "ruining" the White House, within a few years the public forgot the controversy and the balcony seemed like it had always been part of the original plan.

Left: DETAIL OF STATE DINING ROOM,
WITH 1902 ALTERATIONS BY CHARLES F. MCKIM

RENOVATION DURING THE TRUMAN ADMINISTRATION

Another sweeping makeover took place under President Truman between 1948 and 1952. In late 1947 the Trumans became alarmed over severe vibrations they felt in the second-floor family quarters. A team of structural engineers made a thorough study, and in 1948 recommended a complete rebuilding of the interior using structural steel. Congress appropriated $5.4 million for the project. The Trumans lived in Blair House across Pennsylvania Avenue during the renovation. McKim's original floor plans created in 1902 were retained, with the exception, made at the president's request, of redesigning the grand staircase at the east end of the transverse hall, to allow more graceful descents to visiting heads of state. During the renovation the outer walls were carefully preserved, and extra service space was acquired by adding two new subbasements. The Philadelphia firm of John McShain managed the construction, which began in December 1949 and was completed in March 1952. This major renovation increased the total number of White House rooms from 68 to 134. The steel framing should preserve the stability of the White House for the next century. Strangely, there was little public criticism when the White House was gutted in this last project, compared to the uproar over construction of the South Portico balcony.

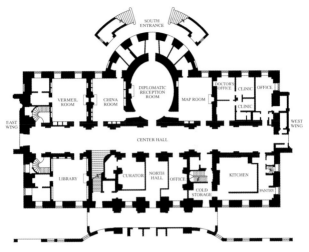

GROUND-FLOOR PLAN

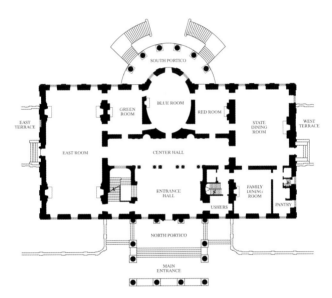

STATE-FLOOR PLAN

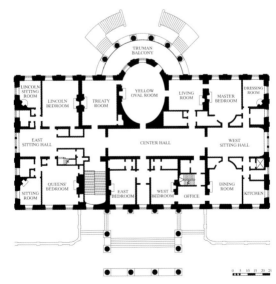

SECOND-FLOOR PLAN

THE OCTAGON

1799 NEW YORK AVENUE, N.W.
WASHINGTON, D.C.

1799–1801

Architect: William Thornton
Neighborhood: Foggy Bottom
Status: Historic House Museum and Offices

ENTRANCE FACADE

B OTH AN UNUSUAL DESIGN AND RICH HISTORY make The Octagon one of the most important houses in the city. Dr. William Thornton designed it in 1799 as the winter town house in the new city of Washington for Col. John Tayloe III (1770–1828), a wealthy tobacco planter and breeder of racehorses in Richmond County, Virginia, whom George Washington had convinced to build a house to encourage development in the nation's capital. For himself, Washington commissioned Thornton to build a double house for rental property near the Capitol on North Capital Street between B (now Constitution Avenue) and C Streets, N.W.

John and Anne Tayloe lived most of the year at Mount Airy, their imposing Tidewater plantation house. While John Tayloe's grandfather, John Tayloe I, established the plantation in 1682, his father, John Tayloe II (1721–1779), built a grand Georgian house at Mount Airy between 1748 and 1758. The five-part stone mansion was considered one of the finest residences in Virginia in the 18th century. It, too, incorporated innovative design, being the first mansion in Virginia to have a completely open central hall with the staircase placed to the side and curved corridors connecting the two-story wings to the central block. John Tayloe II also built a two-story wooden house in Williamsburg to use while attending the King's Council, the upper chamber of the Virginia Colonial General Assembly. John Tayloe III was educated at Eton and Cambridge and, on his return to Virginia, married Ann Ogle, a daughter of the governor of Maryland.

The young couple moved into the newly completed Octagon in the spring of 1802. The Octagon was spacious enough to accommodate their brood— eventually numbering 15—as well as a tutor and a staff of servants and slaves, a few of whom lived in the main house. The estate also included an icehouse, a two-story stable, a cow shed, a two-story laundry, and a smokehouse. A large, handsome brick stable, dating from 1801 and then still in good condition, was demolished in 1968 to make way for the new headquarters of the American Institute of Architects.

GHENT TREATY TABLE

Thornton designed the V-shaped house with a round foyer and two large rooms on the first floor— the dining room faces 18th Street to the left, and the drawing room faces New York Avenue on the right. The front entrance with its raised Ionic porch faces the apex of 18th Street and New York Avenue. The circular foyer's floor is laid in gray-and-white squares of marble, set diagonally. The six-panel original front door curves outward in a gentle swell to follow the entry hall's contour. Other doors in the foyer are shaped to continue the curved walls as well. A pair of large niches set in the foyer walls hold the original neoclassical cast-iron stoves still crowned with stately neoclassical urns.

The house retains its original stone steps, wrought-iron balustrades, and pair of lampposts. Each of the major first-floor rooms has a fireplace at its north end decorated with an English Coade stone mantel and surround. The designs are neoclassical and feature swags, urns, and classical figures in flowing robes. Other similar but less decorative Coade stone mantels are found on the second and third

THE NEOCLASSICAL DINING ROOM COADE STONE MANTEL

floors. Coade stone mantels were cast in fine-grained, off-white terra-cotta in a factory at Lambeth, England, owned by Eleanor Coade and her daughter. The factory operated from 1772 to 1836.

Directly beyond the circular foyer, a large staircase sweeps up three floors, lighted by a central chandelier. The stair hall opens into the drawing room and dining room. To the left of the main staircase hall is a triangular room with doors to the service stairs.

In a sidelight to the aftermath of the War of 1812, on August 24, 1814, following the American defeat at the Battle of Bladensburg, British troops marched into Washington and burned government buildings, including the White House. The British did little damage to personal property, but to guarantee that

The Octagon would be spared, Mrs. Tayloe had the French minister occupy the house while she and her family fled to Virginia.

Soon afterward, President and Mrs. Madison accepted the Tayloes' offer of The Octagon as their temporary quarters; they lived there from September 1814 to March 1817, when Madison's term ended. Madison had his office in Tayloe's study, the circular room on the second floor above the foyer. After American and British diplomats signed the Treaty of Ghent in the Netherlands on December 24, 1814, it was sent to the U.S. Senate, where it was approved on February 16, 1815. The following day, President Madison signed the treaty, with a British diplomat in attendance, in his interim office in The Octagon,

Left: DETAIL OF THE FRONT PORCH

Following Pages: ONE OF TWO ORIGINAL
1801 IRON STOVES IN THE FOYER

officially ending the war. Following the Madisons' departure in the spring of 1817, the Tayloes returned to The Octagon, and members of this large and amicable family used it as a year-round residence for the next 37 years. The last family occupant was Anne Ogle Tayloe, who died in 1855 at the age of 83.

The Tayloe family rented the house in 1860 for a girls' school. After the Civil War it was rented for various offices and housed indigent families. A major change took place in 1899, when secretary of the American Institute of Architects, Glenn Brown, leased The Octagon and moved the institute's national

headquarters there from New York City. A few years later the A.I.A. bought the landmark and began restoration. It was a pioneering example of marshaling adaptive use to historic preservation. In the 1970s the first floor and the second-floor treaty room were furnished with period pieces, and architectural exhibitions were held in rooms on the second and third floors. The house was then transferred to the American Institute of Architects Foundation. Although the dining room and drawing room are no longer furnished as period rooms, The Octagon is open for tours several hours each week.

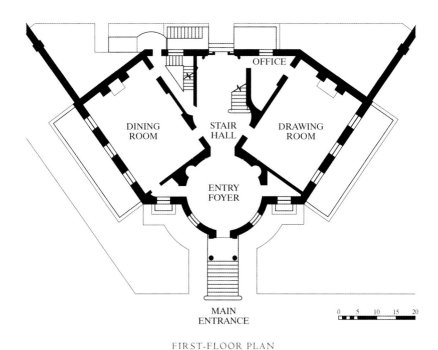

FIRST-FLOOR PLAN

SECOND-FLOOR PLAN

DUMBARTON HOUSE

2715 Q STREET, N.W.
WASHINGTON, D.C.

1798–99
Architect: Unknown
Restoration Architect: Fiske Kimball and Horace W. Peaslee, 1932
Neighborhood: Georgetown
Status: Historic House Museum

MAIN FACADE

DINING ROOM WITH 1789 PORTRAIT OF THE STODDARD CHILDREN

WASHINGTON, D.C., HAS TWO GREAT FEDERAL houses that were constructed in 1799: The Octagon in Foggy Bottom and Dumbarton House on Georgetown Heights. A defining feature of the Federal style is the use of geometrically shaped rooms. Dumbarton House was designed and built with a pair of prominent symmetrical bays on the rear elevation. The large windows of these bow-shaped rooms provide abundant light and garden views.

The facade is embellished with a stone belt course that separates the first and second floors, and a stone coping surrounds the building on the water table above the basement level. A fanlight, side lights, and Ionic pilasters frame the paneled entrance-door. The floor-length second-story windows have shallow iron balcony railings similar to those found at The Octagon. Fiske Kimball added these railings when it was discovered that these projections had originally been balconets.

The first floor plan has a traditional passage with the staircase on the left and a rear door opening onto the garden. To the left of the passage are a parlor in

PARLOR

the front and the dining room in the rear. To the right of the passage are the breakfast room in the front and the "best chamber" or master bedroom in the rear. Two-story wings flank the center block. The spaces in the two wings have been altered from their original use: Today the west wing is used for administrative offices, while the east wing houses an elevator and visitor center, with offices above.

After Peter Charles L'Enfant laid out the city of Washington in 1791, speculators vied for choice building lots, including those on the heights above Georgetown, then a separate city within the District of Columbia. The port of Georgetown had been in operation since 1747, established largely for shipping tobacco to Scotland and England. Investors quickly bought and sold land beginning in the mid-1790s on the blocks north of Back Street (now Q Street).

Most of this land belonged to the Beall family, as part of the 795-acre land grant made to immigrant Col. Ninian Beall by Lord Baltimore. Beall named the land grant Rock of Dumbarton after a site near Glasgow in his native Scotland.

Dumbarton House was built on Georgetown Heights in 1798–99 by Samuel Jackson, a Philadelphia merchant and land speculator. He sold it in 1800 and moved to Tennessee. The house rapidly changed hands several times before Joseph Nourse (1754–1841) and his wife, Maria, purchased it for nearly $7,500 in 1805. This was a bargain compared to the $28,000 that it cost to build The Octagon.

Nourse quickly increased the estate from 4 to 8 acres and built a carriage house, barn, stables, dairy, and smoke house, and moved his icehouse to the property. He kept 10 servants, including six slaves.

PUNCH AND GOUGE MANTEL

Nourse supplemented his income by farming the added land in wheat and hay. During his eight years here he rented a room to Robert Mills, an architect who would become nationally famous as the designer of the Washington Monument.

Although Nourse lived here only eight years he was perhaps the most noteworthy resident in the house's two-century history. Nourse is perhaps best known as the first civil servant in America, beginning his career at the onset of the Revolutionary War at the War Department as military secretary to General Charles Lee. In recognition of his superior service, he was commissioned register of the Treasury in 1781, a position he held for 50 years. His son Charles followed his example by working for the federal government; he became chief clerk of the War Department.

Nourse sold the house in 1813 after losing considerable money when the Bank of the United States suddenly closed. It was bought by Charles Carroll, who named the house Bellevue after his plantation in Hagerstown, Maryland. His brother, Daniel Carroll of Duddington, who lived on Capitol Hill, was the largest proprietor when the Federal City was laid out in 1791. Dolley Madison stopped here after the British burned the White House on August 24, 1814. Various owners during the 19th century renamed the house. The present owner, the National Society of the Colonial Dames of America, gave it the name Dumbarton House.

REAR ELEVATION

The last private owner was Emily Newbold, who purchased it in 1912. She and her husband, John, moved the main house slightly north when Q Street was cut through their property in 1915, joining Georgetown to Washington via the new Dumbarton Bridge. The original wings and hyphens of the five-part house were dismantled and rebuilt. It took three weeks to jack the main house up off the ground, and then several months to slowly move it by horses 100 feet to the north. Civil War veteran and engineer Caleb L. Saers, who owned a local business in the late-19th and early-20th centuries moving Washington houses, carried out its relocation. After this move, the property was reduced to six-tenths of an acre.

In 1928 Newbold sold the house to The National Society of the Colonial Dames of America for their national headquarters. The society was founded in 1891 to preserve historic sites and objects and to educate the public about the nation's early history. In 1930 the Society commissioned noted historian Fiske Kimball and local architect Horace Peaslee to restore the house. Kimball, considered the first professional American architectural historian, was widely experienced, having worked on the restorations of Colonial Williamsburg, Stratford Hall, Gunston Hall, Monticello, and the Fairmont Park houses in Philadelphia. In 1916 he published the monumental study *Thomas Jefferson, Architect*. From 1925 until his death in 1955, Kimball served as director of the Philadelphia Museum of Art. Horace Peaslee was also an experienced restoration architect. During his career he restored St. John's Episcopal Church opposite Lafayette Park and Belle Grove Plantation near Winchester, Virginia, and reconstructed the original Maryland State House in St. Mary's City.

As part of the restoration plan for Dumbarton House, Kimball removed seven Victorian fireplace mantels and replaced them with elegant early-19th-century American mantels, four of them punch and gouge. Four came from houses in Georgetown and one from Philadelphia. The most interesting mantel, with a carving of the frigate U.S.S. Constitution, is reputed to have come from a boardinghouse that stood on Judiciary Square and was once occupied by Chief Justice John Marshall. The passage, parlor, and dining room all have elegant Adamesque plaster cornices of classical urns, swags, garlands, and geometric patterns. The two first-floor rooms on the east side of the house lost their plaster friezes during an early-20th-century remodel.

A remarkable painting in the collection of the Colonial Dames is Charles Willson Peale's 1789 portrait of the children of Benjamin Stoddert, a successful tobacco merchant and the first secretary of the U.S. Navy, under President John Adams. It was painted on the porch of the Stoddert residence, Pretty Prospect, since renamed Halcyon House, at the corner of 34th and Prospect Streets, overlooking the Potomac River. The group includes Benjamin, age seven, on the right, Elizabeth, age five, on the left, and Harriet, a baby five months old in the cart. In the distance is the thriving port of Georgetown and the Analostan Island beyond. It has hung in the house since it was purchased in the 1930s.

The Colonial Dames enlarged the house in 1991 with a below-grade ballroom that is not visible from the street but opens onto a walled courtyard on the east. This addition provides a much-needed meeting room where lectures and other events are held on a regular basis. Dumbarton House has been open to the public for tours, special events, and lectures since 1932. Efforts began in 2010 to redecorate and refurnish the first floor so that it resembles as closely as possible its appearance when Joseph and Maria Nourse lived there.

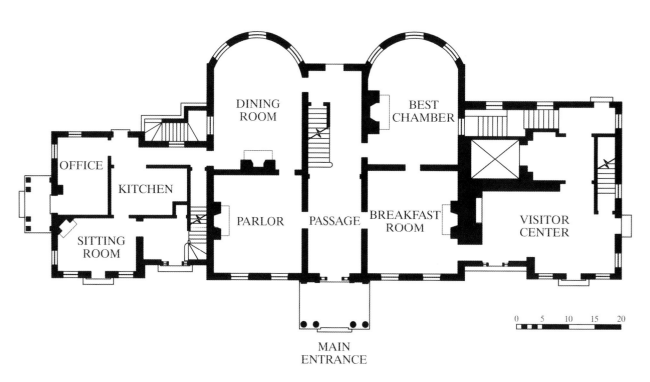

FIRST-FLOOR PLAN

EVERMAY

1623 28TH STREET, N.W.
WASHINGTON, D.C.

———————————

1801

Designer: Nicholas King
Renovation Architect: George N. Ray
Neighborhood: Georgetown
Status: Used by Nonprofit Foundation for Musical Concerts

SOUTHERN, OR GARDEN ELEVATION (ORIGINAL FRONT FACADE)

ONE OF THE STATELIEST FEDERAL HOUSES IN
Washington, Evermay sits on 3½ acres at
28th and R Streets, N.W. Its Georgetown Heights
location afforded splendid views of the newly completed White House, as well as Georgetown and the
Potomac River. Maritime merchant and real estate
speculator Samuel Davidson (1747–1810) carefully
planned the estate over an eight-year period before
starting construction; he acquired the original 15
acres for the house in four purchases from Thomas
Beall, of Georgetown, beginning in 1792. Davidson's
many lucrative business ventures included a brickyard,
which he operated from 1792 to 1794 on the site of
the future Lafayette Park, across from the White
House. He reserved 200,000 bricks for the construction of Evermay, while supplying part of the brick for
the White House and the new bridge over Rock Creek
connecting Georgetown to Washington at Pennsylvania Avenue and M Street, N.W.

Davidson commissioned his friend, Nicholas
King, surveyor of the City of Washington, to design
the 2½-story gabled brick house, five bays wide, with
an elegant fan-lighted doorway on the south front.
The plan also featured three narrow dormer windows
and a pair of chimneys at each end of the roof. King
(1771–1812), a native of Yorkshire, England, became
one of the most prominent surveyors of the young
city of Washington. In a rare instance, his elevation
drawing, floor plan, and site plan for this property
all survive.

Originally, one arrived at Evermay by a steep
carriage drive from 28th Street to the main facade
on the south, which was built with hand-rubbed red
brick laid in Flemish bond. The original rear elevation, which faced the service buildings to the north,
was laid in rough brick in an American bond. In the
late-19th century, the main entrance was changed,
with a circular drive connecting the north elevation
to 28th Street.

Davidson came from Scotland to Annapolis,
Maryland, in 1767 to work in his brother's tobacco

DOUBLE PARLOR

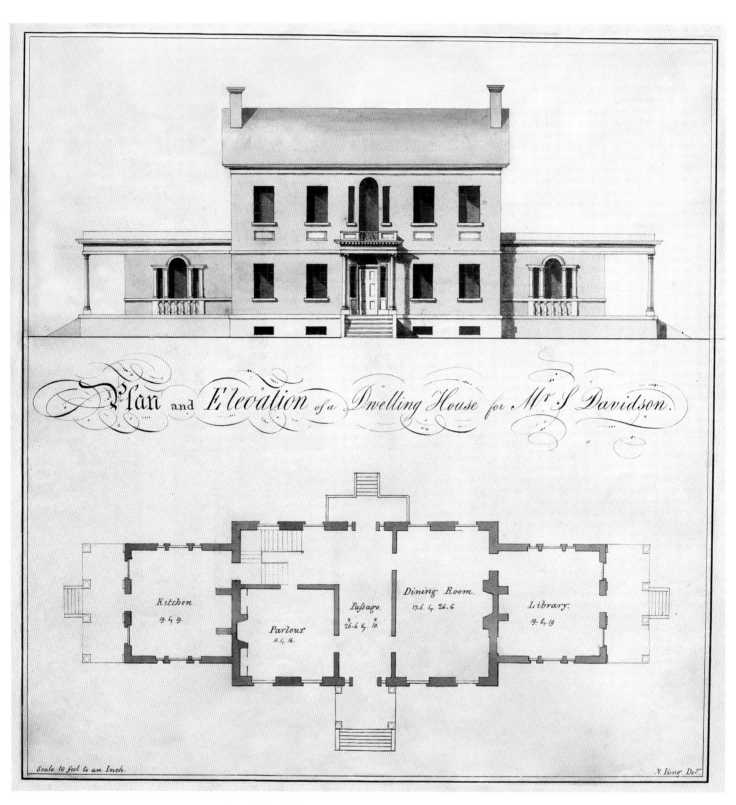

Plan and Elevation of a Dwelling House for Mr S Davidson.

Kitchen
13. by 19.

Parlour
16. by 16.

Passage
26.6 by 10.

Dining Room.
17.6. by 26.6

Library.
19. by 19.

Scale 10 feet to an Inch.

N. King Delt.

RENDERING OF ORIGINAL FACADE AND FLOOR PLAN
WATERCOLOR BY NICHOLAS KING, CA. 1792

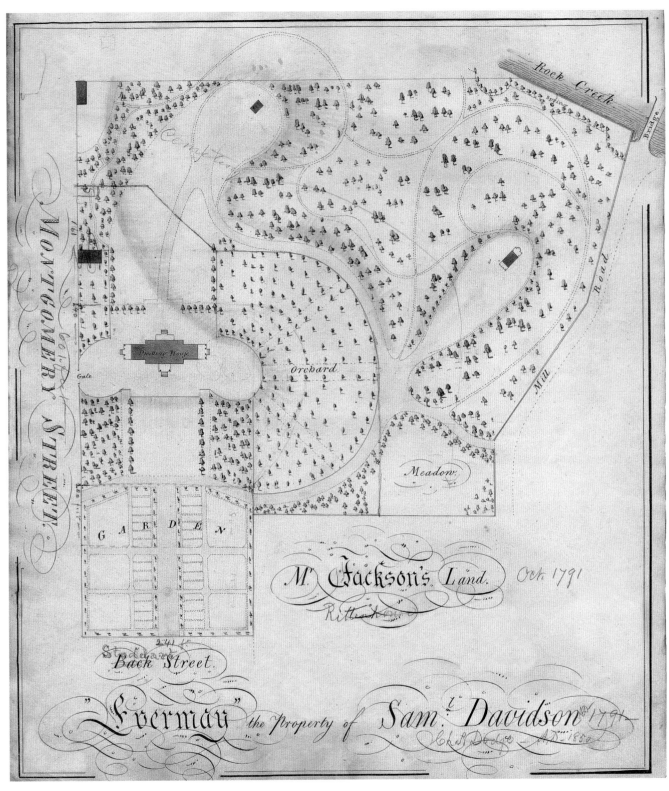

ORIGINAL SITE PLAN, INK DRAWING
BY NICHOLAS KING, CA 1792

shipping business. By 1783 he had accumulated enough capital to open his own shipping business in Georgetown. Davidson divided his time between Evermay and his rooms at Union Tavern on today's M Street, near the Georgetown waterfront.

Davidson spent much of his leisure time developing the gardens at Evermay, which were also designed by King, with the assistance of local horticulturist Theodore Holt. Half of the original 15-acre site was developed as orchards and flower gardens. Davidson died a bachelor and left Evermay to his nephew, Lewis Grant (1779–1832), who took the surname of Davidson as required by the will.

Lewis Grant Davidson continued his uncle's role as a leading businessman in Georgetown and Washington City, investing in local banks, turnpikes, the Chesapeake & Ohio Canal, and shipping. At his death in 1832, his wife, Eliza Grant Davidson, inherited Evermay. She married Charles Dodge, the son of a major Georgetown merchant and shipper, Francis Dodge, in 1849. Eliza and Charles Dodge sold 11½ acres of Evermay in 1858 to banker William Wilson Corcoran for the expansion of the adjacent, newly developed Oak Hill Cemetery.

The fourth owner of Evermay, Georgetown attorney John D. McPherson (1818–1897), began to alter the house soon after he bought it in 1877. McPherson added Victorian porches on both the south and north sides, removed the dormer windows, built an unsightly sleeping porch on the roof, and changed the driveway orientation from the south to the north. After McPherson's death, his heirs rented the estate and eventually sold it to a developer, Francis H. Duehey, in 1919. Duehey planned to raze Evermay and build either a hotel or an apartment house on the site when the adjacent Q Street Bridge was finished. Alarmed Georgetown citizens hurried to alter the zoning regulation and limit building heights in that area to 40 feet. Defeated in his development plans, Duehey sold Evermay to F. Lammot Belin in 1923.

A native of Scranton, Pennsylvania, Ferdinand Lammot Belin was a diplomat who had previously served in Peking and Paris. During President Herbert Hoover's administration, he was appointed chief of protocol, and then in 1932, U.S. ambassador to Poland. Belin initiated a major project in 1923 to restore the exterior of Evermay to its original condition. Since he was on assignment at diplomatic posts in England and Turkey, he hired Washington architect George N. Ray to oversee the restoration. The Victorian veranda and balconies were removed, the dormer windows reconstructed, a west service wing added, and the grounds completely redesigned. Mrs. Belin, an avid tennis player, was delighted to find that the estate already had a tennis court, which she retained. The Belins had Ray design the decorative wrought-iron gates at the entrance to the driveway.

Belin also changed the interior of Evermay. The house originally had a passage on the first floor with two rooms on each side. Belin had the walls between each pair of rooms removed to create a long, open dining room and drawing room. The elegant 12-foot 9-inch ceilings in these rooms were preserved. The four rooms on the second floor and the two in the attic were also left intact. In 1930 Belin purchased handsome early Georgian pine paneling and a pair of mantels for the drawing room. The seller, a London antiques dealer, had these items removed from a room at Sprotbrough Hall in Yorkshire shortly before it was razed by an English developer for a complex of row houses.

Peter Belin, the son of Lammot Belin, inherited the house in 1965, to become the fifth owner. While a student at Yale University in 1937, he had traveled through Europe with a fellow student. They returned from Germany on the ill-fated zeppelin *Hindenburg*, which exploded while attempting to land at Lakehurst, New Jersey. Peter and his friend were saved by jumping from the burning aircraft 30 feet into a sandy section of ground next to the landing field. After graduation, in 1938, Peter Belin served as private secretary to Hugh R. Wilson, U.S. ambassador to Germany, followed by a career in naval intelligence. He added to the comfort and beauty of Evermay by building the large east wing. It helped to balance the west service wing. This impressive room, 26 by 40 feet and 17 feet high, now serves as a living room and orangery. In addition, Belin erected a small freestanding office building to the west, and in the center of the north entrance courtyard, a bronze fountain by Carl Milles, the prominent Swedish sculptor.

Harry Lammot Belin, the son of Peter Belin and a veteran of the U.S. Navy, as well as a noted land-scape architect, inherited the estate in 1996. He rented Evermay for private conferences and parties. Because of high taxes, rising maintenance costs, and complaints by neighbors about the constant noise from the nightly receptions, Belin sold the property in 2010. It is now owned by the S & R Foundation, established by Japanese industrialists who regularly open it to the public for musical concerts.

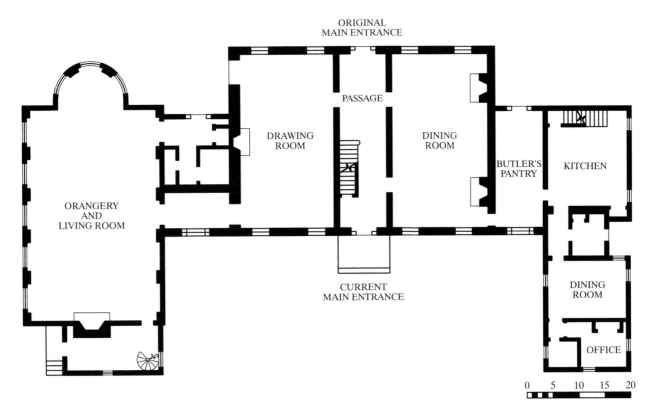

FIRST-FLOOR PLAN

TUDOR PLACE

1644 31ST STREET, N.W.
WASHINGTON, D.C.

———————————

WINGS 1794
MAIN HOUSE 1815–16

Architect: William Thornton
Neighborhood: Georgetown
Status: Historic House Museum

GARDEN FACADE

DRAWING ROOM, WITH THE CONSERVATORY SEEN THROUGH THE DOOR ON THE RIGHT

Thomas Peter, a wealthy Georgetown merchant, and his wife Martha, the namesake and granddaughter of Martha Dandridge Custis Washington, were the builders of Tudor Place. They purchased the 8½-acre Georgetown Heights property with funds acquired from the sale of land that Martha Peter inherited from George Washington, her step-grandfather. The Peters commissioned William Thornton, the original architect of the U.S. Capitol, to design the house. The first owner of the original structure, Francis Lowndes, had in 1794 built two wings and planned to build a central block to connect them but went bankrupt before the house could be finished. Thornton's 1805 plan consisted of a central section connecting the two existing wings. The west wing contained the living quarters and kitchen, while the east wing accommodated a stable and carriage house. From 1805 until 1983, six generations of the Peter family owned and continuously occupied Tudor Place. Endowed as a historic house museum, the building and its original furnishings are the best preserved of any early residence in Washington.

The main entrance on the north opens to a vestibule and then the central reception room or saloon that connects to the south lawn. At the south end of the saloon is the famous temple portico (based on the Temple of Vesta at Tivoli, Italy), which protrudes halfway into the house. Tall curved windows in the saloon face the sloping south lawn. Pocket doors, which recess into the walls to conserve space, open

PARLOR LEADING TO DINING ROOM

from the saloon to rooms on the east and west. They are thought to be the oldest surviving examples of pocket doors in Washington. On the east side of the saloon is the drawing room as well as the conservatory, or greenhouse, and the library (now used as the visitors' entrance and shop). To the west are the parlor, dining room, office, and kitchen (added in 1876). The north side of the first floor, adjacent to the front door, encompasses hallways and service rooms.

Left: INTERIOR VIEW OF
THE CIRCULAR TEMPLE PORCH

Britannia Peter (1815–1911), who married Commodore Beverley Kennon in 1842, was one of the longest-lived residents of Tudor Place. She was widowed less than two years after her marriage, when her husband died from a cannon explosion on the naval ship *Princeton* during tests on the Potomac River. Britannia Peter Kennon rented the house in 1858, but returned in early 1862 and rented out rooms to Union officers to prevent the government from seizing it for

DINING ROOM

an army hospital. Britannia died at age 95 in 1911 and left the estate to her five grandchildren.

Armistead Peter III (1896–1983), the last member of the Peter family to own the house, bought out his siblings' interest in the property and began an important renovation of the house in 1914, adding plumbing, a steam heating system, electricity, and bathrooms, and updating the kitchen. One of the more important contributions Armistead made was to restore the antebellum north garden according to the original plan.

In 1969 he co-authored with Frederick Doveton Nichols the substantial publication *Tudor Place*, which recounts the house's history. The house appears much as Armistead left it, filled with furniture and art that

the family acquired over six generations. Thomas and Martha Peter bought a significant number of objects from the estate of Martha Washington in 1802. By gift, bequest, or purchase, more than 200 objects remain, so that Tudor Place has one of the largest collections of objects that belonged to the first president outside Mount Vernon.

The Tudor Place property once covered the entire block bounded by Q, R, 31st, and 32nd Streets. The open land north of the house held orchards, with vegetable and flower gardens set closer to the house. Armistead spent his life preserving the house and the surviving 5½ acres of grounds. The interior furnishings include a miniature portrait of George Washington by itinerant Irish painter Walter Robertson;

a chest purchased by George Washington from Lord Fairfax; several garments or pieces of garments owned by Martha Washington; and Sèvres tableware owned by the Washingtons at their presidential house in New York. Armistead's maroon-colored 1919 Pierce-Arrow roadster still sits in the 1914 garage.

Armistead Peter III left a significant, lasting legacy by granting a scenic easement for Tudor Place to the Department of the Interior in 1966—the first in the United States. He left the estate itself to the Carostead Foundation, later changed to the Tudor Place Foundation, which since his death in 1983, has continued to preserve the house, contents, and grounds for future generations to enjoy. The foundation ordered conservation and structure reports and then made improvements to the house. It replaced drain lines, removed Portland cement stucco from the exterior walls and replaced it with the more appropriate lime stucco, restored the roofs of the temple portico and the north entrance porch, and repointed the chimneys (replacing the worn mortar between the bricks). Plans are being discussed for a separate building on the grounds to better house the extensive archives.

The foundation has also inventoried and professionally housed the estate's collection of 15,000-plus objects and 5,000-volume library. In addition, it has cataloged the archive, consisting of more than 250,000 items, including correspondence, diaries, financial records, photographs, inventories, blueprints, architectural drawings, and ephemera pertaining to Tudor Place and the Peter family.

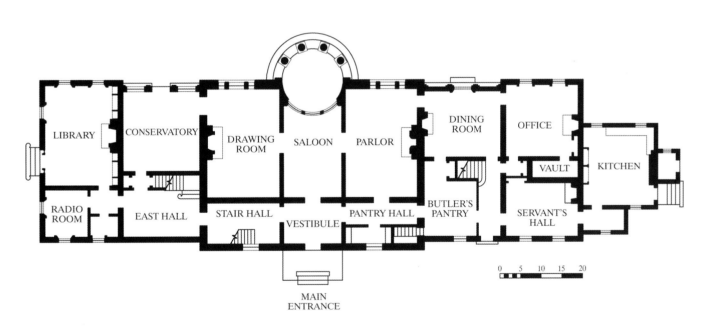

FIRST-FLOOR PLAN

WOODLEY

3000 CATHEDRAL AVENUE, N.W.
WASHINGTON, D.C.

1801
Additions 1867; 1892; 1930

Designer: Philip Barton Key
Neighborhood: Woodley Park
Status: Private School

FACADE

WOODLEY HAS LONG BEEN A SIGNIFICANT part of the architectural and historical fabric of Washington. It is one of the few surviving country estates, along with Arlington House, that were built in the area before the Civil War. It housed many important residents, including three United States presidents, and is one of the few Washington houses after which a neighborhood is named—Woodley Park.

The Woodley site was part of a larger, 795-acre tract in Prince George's County, Maryland, that wealthy Maryland planter Ninian Beall acquired in 1703. Beall named the tract, located on the Potomac River where Georgetown would one day lie, the Rock of Dumbarton, after a natural fortification near his native Glasgow, Scotland.

Two prosperous Georgetown businessmen, Uriah Forrest and Benjamin Stoddert, partners in a tobacco-shipping firm, purchased much of the 500-acre Woodley tract from the Beall family in 1792. Forrest proceeded, in 1793–94, to build his own house, Rosedale, on the northern half of the property—now 1351 Newark Street, N.W. He soon bought out Stoddert, whom President John Adams was to select as the first secretary of the Navy. A severe recession in 1797 forced Forrest to sell off most of the land; he kept only the house and a few acres. His brother-in-law, Philip Barton Key, a successful lawyer, bought 230 acres of Rosedale land from Forrest and took a mortgage on Rosedale to keep Forrest from losing it.

Philip Barton Key was born into a prominent family of planters from Cecil County, Maryland. When the American Revolution began, Philip joined the Maryland Loyalist Regiment in Philadelphia, while his brother John Ross Key became a member of George Washington's Continental Army in Boston. Philip was eventually captured, paroled, and sent to England, where he began to study law in 1784 at the Inns of Court. Five years later he returned to Maryland and publicly apologized for fighting for the British; Philip was one of the few Loyalists to redeem his reputation after the Revolution and reestablish his former prominence. He rose quickly in the legal profession because of his education in London and became a federal judge and member of the U.S. House of Representatives. Key married Ann Plater, the daughter of Maryland's governor and an heir to Sotterley plantation, near present-day Hollywood, Maryland.

Key designed Woodley in 1801, based on his knowledge of Woodley Lodge, the country house near Reading, England, owned by his good friend Henry Addington, later Viscount Sidmouth. The name Woodley means "clearing in the woods." Unfortunately Woodley Lodge was razed in 1962.

The original plan of Woodley had six rooms on the first floor, including the two small wings, and three rooms on the second floor. The rear of the two wings has a typical Federal architectural feature in the large rounded bays. The house was lively with Philip and Ann Key, their three daughters, and frequent houseguest Francis Scott Key, Philip's nephew. Francis, later to become author of "The Star Spangled Banner," written during the bombardment of Fort McHenry in the War of 1812, honored his uncle by naming his son for him. The second Philip Barton Key, a successful Washington attorney, was felled by an infamous scandal shortly before the Civil War. He was shot and killed in Lafayette Park by Congressman Daniel Sickles of New York, who took issue with Key's affair with his wife.

A number of prominent Americans, including U.S. presidents John Tyler, James Buchanan, and Grover Cleveland, rented Woodley as a summer residence. In 1858 Woodley became the property of General Lorenzo Thomas, chief of staff of the U.S. Army. The next noteworthy owner was Robert Walker, a former secretary of the treasury under President James K. Polk, who bought Woodley in 1865. At the time he was the chief lobbyist for Czar Alexander II of Russia, who gave him $36,000 to distribute to members of Congress to persuade them to vote to buy Alaska. He was able to renovate and

Following Pages: REAR ELEVATION

enlarge Woodley with the money he made from the deal, adding a third floor to the central block and second floors to the two small wings in 1867. Walker died in the house only two years later, and it still exhibits the floor plan that he established.

Walker's heirs sold Woodley in 1892 to one of the most significant developers in the history of Washington—Francis Newlands, the former senator from Nevada whose wife was one of the heirs to the Comstock Lode silver and gold mines. He bought Woodley with its surviving 40 acres for speculation. At the time he was developing Chevy Chase, Maryland, as an upscale suburb. Newlands rented Woodley to President Grover Cleveland, his wife, Frances Folsom, and their young child, Ruth, from 1893 to 1897. (Cleveland had sold his nearby summerhouse, Red Top, when he left office at the end of his first term, in 1889. When he returned to office in 1893, the value of the neighborhood, now called Cleveland Park, had escalated so rapidly in the previous four years that the former president could not afford to buy back into the area.) Newlands and his second wife, Edith, then used Woodley as their own residence from 1900 to 1916. Shortly after moving in, Newlands added a long, one-story east wing for guest bedrooms and servants' quarters. Capt. Hayne Ellis of the U.S. Navy and his wife, Sallie Long Ellis, owned the house from 1918 to 1929. On their frequent overseas tours, they also

rented it—the last time to Maj. George Patton, who chose the property because the large stable could accommodate his polo ponies.

The last private owner of Woodley was Henry L. Stimson, who purchased the house with the adjoining 8 acres in 1929. During his remarkable public career, Stimson served in the cabinets of four presidents. His longest tenure was as secretary of war under presidents Franklin D. Roosevelt and Harry S. Truman, from 1933 to 1945. He retired at the age of 78 to his large Long Island estate, Highhold. In 1946 Stimson gave Woodley to his alma mater, Philips Andover Academy. In 1950 the Maret School acquired Woodley and almost half of the total 7¼ acres for its new campus. The remaining southern half of the land was sold to the Swiss Embassy.

The Maret School was founded in 1911 by a French-speaking Swiss immigrant, Marthe Maret. Soon afterward, her two sisters, Jeanne and Louise, came to help her with the growing school. By 1923 the school had moved from Dupont Circle to a new school building at 2118 Kalorama Road, N.W. At the beginning of World War II, enrollment had risen to 169 students. In 1952 the school began operating from the Woodley site. Today the school has 650 students and 110 faculty members with an average class size of 15. It is one of the few schools in Washington to include all grades from 1 to 12.

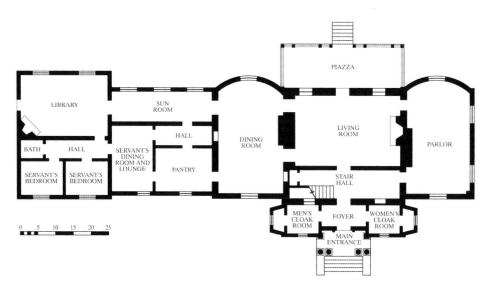

FIRST-FLOOR PLAN

CALDWELL HOUSE

2017 I STREET, N.W.
WASHINGTON, D.C.

1802–08

Designer: Timothy Caldwell
Neighborhood: Foggy Bottom
Status: Private club

FACADE

DRAWING ROOM, TODAY USED AS THE CLUB'S DINING ROOM

THE FINEST SURVIVING FEDERAL HOUSE IN downtown Washington was built as a rental property by the Philadelphia developer Timothy Caldwell in two phases. The first, 25 feet wide and set back 40 feet from the street, was built in 1802. In 1805 Caldwell bought a small adjoining lot and erected a 32-foot-wide addition in the front, which was completed in 1808.

The elegant three-and-a-half-story facade, four bays wide, includes an Aquia stone trim for the keystones, windowsills, belt courses, fanlight, and water table. The belt courses define the individual floors. The front door is embellished with side lights and a large fanlight crowned by a stone arch and decorative keystone. The entrance leads to a long hallway that extends to the original staircase on the left. The hall opens on the right to a pair of connecting rooms; the north one later became the dining room. The original dining room was located in the rear, in the 1802 section, and was later converted into the kitchen. The staircase rises sequentially to the fourth floor, with landings set halfway between the floors. A pair of dormer windows lights the attic.

The house has a history of notable residents. Caldwell sold the just-completed house in 1808 to the new United States postmaster, Gideon Granger, for $10,000. When Granger was preparing to leave office in 1813, he sold it back to Caldwell for the same price. Caldwell then rented out the house until he sold it in 1840.

Right: ENTRY FOYER

STAIR LANDING BETWEEN THE FIRST AND SECOND FLOORS

The most prominent resident was James Monroe, who lived here while he served as secretary of state and later as secretary of war to President James Madison, most notably during the British invasion of Washington and burning of the government buildings in August 1814. Monroe continued to reside at the house as president, from March 4, 1817, until he moved into the rebuilt White House on September 17, 1817. The office that Monroe had built on the east side of the house is no longer extant. The Caldwell House served as the British legation from 1821 to 1831. Before Caldwell sold the house, it also served as the residence of Charles Francis Adams, the son of President John Quincy Adams, as the Austrian legation, and as a boardinghouse and girls' school.

Another Philadelphia investor, Francis Marko, purchased the house from Caldwell. His family rented it until 1877, when it was sold to Cleveland Abbe, founder of the United States Weather Bureau. Abbe taught mathematics at the U.S. Naval Academy and engineering at the University of Michigan before he turned his attention to weather research, using the telegraph to predict weather conditions for Washington. By collecting information on weather conditions in places hundreds of miles away Abbe could predict when and how much the temperature and precipitation would change in the nation's capital. As a result the Signal Corps hired him to develop its Weather Bureau in 1871. In 1890 Abbe was instrumental in the transfer of the Weather Bureau from the Department of the Army to the Department of Agriculture. He died shortly after retiring in 1916 and his heirs sold the house.

The new owner, the Arts Club of Washington, had just been founded that same year by a group of 25 local artists. It first rented Caldwell House and then bought it by the end of the year. In the first year membership grew to 450. In 1929 the club expanded by buying the adjacent Victorian row house to the east—2015 I Street, N.W. This house, built in 1876, was first rented and then purchased by Brig. Gen. Robert Macfeely, who lived there until his death in 1901. To serve the needs of the club, several of the first-floor interior walls were demolished to create a small auditorium for exhibitions, plays, and concerts. Steel beams were used to replace the load-bearing walls. A set of first-floor stairs was built to join the Macfeely and Caldwell houses, because the floors of the two houses were not at the same level. Doors were also cut in the basement and second floors to link the two structures. The rear lawn became a garden with a terrace for dining in the spring and fall.

The club furnished two of the original bedrooms for members to rent. One of the most prominent renters during the 1930s was architectural photographer Frances Benjamin Johnson. During the Depression the club became fashionable for its annual costume ball, welcoming such luminaries as D.W. Griffith, Claudette Colbert, F. Scott Fitzgerald, and Tallulah Bankhead.

Today, the club retains a stable membership of 230 and has developed additional sources of income. One of the reasons for the club's financial stability is a change in the zoning laws of Washington, D.C. In 1989 the club was able to sell its air rights to a developer for an office building on the same block. In exchange, the two parties signed a 99-year agreement by which the developer pays the club $165,000 annually. The club makes an additional $500,000 a year by renting space for weddings and parties. As a public service, the Arts Club awards college scholarships, prizes for writing and poetry, and holds four exhibitions a year, open to nonmembers.

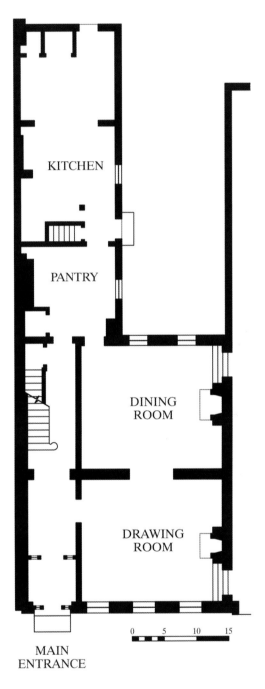

FIRST-FLOOR PLAN

RIVERSDALE

4811 RIVERDALE ROAD
RIVERDALE, MARYLAND

1801—07

Designer: Charles Stier
Status: Historic House Museum

FACADE

SALON

THIS IMPOSING FEDERAL PLANTATION house, built of brick and covered with stucco, was erected by Baron Henri Joseph Stier, a Belgian nobleman who fled to America to escape the dangers posed by the invading armies of the French Revolution. As French troops crossed into Flanders (now part of Belgium) in 1794, Stier abandoned his four estates and many business holdings and sailed to Philadelphia with his large family.

What he didn't leave behind was a remarkable collection of 63 Old Master paintings by Titian, Rembrandt, Jan Brueghel, Anthony van Dyck, and Peter Paul Rubens (of whom Stier was a direct descendant). Stier took the paintings when he and his extensive family moved again, from Philadelphia to Annapolis, Maryland, in 1797.

It was there that Stier's daughter, Rosalie, met George Calvert (1768–1838), grandson of the fifth Lord Baltimore. George Calvert and Rosalie Stier married in Annapolis in 1799. At that time Calvert was serving in the Maryland legislature from Prince George's County. During their wedding trip, the young couple spent two nights with President and Mrs. George Washington at Mount Vernon. George Calvert knew the Washingtons well because his sister, Eleanor, had married John Parke Custis, Martha Washington's son, who died in the Battle of Yorktown.

As troubles in Europe dragged on, Baron Stier tired of renting houses. He purchased 730 acres near Bladensburg, Maryland, only 6 miles from the new city of Washington. The design of the classically inspired mansion he built there came largely from

drawings by Stier's son, Charles, based on one of the baron's former residences—the late-18th-century Château du Mick—located 10 miles north of Antwerp. Several of the house's architectural details have been attributed to friends of George Calvert: the main staircase to William Thornton and the porticoes to Benjamin H. Latrobe.

One originally approached the house from a long driveway on the north that featured a pair of gate lodges situated a mile from the house. The main block of the five-part house consists of two stories, with a full basement. It is flanked on the east and west by one-and-a-half-story gabled wings joined to the main block by slightly lower hyphens, or one-story connections.

The broad expanse of the facade is articulated by a water table above the basement level, a stringcourse between the first and second floors, and a pedimented Tuscan portico over the north-facing main carriage entrance, as well as one sheltering the south garden entrance. The three central bays of the facade are slightly recessed. Arranged in a central line, four chimneys—one of which is not functional but provides symmetry—punctuate the main house's hipped roof. Slightly to the east is a freestanding, two-story dependency, also of stuccoed brick, which contains the kitchen and rooms for house servants.

The arched fanlight over the central entrance is repeated in the arched door of the hyphens, and this arch also occurs in the interior. The first floor of the main house contains a spacious foyer at the principal north driveway entrance, flanked by hallways to the wings. Three public rooms for formal entertaining open sequentially on the south side of the house—the orangery, or glass room, with a series of arches that originally contained mirrors, the drawing room, and the dining room. Elegant double mahogany doors open from the orangery to the drawing and dining rooms. The hallway to the right of the main entrance leads to the library in the east hyphen and originally to the carriage house and stable in the east wing (now

LIBRARY

the ballroom). The dining room connects to the kitchen in the west wing. Both rooms in the east and west wings have impressive 18½-foot-high ceilings. During the summer months, the citrus trees in the orangery were taken out and placed along the principal driveway on the north side of the house. To provide more space for entertaining, Charles Stier located the principal staircase at the northwest corner of the main house—not in the passage.

Baron Stier, his son, and one of his daughters returned to Antwerp in 1803, when Napoleon offered amnesty to all residents who had fled their occupied countries. Rosalie Stier remained at Riversdale with her husband, George, and their two sons. They moved into the east wing of Riversdale in 1802, the first part to be completed. The house was finally finished in 1807. Visitors flocked to see Riversdale, finding the floor plan odd. Even Jefferson rode out from the White House to inspect the mansion.

Riversdale was considered more European than American in its plan because the entertaining, living, and service areas were all situated in distinct, separated spaces. Its plan is thought to have directly influenced William Thornton's design of Tudor Place, which was built soon after Riversdale. Rosalie Stier Calvert wrote to her sister, Isabelle van Havre, in Belgium in 1806, "You are correct that there is a lot of talk about our house, but not because it is so splendid, since many in the Baltimore area greatly surpass it, and even more beautiful ones are being built every year. The reason people talk about our house is because of its distinctive style, and people always much admire anything done by Europeans."

With her husband busy managing the four other plantations they owned, Rosalie often took part in the operation of Riversdale; she learned advanced farming techniques from both her father and her husband. The Calverts practiced crop rotation and devoted part of their 1,500 acres to wheat rather than totally to the soil-depleting tobacco. Rosalie was also instrumental in laying out a large lagoon on the south, or garden, side of the house. The lake,

created by damming a spring, was filled in during the early-20th century, and small houses occupy the site today.

Rosalie and George Calvert had nine children at Riversdale, of which five lived to maturity. Rosalie died in 1822 and George in 1838; both are buried in the family graveyard at Riversdale. After George's death, Riversdale was left to his two sons, George Henry Calvert II and Charles Benedict Calvert. The former moved to Newport, Rhode Island, where he devoted himself to writing and politics, serving as mayor of the city. The younger brother, Charles, stayed at Riversdale and pursued agriculture, ultimately making substantial contributions to both Maryland and the nation in promoting agricultural improvement. Charles helped found the Maryland Agricultural Research College, which would become the University of Maryland. The main campus at College Park is located on 428 acres that Charles and his brother, George, sold to create the campus in 1858. Charles also helped establish the Federal Bureau of Agriculture in 1862, which became the U.S. Department of Agriculture.

One of the most unusual features of Riversdale's farm was the large octagonal barn, which was described in the June 1854 issue of American Farmer magazine. The landmark was later demolished to build an elementary school. After Charles' death in 1864, his eldest son, George Henry Calvert II, managed the plantation; with other Calvert heirs, he sold the estate in 1887 to a real estate company in Riverdale, New York, then as now a fashionable neighborhood of the Bronx. The developer subdivided the land closest to the house as the new town of Riverdale, Maryland. Most of the scattering of late Victorian houses built nearby in the 1890s survive today.

The Riversdale mansion and 6 acres surrounding it were kept intact and rented for many years to a succession of prominent figures, including Senator Hiram Johnson, of California, and Senators Thaddeus Caraway and Hattie Caraway, of Arkansas. The last private owner was Congressman Abraham Lafferty, of Oregon, who lived there from 1933 until

1949. Lafferty sold Riversdale to the Maryland-National Capital Park and Planning Commission in 1949, for both preservation and use as offices. The Calvert family sold the last of the plantation acreage to the federal government during World War II.

In 1986 Maryland historian Margaret Law Call-cott discovered a cache of letters written by Rosalie Stier Calvert to her family in the early-19th century at the Château du Mick. The letters recount the history of Riversdale's construction, and household and land management, as well as its interior decoration. More than 200 of the important letters were edited by Callcott and published in 1991 by Johns Hopkins University Press as *Mistress of Riversdale, the Plantation Letters of Rosalie Stier Calvert, 1795–1821.* This newfound wealth of knowledge about early-19th-century activities at the house prompted the Maryland-National Capital Planning Commission, as stewards of the property, to undertake restoration of the house to that era rather than the plan previously proposed for a Victorian-period house. This decision altered the contract between the Commission and the State of Maryland, the state withdrawing a restoration grant of $250,000 it had offered in 1986. The Riverdale Historical Society appealed, and after considerable trouble, the grant was restored in 1989. Ann Ferguson, a local civic leader who later became mayor of Riverdale, was instrumental in winning the appeal and pushing the restoration forward.

In 2000 the State made a second grant of $300,000 for the restoration of Riversdale. The house has been open to the public for tours on Fridays and Sunday afternoons since the early 1990s. To offset in part the cost of maintenance, the public can rent the first-floor rooms for wedding receptions and other social events.

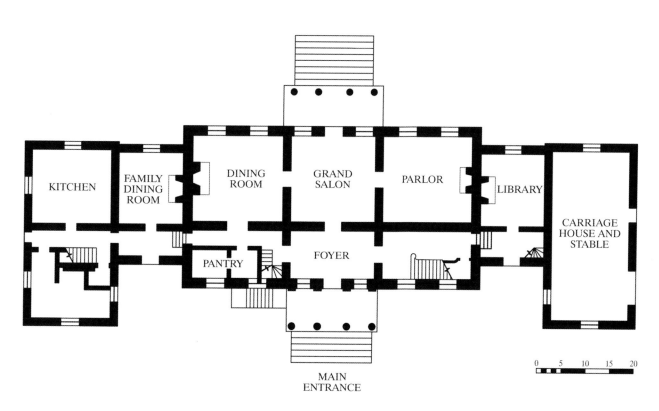

FIRST-FLOOR PLAN

BLAIR HOUSE

1651–1653 PENNSYLVANIA AVENUE, N.W.
WASHINGTON, D.C.

───────────────

1824

Designer: Unknown
Neighborhood: Lafayette Park
Status: Guesthouse of The President of The United States

FACADE

FRONT PARLOR

BLAIR HOUSE IS NAMED FOR FRANCIS PRESTON Blair Sr. (1791–1876), publisher of *The Argus of Western America*, an influential Frankfort, Kentucky, newspaper that helped build the Democratic Party into a national force before the Civil War. Shortly after President Andrew Jackson took office in 1829, Blair moved to Washington at Jackson's request. Jackson had read the many supportive articles Blair published on behalf of his presidential campaign and wanted him to establish a newspaper in the nation's capital to support his views and those of the Democratic Party. Blair started *The Globe* in Washington in 1831, and soon after, the *Congressional Globe* with John C. Rives. The latter newspaper reported daily on the proceedings of Congress, and survives today as the *Congressional Record*.

After renting several houses in Washington, Blair bought the Lovell house at 1651 Pennsylvania Avenue, N.W., in 1836 for $6,500, just as Jackson was about to leave office. Dr. Joseph Lovell (1788–1836), the first United States surgeon general and founder of the Army Corps of Engineers, built the house in 1824.

Following Pages: THE DOUBLE PARLOR
IN THE CONNECTED LEE HOUSE

Lovell chose a site close to major seats of power, directly opposite the earlier War Department building, built by President George Washington, just northwest of the White House. Burned during the British invasion of August 1814, the White House was immediately reconstructed on the same site.

In 1845 Blair sold his newspapers and built Silver Spring, his country house 6 miles from Washington in Montgomery County, Maryland. Over the next decade, he rented Blair House to a number of distinguished civil servants, including George Bancroft, secretary of the Navy under President Polk, and Thomas Ewing, secretary of the interior under President Zachary Taylor.

Francis Preston Blair had three sons: F. P. Blair Jr., called Frank; James, who died young; and Montgomery Blair. By all accounts, however, his only daughter, Elizabeth, was his favorite child. Montgomery Blair studied law in St. Louis and began a practice there in 1837; he and his family returned to Washington in 1852 and took over his parents' house on Pennsylvania Avenue after the elder Blairs moved to Silver Spring. He altered the house considerably, changing the original height from two-and-a-half stories with a gable roof to four full stories with a flat roof. He also had the facade stuccoed and scored to resemble stone. Montgomery Blair then built a country house, Falkland, near his father's estate in Montgomery County.

In 1858 Francis Preston Blair Sr., built a house adjoining Blair on the west for his daughter, Elizabeth, and her husband, Lt. Samuel Phillips Lee, a naval officer and cousin of Robert E. Lee. Since her husband was frequently assigned abroad, Elizabeth's parents stayed with her in Lee House, usually during the winter season, when Congress was in session.

Even though F.P. Blair Sr. owned slaves, he was opposed to the spread of slavery into the western states and territories. His son Montgomery, however, was a confirmed abolitionist. Both father and son were united in founding the Republican Party in 1855, which opposed the spread of slavery. They both supported Republican candidates: John C. Fremont in the election of 1856 and Abraham Lincoln in the election of 1860. Both Blairs were close advisers to President Lincoln throughout the Civil War.

At the beginning of the Civil War, Lincoln called on F.P. Blair Sr. to convey his offer of command of the U. S. Army to Col. Robert E. Lee. Blair and Lee were both slaveholders and Blair's son-in-law was Lee's cousin. After meeting at Blair House, Lee considered the offer for several days and decided that he could not fight against his native Virginia and his own relatives. After resigning his U.S. Army commission, Lee joined the Confederate Army along with 284 other U.S. officers who favored the Southern cause.

Lincoln appointed Montgomery Blair postmaster general in 1861 for his support during the presidential campaign, and Blair set about reforming the Post Office. He compensated postmasters by paying them a salary rather than a commission on the volume of mail handled. Under his direction the railroads reduced rates for carrying mail. Blair also decreased the delivery time for mail by having it sorted on the train between cities. He then introduced machines to make the cancellation of letters more efficient. He instituted a single rate for mailing letters, regardless of distance. To facilitate delivery of mail to soldiers during the Civil War, Blair appointed postmasters for every regiment. He was the first postmaster to have mail delivered to houses and businesses, and he also persuaded European nations to meet in Paris in 1863 to establish international uniform postal rates. Under Blair's tenure, the Post Office eliminated its deficit and earned a healthy return for the government.

Montgomery Blair's brother, Francis P. "Frank" Blair Jr., served as a general under the command of General Sherman. When Confederate General Jubal Early and his army invaded Washington and attacked Fort Stevens in July 1864, he also marched through Montgomery County, Maryland, burning Montgomery Blair's estate—Falkland—but sparing the father's house, Silver Spring.

Montgomery Blair's son Gist returned to Washington from St. Louis in 1897 to practice law, and moved into Blair House. Realizing the house's historical significance, Gist Blair much later fought to prevent the federal government from razing the landmark for federal office buildings; he found a friend in President Franklin D. Roosevelt, who loved old houses and so arranged in 1942 to have the government purchase the house and its historic furnishings for use as the president's guesthouse. The adjacent Lee House was acquired in 1943, and both houses were placed on the National Register of Historic Places in the early 1960s. President Truman and his family occupied Blair House from 1948 to 1952 while the White House was being rebuilt. Doors that separated the interiors of the two houses were eventually removed to join them.

Because of the expanding role of the United States in international affairs after World War II, the federal government needed additional guest accommodations for visiting diplomats. In 1969–70 the government acquired two row houses on Jackson Place and merged them with Blair House as well. Today Blair House contains 120 rooms on five levels, covering nearly 70,000 square feet. In 1985 the federal government spent $8.6 million to restore the building. The handsome antique furniture, paintings, historic prints, and their conservation, are paid for by private contributions to the Blair House Restoration Fund.

The floor plans here are from *Inside Blair House* by Mary Wilroy and Lucie Prinz, published in 1982. Between 1984 and 1988 a new rear wing was added to Blair House. This garden pavilion provides a large reception room and a spacious guest suite. It is flanked by two courtyard gardens that guests use in warm weather. For security reasons the current floor plan of Blair House cannot be published.

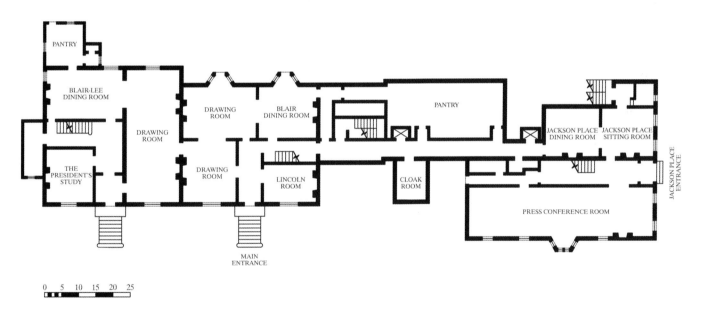

0 5 10 15 20 25

FIRST-FLOOR PLAN

Following Pages: PENNSYLVANIA AVENUE
WITH RENWICK GALLERY AT FAR LEFT

GREEK REVIVAL
HOUSES

Arlington House

McCormick House

Mackall Square

Steedman House

ARLINGTON HOUSE

ARLINGTON NATIONAL CEMETERY
ARLINGTON, VIRGINIA

WINGS 1802–1804
HOUSE 1817–1820

Architect: George Hadfield
Status: Historic House Museum

FACADE

ROBERT E. LEE AND WILLIAM HENRY FITZHUGH "ROONEY" LEE

EW HOUSES IN METROPOLITAN WASHINGTON have a more prominent location than Arlington, which overlooks the nation's capital from the hill that is now home to Arlington National Cemetery. George Washington Parke Custis (1781–1857), the adopted son and namesake of George Washington, built the house in three sections between 1802 and 1818. His father, John Parke Custis, the only son of Martha Custis Washington, died of camp fever while serving in the Continental Army at Yorktown in 1781. Of John Parke Custis' four children, only the two youngest, George Washington Parke Custis and Eleanor, were adopted by George and Martha Washington and raised at Mount Vernon.

When Martha Washington died in 1802, 21-year-old George Custis moved to the 1,100-acre Arlington estate that he had inherited from his father. Temporarily occupying a cottage already standing on the estate, Custis commissioned English architect George Hadfield

(1764–1826), who had superintended construction of the U. S. Capitol (1795–1798), to design Arlington, named from an earlier Custis estate on the Eastern Shore of Virginia. Hadfield had won a number of honors from the Royal Academy in London, where he had studied architecture under renowned architect, James Wyatt. He gained extensive knowledge of classical architecture from studying in Rome from 1790 to 1795. Arlington was one of the first Greek Revival houses in the country—designed with one-story wings and a central two-story section, embellished by a portico with eight massive Doric columns, reputedly based on those of the ancient temple of Theseus in Athens.

Custis built the wings first, in 1803–04, and when funds became available, the central section between 1817 and 1820. After he married Mary Lee Fitzhugh in 1804, he divided the south wing into four rooms as living quarters. The north wing was then used as his office and a large reception area. Of the

DINING ROOM

four children born to the couple, only one, Mary Anna Randolph Custis, lived to maturity.

The interior of the house contains a long central reception hall that extends to the rear elevation. The main staircase rises in the left rear of the hall. On the right side, the principal parlor opens onto the dining room in the rear through three large arches, an unusual arrangement. Custis used the large studio in the south wing for painting Revolutionary War battlefield scenes showing George Washington as the commanding officer. Custis also wrote and published plays and gave public speeches about the Revolution. He encouraged agricultural reforms and made a lasting contribution to the science of husbandry by improving the breeding of sheep.

Custis purchased many of the contents of Mount Vernon when they were sold at auction following the death of Martha Washington in 1802. He displayed them at Arlington House and gave tours of the collection to many prominent visitors, including Sam Houston, Daniel Webster, Andrew Jackson, and the Marquis de Lafayette.

Custis maintained Arlington as a residential estate rather than a working plantation. Most of his income came from two large plantations he owned in Kent County, Virginia, totaling more than 10,000 acres. Much of Arlington was made up of the Park—a virgin forest of hardwoods that extended from the house to the western end of the estate. Custis planted orchards and vegetable gardens along the banks of

PARLOR

the Potomac River to supply his family and staff. He maintained a wharf on the estate for shipping. The two original slave quarters, one of which contains the summer kitchen, still stand behind the mansion, and were built of brick, covered with stucco, and scored to resemble stone.

When Robert E. Lee moved with his mother to live in Alexandria, Virginia, in 1810, he frequently visited Arlington and saw the house under construction. The childhood friendship between Mary Custis and Robert E. Lee matured into love, and the couple was married at the house in 1831, shortly after Lee graduated from West Point. They lived at Lee's first assignment, Fort Monroe, Virginia, for three years. When Lee was dispatched to army duty in Washington, he

lived at Arlington House between 1834 and 1837. Mary spent part of each year with Captain Lee at other assignments in St. Louis, Missouri, and Fort Hamilton, New York. She and the children remained at Arlington House while Lee served in the Mexican War from 1846 to 1848. After his promotion to colonel, Lee took command of West Point in 1852, bringing his wife, three sons, and four daughters with him. Following the death of her father in 1857, Mary Lee returned to Arlington House with her children to manage the estate.

When Virginia seceded and joined the Confederacy in May 1861, Robert E. Lee, then living at Arlington, was commissioned a general in the Confederate Army and moved to Richmond. His wife quickly joined him, taking family portraits, silver, and

WINTER KITCHEN

WINE CELLER

SLAVE QUARTERS AND SUMMER KITCHEN

a few other furnishings with her. Arlington House became the headquarters of the generals commanding the Union troops in northern Virginia, guarding Washington. The estate was seized by the Union government for nonpayment of taxes ($300), after which General Montgomery Meigs in 1863 vengefully directed the burial of Union soldiers at Arlington, close to the house itself, so that the Lees might not want to live there again.

After Lee surrendered the Army of Northern Virginia to Ulysses S. Grant at Appomattox, in April 1865, he accepted the position of president of Washington College in Lexington, Virginia. Although the Lees attempted to reclaim Arlington House, they both died before any action could take place—Robert E.

Lee in 1870 and Mary Custis Lee in 1873. Their son Custis pressed the case in court and won title to Arlington House in 1882. Because of the expense and difficulty of moving thousands of Union soldiers buried there, Custis sold the Arlington estate to the federal government for $150,000 a short time later.

The War Department began restoration of Arlington House in 1928. Most of the work was completed by 1934, when the estate was transferred to the National Park Service. It has remained open to the public as a house museum since then. From 2009 to 2013, Arlington House was renovated with new wiring, plumbing, air-conditioning, and humidity control. It stands as one of the great iconic monuments in American architecture.

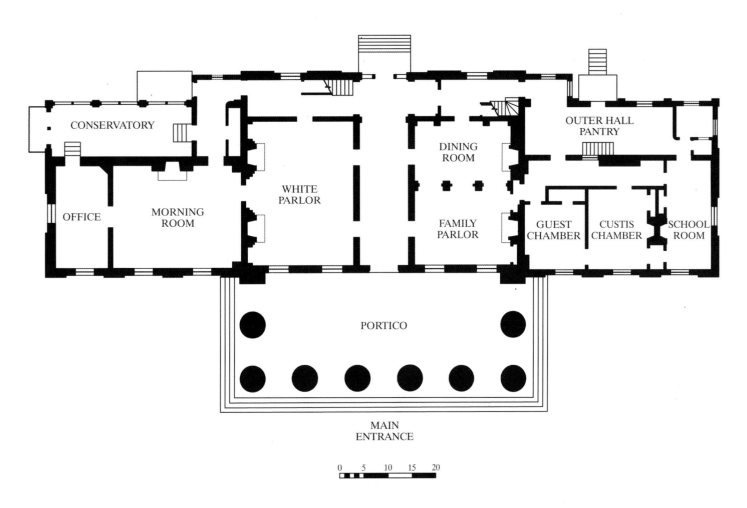

CONSERVATORY

OUTER HALL
PANTRY

OFFICE

MORNING
ROOM

WHITE
PARLOR

DINING
ROOM

FAMILY
PARLOR

GUEST
CHAMBER

CUSTIS
CHAMBER

SCHOOL
ROOM

PORTICO

MAIN
ENTRANCE

0   5   10   15   20

FIRST-FLOOR PLAN

Left: MAIN FACADE FROM
ARLINGTON NATIONAL CEMETERY

McCORMICK HOUSE

1224 30TH STREET, N.W.
WASHINGTON, D.C.

1840
ADDITION 1929

Architect: Unknown
Addition and Alterations: Ward Brown, 1929
Neighborhood: Georgetown
Status: Private Residence

FACADE

McCORMICK HOUSE IN GEORGETOWN IS A good example of restrained Greek Revival architecture, in vernacular form. It was originally built as a pair of attached, three-story houses in 1840. The principal neoclassical features of the original design are the low pediments that cap each window frame, the row of smaller third-floor frieze windows, and the four-pillar-wide porch, which originally sheltered a pair of doors. The original first-floor plan of each house had a small foyer with a narrow staircase directly opposite the front door. The foyer opened into a double parlor leading to a dining room and kitchen in the rear.

In 1929 Congresswoman Ruth Hanna McCormick of Chicago purchased the two houses. She was the widow of Senator Joseph Medill McCormick (1878–1925) of the influential family that owned the *Chicago Daily Tribune.* The residence became known as McCormick House after Rep. McCormick combined the two houses and initiated sensitive additions, designed by prominent Washington architect Ward Brown.

Joseph Medill McCormick (commonly known as Medill McCormick) was the grandnephew of Cyrus Hall McCormick, the 19th-century inventor of the reaper, whose business evolved in the early-20th century into the International Harvester Company. Medill's father, Robert S. McCormick, was a successful businessman, the owner of a major grain business in Chicago, who served as U.S. ambassador to Austria-Hungary as well as to France before World War I. His brother, Robert R. McCormick, was president and publisher of the *Chicago Daily Tribune* for many years. On his mother's side, the younger McCormick was the grandson of Joseph Medill, the mayor of Chicago during the 1870s.

Medill McCormick had an outstanding career before taking his seat in the U.S. Senate in 1919. After completing school at Groton, he graduated from Yale University in 1900 and began a brief career in journalism before he entered politics. In 1903 McCormick married Ruth Hanna, the daughter of U.S. Senator Marcus A. Hanna of Cleveland, Ohio, a great campaigner who helped William McKinley win the presidency. Hanna was a successful businessman involved in wholesale groceries, coal mining, shipbuilding, railroads, and banking. The marriage united two powerful families. The height of McCormick's career came when he served one term (1919–25) in the U.S. Senate from Illinois.

Ruth Hanna McCormick left a more lasting contribution to the American political and cultural scene than her husband. She was born in Chicago in 1880 and educated at Miss Porter's School in Farmington, Connecticut. After her marriage she developed her business skills by purchasing and managing a large dairy and a newspaper in Rockport, Illinois. During this time she exercised leadership as chair of the Congressional Committee of the National American Woman Suffrage Association. During the 1920s, she lobbied for greater inclusion of women in the political process and the abolition of child labor. She remained active in politics after her husband committed suicide

ENTRANCE HALL LOOKING INTO PARLOR

in Washington in 1925. That year she founded the Illinois Federation of Republican Women, which became her power base in 1930 when she unsuccessfully ran for the U.S. Senate.

She began a new life in 1932 when she married Albert G. Simms, a member of the U.S. House of Representatives from New Mexico. During her time in New Mexico she left her mark by founding two prep schools. The Georgetown house on 30th Street occupied much of her time in the 1930s even though she maintained a second residence in Albuquerque. After her second husband died, she informally resumed using the name Ruth Hanna.

Hanna commissioned Ward Brown to combine the Greek Revival attached houses. The architect was the son of Glenn Brown, another important Washington architect, who designed the Joseph Beale House. Brown converted the door to the left house to a window, removed the staircase in the left house, and created a large foyer for the combined house, with a coatroom and bathroom on the right. While he retained the double parlor and kitchen of the left house, he converted the first floor of the house on the right into service rooms: a large kitchen and pantry, storeroom, servants' hall, and coatroom.

Brown then added a large wing to the left of the original two houses. The first floor of the wing opened into the double parlor of the left house, and served as a library—the largest room in the new house, and the most beautiful. Brown framed the library fireplace with fluted pilasters and installed carved acanthus leaves as part of the paneling above the fireplace mantel. The second floor of the wing includes the master bedroom, dressing room, and study. The enlarged house now had eight bedrooms. The two-story wing was painted yellow in keeping with the main house. Brown installed window surrounds on the new wing identical to those on the original house, except for the long library windows that extended to the floor. Hanna purchased the narrow Victorian row house to

the south, or far left, to provide lodging for her staff. The architect added a handsome balustrade for the porch and continued its design in the Greek Revival cast-iron fence that spans the front of the entire ensemble. All these changes were successful in integrating the new brick wing with the main house.

Hanna built a handsome octagonal gazebo with terraced exterior walls for her garden library. After buying seven lots in the rear, she created a spacious three-tier boxwood garden that opens onto an alley leading to N Street on the north. Within this large complex, in the middle of cramped Georgetown, she added a swimming pool, theater, greenhouse, and large rear parking lot for cars for guests. After her death in 1944, the house changed hands several times. The ambassador from India leased it at one time.

The second major change to the house came in 1957, when Mr. and Mrs. Gordon Gray purchased it. A native of Winston-Salem, North Carolina, Gray was a prominent public servant. His brother Bowman was also well-known in Winston-Salem, where he managed the family's business, the R.J. Reynolds Tobacco Company. Gray served under Truman as the first assistant secretary of defense; afterward he became president of the University of North Carolina, and lastly, chairman of the board of the National Trust for Historic Preservation.

The Grays made several changes to the property. They added a second greenhouse for raising orchids, built a garden room with wet bar off the library, extended the dining room 3 feet outward into the south yard, and added a circular breakfast room to the rear of the dining room. The Grays also installed central air conditioning, with the machinery located on the lawn on the north side. To provide additional privacy they also bought the adjacent house to the right (north side) and rented it out.

Gray commissioned Margaret B. Weller, a decorator originally from Charlottesville, Virginia, to assist with the interior design. Their decision to arrange

Right: PARLOR FIREPLACE

Following Pages: MASTER BEDROOM

chintz sofas and chairs amid the antique furniture adds an abundance of color. Mrs. Gray's paintings of ancient Egypt, Italian landscapes, and Oriental scenes are prominently displayed, along with her extensive collection of antique porcelain. A signature feature of her fashionable dinner parties was the glowing ambiance created by mirror-reflected candles arranged throughout the house. After Weller retired in 1983, her daughter Nancy Pierpont continued to assist Mrs.

Gray. The landscape architect Perry Wheeler made improvements to the grounds by redesigning and enlarging the boxwood garden around a new octagonal fountain set on the main terrace level.

Several years after the death of Gordon Gray, his widow married Elben Pyne, a New York investment banker and railroad executive. McCormick House continues to be well preserved and cared for under the ownership of Nancy Gray Pyne.

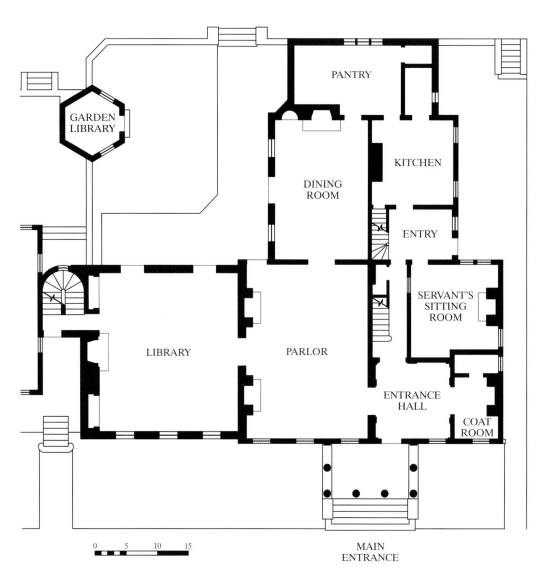

FIRST-FLOOR PLAN

MACKALL SQUARE

1633 29TH STREET, N. W.
WASHINGTON, D.C.

––––––––––––––––

REAR WINGS CA. 1780; 1808; 1818
MAIN HOUSE 1820
PORTICO 1840

Architects: Unknown
Neighborhood: Georgetown
Status: Private Residence

FACADE WITH THE IONIC PORTICO

MACKALL SQUARE, ONE OF THE MOST secluded houses in Georgetown, is located on 2 acres in the center of the block bounded by 28th, 29th, Q, and R Streets, N.W. One enters the property on 29th near R Street through an unassuming entrance with no pillars or gatehouse. The footprint of Mackall Square (pronounced May-kall), including its various additions, suggests a telescope with progressively larger sections. The house was constructed in five stages some time between 1780 and 1840.

The property was originally part of a large tract that ran along the Potomac River in what was then Prince George's County, Maryland. Ninian Beall, who had acquired the land in 1703, named it the Rock of Dumbarton after a landmark on the Clyde River in

SIDE ELEVATION SHOWING THE MANY ADDITIONS

his native Scotland. His son George and other Beall heirs farmed the land and built a crude one-story frame cottage with a large open fireplace for the use of their tenant circa 1780. This structure forms the northern end of the complex and is the smallest of the five sections. The adjoining one-story frame section with a door and two narrow windows facing the present driveway was probably added in 1808. The third part, a two-story frame section, was built about 1818, while the fourth section, the main brick house, dates from 1820, according to tax records. The fifth and most recent addition is the elegant Greek Revival portico, which was added in 1840, shortly after Louis Mackall inherited the property.

When the port of Georgetown was established on the Potomac River in 1751 for shipping tobacco

NEW POOL AND POOL HOUSE

to England and Scotland, the town's northern boundary was established at Back Street—later renamed Stoddert Street, and known today as Q Street. By 1790 the boundary had been extended to allow streets to be cut farther north, which enabled the Beall family to sell very desirable building sites on a high elevation for the construction of large houses. In 1805 Col. Brooke Beall deeded an 8-acre plot of land, or double square, between Q and R Streets, to Benjamin Mackall II and his wife, Christiana, Beall's own daughter.

Benjamin Mackall II was the son of Col. Benjamin Mackall, a wealthy planter from Calvert County, Maryland, who was chairman of the Maryland Convention in Annapolis that sent delegates to the Continental Congress in Philadelphia; some of these delegates eventually signed the Declaration of Independence. The elder Mackall raised eight battalions of regular troops for the Continental Army, the quota assigned Maryland by the Continental Congress. Mackall put much of his own fortune into purchasing arms for the Maryland troops, funds that were never reimbursed despite petitions to the U.S. Congress after the war. Col. Mackall died in 1807 on his plantation, Godsgrace, in Calvert County, and was buried there in the family graveyard.

Originally the only entrance to Mackall Square was from a driveway that opened on Q Street. When the city of Georgetown revised its regulations in the 1790s to allow additional streets to be opened north of Q Street, the younger Mackall donated land to the city for streets. To his utter dismay, Mackall found his house isolated from his neighbors when the city steeply graded 28th Street on the east and 29th Street on the west.

It is not clear exactly when Benjamin Mackall II and his wife moved into Mackall Square: after the 1808 one-story frame addition was put up or after the more prominent two-story frame addition to the south was completed in 1818. Mackall, a shipping merchant in Georgetown, added the main brick house in 1820. It features a handsome wide fanlight over the front door, flanked by a pair of simple pilasters. He died in the house two years later at the age of 57. Mackall's widow inherited the property and left it to their son Dr. Louis Mackall on her death in 1839. The next year Dr. Mackall built the imposing Greek Revival portico—marking the fifth addition to the house. Four large fluted columns with cast-iron Ionic capitals support the portico. The wooden balustrade above the porch is original. After completing his medical training in 1824 Dr. Mackall practiced in Georgetown but retired early to devote himself to research and writing on scientific subjects.

Shortly after Louis Mackall's death in 1876, his heirs began to sell off parts of Mackall Square. They sold the northern section in 1878 to Oak Hill Cemetery for construction of a stable and greenhouse. This land was opposite the cemetery on the south side of R Street (then Road Street) between 28th and 29th Streets, N.W. (In 1959 the cemetery's board of directors sold this land to a developer who built a range of brick row houses on the site.) The heirs next sold off the southern portion of Mackall Square to developers, who built eight Victorian row houses on

the north side of Q Street between 28th and 29th Streets in the 1880s.

In 1911 the Mackall heirs sold the rest of Mackall Square to Herman Hollerith (1860–1929), a native of Buffalo, New York, and son of German immigrants. After graduating from Columbia University in engineering, Hollerith moved to Washington in 1879 and joined the U.S. Census Bureau. He soon began to think of a way to mechanize census tabulations to reduce working time and prevent errors. Observing the Washington streetcar conductors punching tickets inspired Hollerith to experiment with compiling data by a similar method.

By 1884 Hollerith had patented the first punched-card electrical tabulating machines; they were used for the 1890 census, to immediate success. Twice as fast as any other such system, it saved the government about $5 million. In 1896 he founded the Tabulating Machine Company and opened a shop to manufacture his machines at 29th Street and the C&O Canal, near the foot of Georgetown. Hollerith's real wealth came from renting his tabulating machines to railroads, department stores, and other large businesses. His first fortune came in the 1890s when European countries rented his machines for their national censuses.

In 1911 Hollerith merged his business into the Computer-Tabulating-Recording Company, a conglomerate of the four leading tabulating firms in the United States. He remained a major stockholder in the new corporation and served as its chief engineer for the next decade, before retiring in 1922. In 1924 the firm was renamed the International Business Machine Company.

When Hollerith purchased Mackall Square, he planned to enlarge the house for the eight members of his family. His architect, Frederick Pyle, recommended that he raze Mackall Square to provide room for a much larger house. Mrs. Hollerith, a great lover of trees, would not consider this option because it entailed cutting down the century-old oaks next to the house. The Holleriths decided to build in a different location and subsequently rented Mackall

Square to Thomas Bradlee and his family for many years; it was here that Ben Bradlee grew up. He later earned fame as vice president and executive editor of the *Washington Post*, which led news coverage of the Watergate scandal.

The Hollerith family built their 30-room, four-story Georgian Revival mansion on the southwest corner of Mackall Square, where they lived from 1915 to 1993. Hollerith devoted the last years of his life to raising Guernsey cattle on a large farm on the Eastern Shore of Maryland and sailing in the Chesapeake Bay. He told one friend that his life was devoted to "boats, bulls, and butter."

After Hollerith died in Washington in 1929 his three unmarried daughters continued living in the 29th Street house. The youngest daughter, Virginia Hollerith, was anxious to preserve the old house and placed a scenic easement on Mackall Square in October 1984. She did not include the northern section of the lawn, however, since it was removed from the house.

The heirs of Virginia Hollerith sold both houses in 1995. Ben Johns, a Georgetown businessman, bought Mackall Square; he restored the house and added a swimming pool and guesthouse on the north lawn. Today the house looks much as it did in the 19th century.

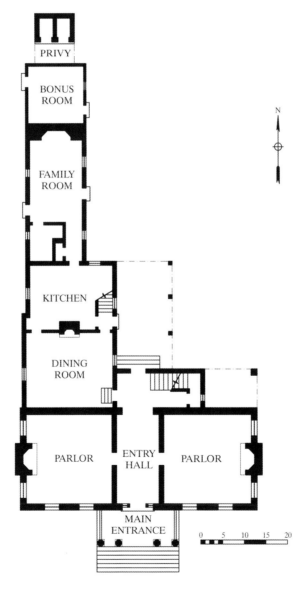

FIRST-FLOOR PLAN

STEEDMAN HOUSE

1925 F STREET, N.W.
WASHINGTON, D.C.

1849

Architect: Unknown
Neighborhood: Foggy Bottom
Status: Residence of the President of George Washington University

20TH AND F STREET ELEVATION

USED DURING THE CIVIL WAR FOR UNION ARMY OFFICES

STEEDMAN HOUSE IS ONE OF ONLY A FEW surviving Greek Revival residences in the city of Washington. Dozens of them were built in the heart of the city, along F, G, and H Streets, between 7th and 18th Streets, N.W., during the 1840s and 1850s, when that was a prime residential neighborhood. Almost all were razed in the early-20th century for the construction of office buildings and hotels. Capt. Charles Steedman, a distinguished naval officer who worked in the nearby Naval Observatory on 23rd Street, built this Foggy Bottom example. During the Civil War he commanded the iron steamers *USS Maryland* and *USS Ticonderoga* and helped enforce the blockade of the South Carolina and Georgia coasts. After the war Steedman commanded the Boston Navy Yard and then the South Pacific Squadron before retiring from active duty in 1873. His last years were spent in Washington, where he died in 1890.

This three-story, low-gabled brick house has a width of five bays. Five small Greek Revival frieze windows on the facade, highlighted above by a decorative terra-cotta cornice, light the third-floor rooms.

The first-floor plan includes a central hall with the staircase in the rear. On the left front is the library, which opens into the dining room in the rear. On the right were originally double parlors, later made into one long drawing room. There are four bedrooms on the second floor, as well as others on the third.

When the Civil War broke out, the Foggy Bottom neighborhood, bounded by Pennsylvania Avenue on the north, 17th Street on the east, the Potomac River on the south, and Rock Creek on the west, was basically divided into two parts by 23rd Street. The area west of 23rd was mostly industrial, with German immigrants working in breweries and glass factories, and Irish immigrants working at the Washington Gas Works. Most lived in the same neighborhood in modest narrow row houses. East of 23rd Street, however, there were more spacious freestanding houses with lawns and trees. The elegant Naval Observatory building, on the west side of 23rd, was the only "industry" close to this more desirable part of Foggy Bottom. In 1860 the dedication of a bronze equestrian statue of Gen. George Washington enhanced the

CONSERVATORY

neighborhood. Designed by Clark Mills, the sculpture was installed in the newly created Washington Circle, a public park at the intersection of Pennsylvania Avenue and 23rd Street.

Foggy Bottom underwent substantial change during the Civil War, when many of the dwellings west of the White House were rented as offices for the Union army. The original Corcoran Gallery, at Pennsylvania Avenue and 17th Street, then a private building owned by Confederate sympathizer William Wilson Corcoran, was seized for the Quartermaster General's headquarters. Major General Hancock and General U.S. Grant, as well as the adjutant general, the signal corps commander, and the medical director of the army similarly took over other houses. Wooden barracks were erected in Foggy Bottom just south of Washington Circle along 23rd Street for the Invalid Division, comprising injured soldiers who were unfit for battle but able to guard government buildings in the city. Between those barracks and the Potomac

Following Pages: DINING ROOM, WITH CHAIRS, TABLE, AND PORTRAIT WHICH ORIGINALLY BELONGED TO GENERAL U. S. GRANT

River, in an area known as Camp Fry, many wooden warehouses were built to store uniforms and supplies, overseen by the quartermaster general.

With her husband away at war, Mrs. Steedman rented their house for $100 a month to the Office of the Commissary-General of Prisoners of the War Department from 1862 to 1865. During the war Brig. General William Hoffman headed this office; he supervised the Union prisons that housed Confederate officers and soldiers, and the exchange and parole of Confederate and Union prisoners. After Mrs. Steedman sold the house to the U.S. government in 1865, the commissary-general continued to occupy it until the department was dissolved in 1867.

The second owner, Alexander Ray, a wealthy coal shipper and flour mill owner, made major alterations in 1868. The recessed Greek Revival entrance is original to the house, but an elaborate pediment supported by bold consoles replaced the simple flat entrance frontispiece. A sash with six-over-six lights was changed to the then fashionable two-over-two lights. A prominent three-sided bay window was added to the dining room facing 20th Street, as well as a large rear wing, which provided more service rooms on the first floor and bedrooms on the second floor. The exterior was painted white in the late-19th century.

The appearance of the house changed again in 1872, when the city's board of public works graded F Street, N.W., lowering it 5 feet at this location. Consequently, front steps and a stone retaining wall were added to support the front and side lawns. An 1863 photograph of the Steedman House, with Union soldiers and civilian clerks standing in front, documents the original siting of the house, which was level with the street. After Ray's death in 1878, the family continued to own the house until 1909. They rented it as an investment to many prominent people, including congressmen, army officers, and cabinet members.

In 1921, American University, located at the intersection of Massachusetts and Nebraska Avenues at Ward Circle, purchased Steedman House for use as a downtown campus. When that plan was abandoned,

the university rented the house briefly to the Lithuanian Embassy in 1923, and then to Mr. and Mrs. James F. Curtis in 1924. Curtis, a Harvard-educated lawyer, came to Washington to serve as assistant secretary of the Treasury Department under President Coolidge. Laura Curtis, his wife, was a leading figure in the Republican Party social scene throughout the 1920s and 1930s. She was well connected socially in the nation's capital before her marriage: President McKinley had appointed her father, William Rush Merriam, a former governor of Minnesota, director of the U.S. Customs Bureau. She married James Freeman Curtis in 1913 and had four children with him. Laura entertained graciously in the Steedman House, which she transformed into a showplace for her collection of family portraits, paintings, tapestries, oriental rugs, and American and English antique furniture.

When the Great Depression began, Laura Curtis, then separated from her husband, could not afford the rent for Steedman House. Friends persuaded her to stay—by living on the second and third floors and transforming the first floor into a social club. The furniture and atmosphere had not changed and the servants all remained, and Mrs. Curtis was able to make ends meet as manager of the new F Street Club. Privacy was key to the club's success, as the names of the 300 members were never published, nor was photography allowed at dinner parties given there by luminaries such as Mamie Eisenhower, Jacqueline Kennedy, Pamela Harriman, and Katherine Graham.

In 1938 Laura Curtis divorced her husband and married John Messick Gross, vice president of Bethlehem Steel Company. Even though she moved to Bethlehem, Pennsylvania, to be with her husband, she continued to manage the F Street Club by commuting monthly to Washington, D.C. When her husband retired, they moved to Washington to live in their apartment at the Watergate, where she died in 1973, while still managing the F Street Club.

George Washington University acquired Steedman House in 1974. Several years later, the university planned to sell the landmark to the adjacent World

Bank as part of land for its new office building. Citing its historical and architectural importance, city review agencies denied the university's request to raze it. In its last years the F Street Club admitted the university's faculty until 1999, when it became the Alumni House.

After the property was renovated and a sun room added to its east side, Steedman House became the university President's House in 2008, its first resident being Steven Knapp, the university's 16th president.

Knapp thus became the first president to live on campus since the university had moved to Foggy Bottom in 1912. His predecessor, Stephen J. Trachtenberg, lived for 19 years in a university-owned house on Bancroft Place, just west of Connecticut Avenue, above Dupont Circle. When President Knapp elected to live on campus, the Bancroft Place house was sold for $3 million and the funds allocated to an endowment for Steedman House.

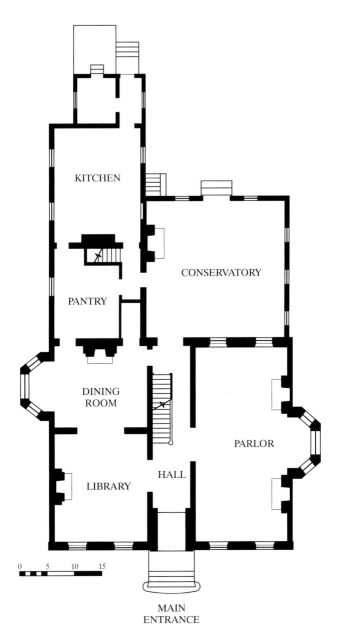

KITCHEN

CONSERVATORY

PANTRY

DINING ROOM

PARLOR

HALL

LIBRARY

0 5 10 15

MAIN ENTRANCE

FIRST-FLOOR PLAN

VICTORIAN
HOUSES

Oak Hill Cemetery Gatehouse

Cedar Hill

House One

Cooke's Row

Breiding House

Denman–Werlich House

Brown–Toutorsky House

Clara Barton House

Heurich House

OAK HILL CEMETERY GATEHOUSE

3001 R STREET, N.W.
WASHINGTON, D.C.

———————————

1850

Designer: George de la Roche
Neighborhood: Georgetown
Status: Residence of the Cemetery Manager

MAIN GATEPOSTS

MANAGER'S FRONT PARLOR

THE OAK HILL CEMETERY GATEHOUSE IS ONE of the most unusual residences in Washington, among the few surviving cemetery gatehouses on the East Coast that are still used as residence and office. One of the longest-termed cemetery superintendents was Joseph Pozell, who served from 1985 to 2005. His widow, Ella Pozell, succeeded him, from 2005 to 2012, and in 2013, her niece's husband, David Jackson, a former manager of the Army/Navy Club, succeeded Ella.

The redbrick, three-story Italianate-style house is quite picturesque, with various gabled roofs with wide eaves and wooden brackets, and a tall corner hipped-roof bell tower. Red Seneca sandstone accentuates many of the exterior details, including the hoodmolds around the arched windows and doors, as well as the water table, steps, buttress caps, and stringcourse around the tower. The architect successfully rebelled against the symmetry of Greek Revival houses.

The original 1850 design consisted of a two-story house and a three-story bell tower. A number of alterations were made after the Civil War. The main change came in 1867, when it was found that the timbers in the bell tower had rotted. The tower was removed and rebuilt, and a third floor was added to the house. The first floor was enlarged shortly afterward. By 1881 the additions to the Gatehouse were complete, and it has remained the same since, with nine rooms. The first floor contains the main staircase, two office rooms, a walk-in safe, a library, dining room, parlor, small rear staircase, and kitchen. The second floor has two bedrooms, two baths, a sitting room, and a dressing room. The third floor comprises one bedroom and the bell tower.

Following Pages: R STREET ELEVATION

MAIN STAIRCASE

Following the Civil War a detached two-story staff building was put up immediately west of the Gatehouse. On the first floor is a workshop, locker room, and bath; on the second are the groundskeeper's office and a kitchen and lunchroom.

Washington banker, real estate investor, and philanthropist William Wilson Corcoran (1798–1888) paid $3,000 for 15 acres at the highest point of Georgetown on Road Street, renamed R Street about 1900, on which to found Oak Hill Cemetery in 1849.

Corcoran met New York architect James Renwick Jr. when he won the competition to design the Smithsonian Castle in 1846. Corcoran hired Renwick three years later to enlarge and redesign his house facing Lafayette Park in an exuberant Italianate vein and in 1858 to design his private art gallery in the Second Empire style at Pennsylvania Avenue and 17th Street. In 1850 Corcoran commissioned Renwick to build an elegant Gothic Revival stone chapel for Oak Hill Cemetery. This small building, 23 by 41 feet, is sheathed in local gray Potomac gneiss. The chapel is decorated with local Seneca sandstone on the window surrounds, frieze, front door moldings, caps for the buttresses, belt courses, water table, and finial. After the Civil War, the clear glass windows of the chapel were replaced with stained glass. The large east window portrays an angel, the west elevation has a rose window, and the north and south elevations each contain three identically patterned stained-glass windows. Among the most decorative features of the interior are the dozens of elaborately carved quatrefoils on the vertical boarding of the ceiling.

An elegant 10-foot-high cast-iron Egyptian Revival fence was added in 1852–53 along the north side of R Street between 30th and 31st Streets. It was cast from the original mold used in 1844 by Dr. Joseph Bigelow for his Mount Auburn Cemetery in Charlestown, Massachusetts. The top of the fence features three-tiered lotus flowers as finials. Mount Auburn, founded in 1831 in the then undeveloped Boston suburbs and landscaped as a park, was the first noteworthy rural cemetery in the United States. The layout of dozens of other American cemeteries, including Oak Hill, are based conceptually on Mount Auburn, with its elegant monuments, impressive vistas, and carefully tended landscaping. Fortunately, Oak Hill's fence still stands, for Mount Auburn's board of directors voted to demolish the entire 4,000-foot length of theirs in the 1960s, its upkeep having become too costly.

Ten of Oak Hill's 11 superintendents have served with industry and integrity. The one exception was the first superintendent, John A. Blundon of Ohio, who was employed from 1851 to 1869. Blundon greatly expanded Oak Hill by purchasing additional land on the east in 1865 and 1867 from Charles Dodge of Evermay, an adjacent estate. Blundon paid Dodge a total of $18,000 for the additional "13 acres," which turned out to be only 7½ when it was surveyed after the sale. The elegant iron fence was extended, and a second pair of sandstone gate piers and iron gates were installed at the corner of R and 28th Streets to enclose the additional property. An investigation in 1868 revealed that Blundon had mismanaged

CORCORAN-EUSTIS MAUSOLEUM

recordkeeping, failing over the years to collect more than $8,000 in annual dues from the lot owners and allegedly receiving kickbacks from stone carvers and florists. Blundon effectively exercised control over the board of directors during the Civil War, when Corcoran, a Southern sympathizer, moved to Paris. The superintendent's duplicity infuriated Corcoran, who collected enough proxies from plot owners to regain control of the board in 1869. William Barker immediately succeeded Blundon as superintendent.

Oak Hill is endowed with many outstanding stone monuments and sculptures. On the Ellipse, the 135-foot-long front lawn between the gatehouse and the chapel, is a statue of the Episcopal bishop of Maryland William Pinkney (1810–1883) and a bust of John Howard Payne, the American diplomat who wrote the beloved song, *Home Sweet Home.* Between them is a small bronze crane that serves as the centerpiece of a Victorian fountain. Several large neoclassical mausoleums here are noteworthy, including one

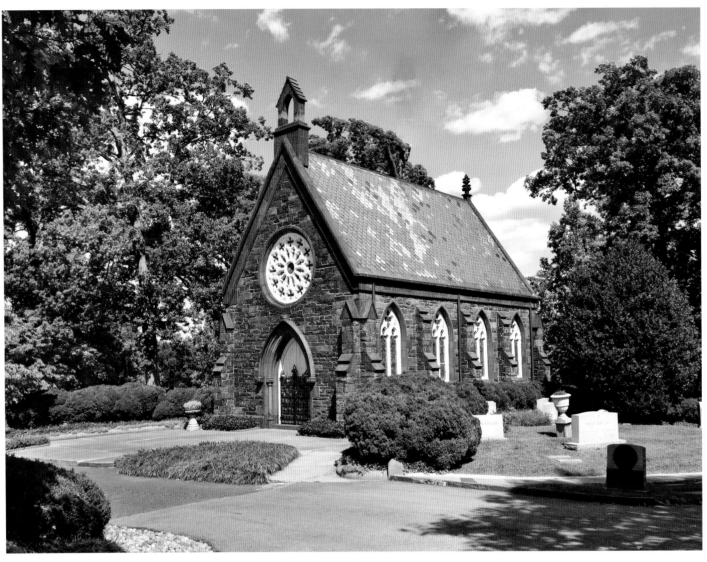

CHAPEL

designed for Corcoran's family by Philadelphia architect Thomas U. Walter in 1852, while he served as architect of the U.S. Capitol extension. The Corcoran name is carved on the frieze on one side, while on the other side is carved "Eustis," the family into which Corcoran's daughter, Louise, married. The Corcoran mausoleum is located north of the chapel. Another prominent early neoclassical mausoleum, east of the stone chapel, is that designed for John Peter van Ness in 1824 by George Hadfield, who had earlier designed the first War and Treasury Department buildings adjacent to the White House. John Peter van Ness was a former congressman from New York and an

early Washington banker. The mausoleum, originally sited at a downtown cemetery that was razed for business development in 1872, was moved to Oak Hill Cemetery for preservation. The local Evergreen Garden Club restored it in 1992.

In addition to these prominent sculptures and monumental neoclassical mausoleums, there are more than two dozen eminent Victorian stone mausoleums. Gradually, as most downtown graveyards were razed for development, many other graves were moved to Oak Hill, including that of Gen. Uriah Forrest (1746–1805), a delegate to the Continental Congress in 1786–87 and U.S. Congressman from Maryland

Right: INTERIOR OF CHAPEL

(1793–94). Although Forrest's Georgetown residence has long since been demolished, his 18th-century country house, Rosedale, one of the oldest buildings in Washington, still stands in Cleveland Park at 34th and Newark Streets, N.W. Other prominent antebellum notables buried at Oak Hill include Secretary of War John H. Eaton and Joseph Henry, a friend of Corcoran's, who became the first secretary of the Smithsonian Institution in 1846.

Among the important Civil War figures interred here are 16 Union generals and admirals, including the well-liked Major General Jesse Reno (1823–1862) and one Confederate general, Cadmus Marcellus Wilcox (1824–1890). Also buried at Oak Hill is Edwin Stanton (1814–1869), secretary of war under Presidents Lincoln and Johnson, who opposed lenient terms for the South during Reconstruction.

More than 19,000 burials have taken place at Oak Hill and hundreds more vacant plots remain, still owned by local families. However, fewer than 500 burial sites remain for both interment and cremation urns. Oak Hill today is one of the few historical American cemeteries that do not require perpetual care fees from plot owners. The cemetery relies on the original endowment established by W. W. Corcoran in 1849, which is currently assessed at $3 million. Even so, Oak Hill relies on annual gifts to maintain upkeep of the grounds and perform funerals.

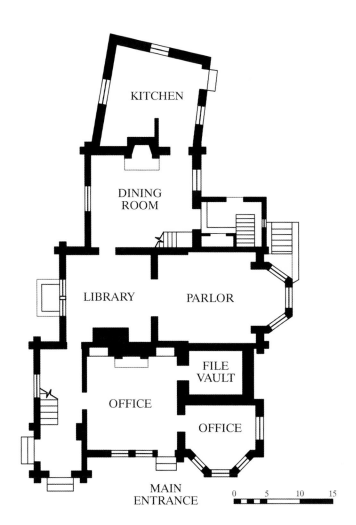

FIRST-FLOOR PLAN

CEDAR HILL

1411 W STREET, S.E.
WASHINGTON, D.C.

1855
WINDOW BAYS AND REAR WING 1878

Architect: John Welsh van Hook, 1855
Neighborhood: Anacostia
Status: Historic House Museum

FACADE

FREDERICK DOUGLASS WITH HIS SECOND WIFE, SEATED, AND HER SISTER

THE U.S. NATIONAL PARK SERVICE MAINTAINS as historic house museums the properties of four prominent African Americans: Frederick Douglass, Booker T. Washington, George Washington Carver, and Mary McLeod Bethune. While the latter three were important leaders in black education in the late-19th and early-20th centuries, Frederick Douglass, a former slave, played the central role in the fight for both abolition and women's rights.

Douglass lived at Cedar Hill from 1877 until his death in 1895. He was absent for short periods of time: while campaigning for Republican presidential candidates in 1880 and 1888; during a trip to Europe in 1886–87; and when he served as U.S. minister to Haiti, from 1889 to 1891. Douglass and his first wife, Anne Murray Douglass, a native of Baltimore and also

a free black, and his second wife, Helen Pitts Douglass, a white woman originally from Rochester, New York, lived comfortably at Cedar Hill, attended by a housekeeper, butler, and carriage driver. In his later years Douglass made a good living from his positions as marshal and recorder of deeds of the District of Columbia, as well as a considerable income from speaker's fees.

The origins of Cedar Hill trace back to 1854, when three Washington investors, John Welsh van Hook, John Fox, and John Dobler formed the Union Land Association to develop a new subdivision in far southeast Washington called Uniontown. That year they purchased 100 acres of a 240-acre farm owned by Enoch Tucker on the east side of the Anacostia River, directly across from the Washington Navy

WEST PARLOR

Yard. The subdivision was laid out with 700 lots covering 15 blocks. The developers expected many Washington Navy Yard mechanics to build houses in Uniontown since it was an easy walk across the Navy Yard Bridge (now the 11th Street Bridge) that spanned the Anacostia. Though many of the lots, priced at $60, sold within the first three years, speculators who held lots but did not build on them crippled the town.

Cedar Hill, originally known as Van Hook's Hill, was the most substantial house in Uniontown. Constructed in 1855 by John W. van Hook, it served as a sales office for Uniontown lots and then became his residence. The imposing brick house stands 51 feet above street level, giving it a commanding view of the city and the U. S. Capitol in the distance. Van Hook, who trained as an architect in Philadelphia, moved to Baltimore as a young man to work for Johns Hopkins, a prominent merchant and entrepreneur, in developing that city's early suburbs. In 1852 he moved to Washington and entered the real estate business.

He very likely designed his Uniontown house, embellishing it with a broad front porch supported by four fluted Doric columns crowned with a latticework frieze. The main roof has a central gable. The two first-floor bays on the east side of the house were added in the late 1870s. The imposing front entrance, with a pair of paneled doors flanked by

Following Pages: EAST PARLOR

LIBRARY AND DESK OF FREDERICK DOUGLASS

sidelights and crowned by a wide transom, opens onto a central hallway. On the second floor, the hallway terminates in the front with a three-sided bay with a French door framed by two windows.

At the end of the Civil War, Van Hook took out a mortgage on the house with the newly established Freedman's Bank. When the developer's real estate business and produce firm both failed, he lost the house in early 1877 to the bank. In September 1877 Douglass, former president of the Freedmen's Savings Bank, purchased the 9½ acres of Van Hook's Hill from the bank for $6,700. He renamed it Cedar Hill for the great number of cedars on the lawn. Douglass and his family moved in the following year and bought additional adjoining land, increasing the property to 15½ acres.

The plan of the original 1855 house has a first-floor central hall with a staircase on the left. The east, or left, side of the hall contains a formal front parlor

for receiving guests and a small library at the rear. To the west, or right, of the central hall is the more informal family parlor with a piano and a dining room behind. The second floor has seven bedrooms, and the third floor has five small rooms whose use remains unknown. In 1877–78, Douglass built a two-story, wooden rear wing with a kitchen, pantry, laundry room, and storage room on the first floor and three bedrooms on the second floor. Over the following decade he added seven outbuildings to the grounds, including a small office, stable, and carriage house.

Cedar Hill has a remarkable collection of Douglass' prints, photographs, busts, and other artifacts relating to the history of the abolition of American slavery, and to a lesser degree, women's rights in the United States in the 19th century. Prints of Abraham Lincoln and Douglass himself are displayed with portraits of other abolitionists—Wendell Phillips, Gerrit Smith, William Lloyd Garrison, Elijah P.

Lovejoy, as well as Blanche K. Bruce, the first black U.S. senator, who served during Reconstruction from Mississippi. A good friend of Douglass', Bruce witnessed his marriage to Helen Pitts and served as a pallbearer at his funeral. Other prints show pivotal historical events, such as John Brown being led to his execution after his failed attempt to arm the slaves in Harpers Ferry, Virginia.

During the 17 years that Douglass lived here the house was full of relatives. The 21 grandchildren of his three children with Anne Murray were occasional visitors, while other family members stayed for long periods, including Douglass' half-brother, and the mother and sister of his second wife. Douglass also welcomed the many strangers who came to pay their respects.

When Douglass died in 1895, his second wife was intended to inherit the house. His will proved invalid, however, because it bore only two of the required three witness signatures. His children put the house and grounds up for auction, but his widow was able to acquire it with a mortgage for $12,000. Helen Pitts Douglass devoted the remaining eight years of her life to preserving Cedar Hill. She bequeathed it to the Frederick Douglass Memorial and Historical Association, which tried to maintain the house and the original furnishings despite meager funds. In 1916 the National Association of Colored Women's Clubs paid off the $4,000 mortgage.

The National Association of Colored Women's Clubs began to raise funds in the 1920s when the foundation could no longer maintain the house. In 1922 the Colored Women's Clubs also paid for the construction of a separate, one-story brick building for a caretaker behind the house. When the members could no longer afford the upkeep and repairs, they gave Cedar Hill to the U.S. government in 1962. The National Park Service undertook an extensive restoration of the 20-room house, opening it to the public as a museum in 1972. Much of the roof had to be replaced, the walls and floors were strengthened, and interior furnishings, many stored in the attic, were returned to their late-19th-century appearance.

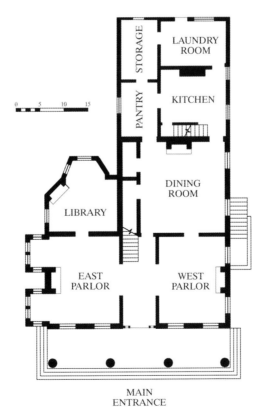

MAIN ENTRANCE

FIRST-FLOOR PLAN

HOUSE ONE

GALLAUDET UNIVERSITY
800 FLORIDA AVENUE, N.E.
WASHINGTON, D.C.

───────────────

1867–68

Architect: Frederick C. Withers
Landscape Architects: Frederick Law Olmsted & Calvert Vaux
Neighborhood: Trinidad
Status: Residence of the President of Gallaudet University

EAST PORCH

MAIN ENTRANCE

IN 1855 AMOS KENDALL ESTABLISHED A SCHOOL for five deaf children on his large estate, Kendall Green, one mile north of the U.S. Capitol. A prominent Washingtonian, Kendall was incensed by the actions of P. H. Skinner, a teacher from New York. Skinner abused deaf-mute children in his school for the disabled and committed financial fraud. He would display the children to attract donations and then travel to a new location and use the same ploy. Kendall made a case against him in court, and as a result the judge removed the children, ages 6 to 13, from Skinner's charge and appointed Kendall their guardian.

Amos Kendall was the editor of the influential Washington newspaper, *The Argos of Western America*, as well as a major figure in the Democratic Party, having served as a close adviser to President Andrew Jackson. He was appointed to President James Buchanan's cabinet as postmaster general. Kendall had become financially independent through shrewdly investing in Samuel F. B. Morse's new invention, the telegraph, and serving as Morse's business manager during its development and marketing.

Kendall donated 2 acres for the school from his estate in 1856, and in 1857 Congress chartered the

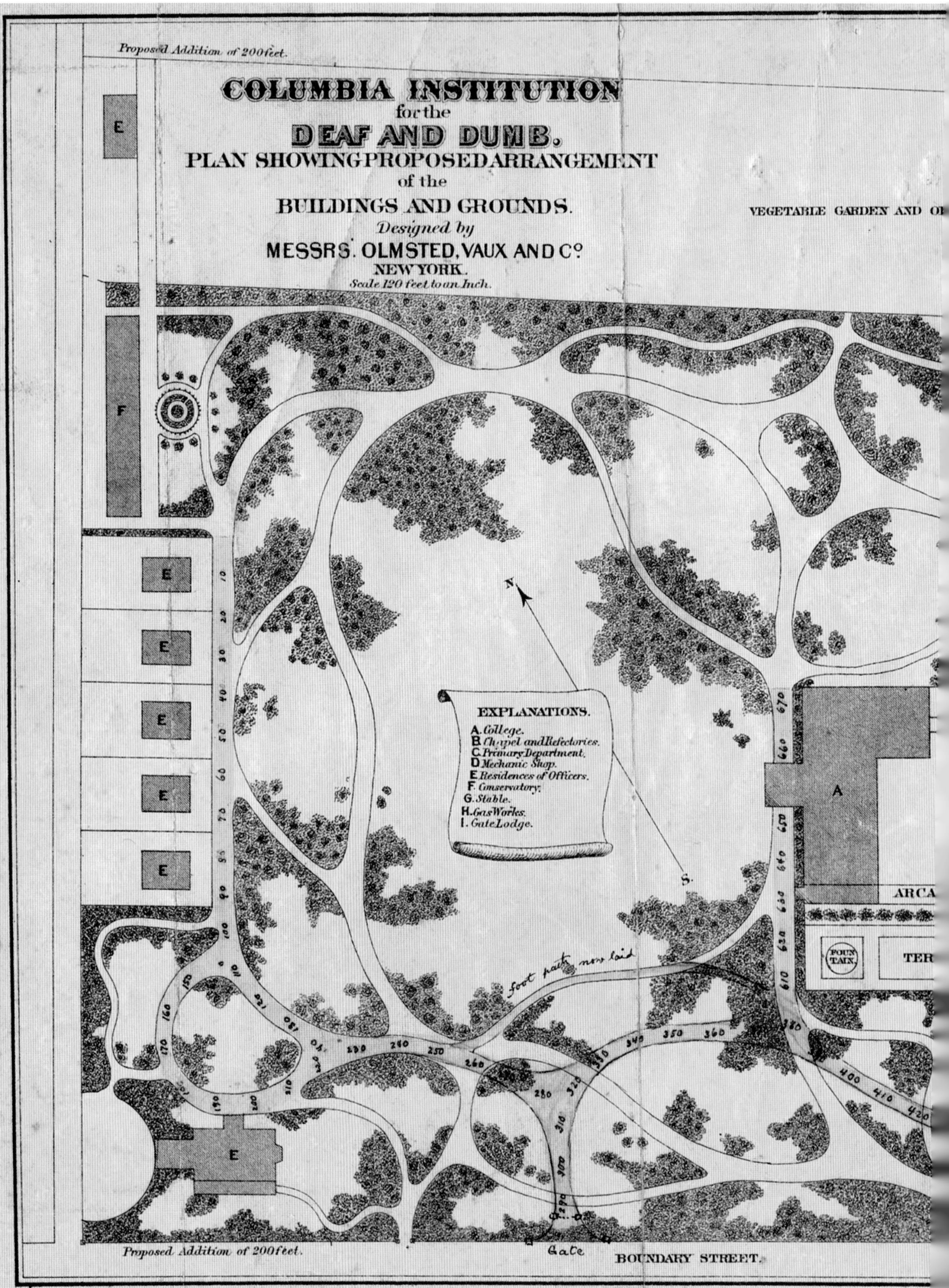

Proposed Addition of 200 feet.

COLUMBIA INSTITUTION
for the
DEAF AND DUMB,
PLAN SHOWING PROPOSED ARRANGEMENT
of the
BUILDINGS AND GROUNDS.
Designed by
MESSRS. OLMSTED, VAUX AND Cº
NEW YORK.
Scale 120 feet to an Inch.

VEGETABLE GARDEN AND O

E

F

E

E

E

E

E

N

EXPLANATIONS.

A. *College.*
B. *Chapel and Refectories.*
C. *Primary Department.*
D. *Mechanic Shop.*
E. *Residences of Officers.*
F. *Conservatory.*
G. *Stable.*
H. *Gas Works.*
I. *Gate Lodge.*

S.

A

ARCA

FOUN TAIN

TER

foot path now laid

E

10
20
30
40
50
60
70
80
90
100
110
120
130
140
150
160
170
180
190
200
210
220
230
240
250
260
270
280
290
300
310
320
330
340
350
360
370
380
390
400
410
420
610
620
630
640
650
660
670

Proposed Addition of 200 feet.

Gate   BOUNDARY STREET.

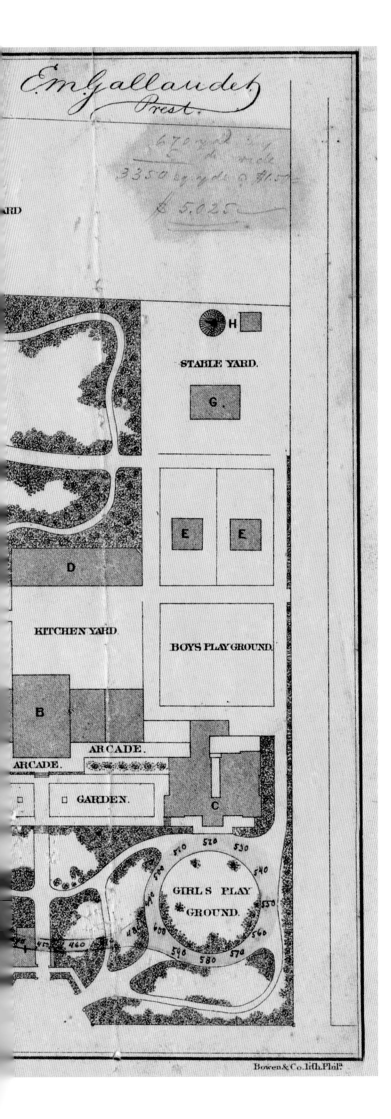

Columbia Institution for the Deaf, Dumb, and Blind. Kendall began searching for a school principal, and hired 20-year-old Edward Miner Gallaudet, a teacher at the Hartford School for the Deaf, as the first headmaster. Edward was the son of the Hartford School's founder, Thomas Hopkins Gallaudet. Edward's widowed mother, who was deaf, accompanied him to Washington to supervise the children when they were not in the classroom. Gallaudet designed and Kendall financed a handsome three-story Greek Revival school building on the new campus to replace two crowded, temporary buildings.

Operation of the Columbia Institution was interrupted during the Civil War by the temporary takeover of the campus for use as an army hospital in the summer of 1861. Gallaudet successfully petitioned Congress and President Lincoln to elevate the Columbia Institution for the Deaf, Dumb, and Blind to Gallaudet College in 1864. Shortly thereafter, the blind students were transferred to a school in Baltimore, and the institution focused exclusively on the deaf.

President Edward Miner Gallaudet took a very active role in advancing the college's physical size and academic standing during his 46 years there. He commissioned Frederick Law Olmsted, a native of Hartford, Connecticut, and a longtime friend of the Gallaudet family, to prepare a master plan for landscaping the campus and siting future buildings. Olmsted and his partner, Calvert Vaux, had landscaped the grounds of the Retreat for the Insane in Hartford in 1861. After Amos Kendall died in 1869, Gallaudet was able to acquire $85,000 in government funds to buy the 81-acre campus from the Kendall estate.

In 1867 Gallaudet persuaded Congress to grant $51,000 for new buildings on the campus, which were built between 1867 and 1885, and included the president's 20-room residence (House One), five professors' houses, Chapel Hall, College Hall (the main building for classrooms and offices), the gymnasium, and a small classroom building. Frederick Clarke

EDWARD GALLAUDET AND FAMILY ON THE EAST PORCH IN THE 1880S

Withers, a prominent English-born architect, designed the buildings in a High Victorian Gothic vein, influenced by the writings of John Ruskin. Withers was an associate in Olmsted and Vaux's New York firm, well known for designing Central Park.

House One is located in the southwest corner of the campus, facing a row of faculty houses (named House Two to House Six). A steeply pitched gabled roof crowns the facade, which features a tall, projecting entrance pavilion. Delicately carved flowers and leaves ornament the brownstone entrance. Withers created a picturesque effect by designing steep gabled and hipped roofs, dormers with wide overhangs that project past the walls, and carved wooden brackets on both the dormers and the east porch. A polychromatic effect results from bands of stone set into the brick walls and the use of horizontal rows of colored slate on the original roof (since replaced with modern shingles). The spacious east side porch, with bowed

entrance, retains its original balustrades as well as triangular brackets set on the sides for the pillars.

The first floor of House One provides easy circulation for large numbers of guests, as well as more intimate spaces to receive visitors on business. From the foyer one enters a wide central hall that leads at the far end to the conservatory (labeled "plant cabinet" on the original plans). The sidelights of the conservatory door were originally large lithophanes—decorative Victorian colored glass scenes, which were removed by a former occupant and are now in storage on the campus.

To the left of the central hall is the parlor, which connects to the library. These two rooms were designed to have the best views of the grounds and main buildings—Chapel Hall and College Hall. To the right is the reception room for visitors and the dining room, with a bowed end. A stair hall separates the reception and dining rooms and connects to the

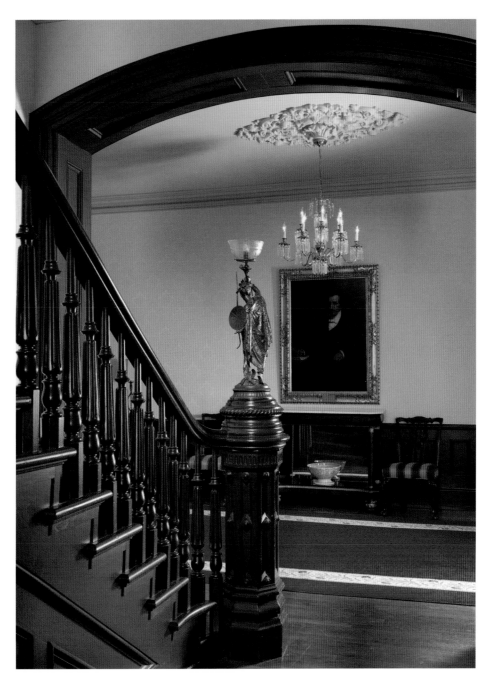

MAIN STAIRS AND CENTER HALL

service wing on the right. Here are found the large kitchen, laundry room, storerooms, and butler's pantry adjacent to the dining room, and the kitchen pantry.

Most of the rooms on the first, second, and third floors have working fireplaces, which retain their original wooden mantels and handsome ceramic tile surrounds. The library fireplace surrounds are Minton tiles from Stoke-on-Trent, England. The top ones depict scenes from the Biblical parables, while those on the sides illustrate Aesop's fables. Many of the original Victorian furnishings are still in place throughout the house. Most are Renaissance Revival, including a massive walnut bed reminiscent of the Lincoln bed at the White House, while others are the simpler Eastlake style. The dining room contains a handsome ceiling medallion as well as an American Federal sideboard circa 1790, which was given to Gallaudet by Kendall when he first occupied the house in 1868.

PARLOR

LINCOLN BEDROOM

After his first year at the school, Gallaudet married Jane Fessenden of Hartford in 1858. Their two surviving children were named Katharine and Grace. Jane died in 1864, and two years later Gallaudet wed 20-year-old Susan Denison of Vermont, 10 years his junior. She presided over the daily and social affairs at House One with grace and poise. The house was full of activity—Susan's 12-year-old orphaned nephew, Will Denison, came to live with them and during the 1870s the Gallaudets had three more children, Eliza, Herbert, and Denison. Even with six children the nine-bedroom house was large enough to temporarily accommodate the first six women students who were admitted in 1887. They resided on the third floor for several years until a separate building could be built for them. A striking 1885 photograph shows the entire family assembled on the lawn in front of the east porch, complete with newly fashionable bicycles and tricycles.

Edward Miner Gallaudet's skillful lobbying of Congress resulted in funds for new buildings on campus as well as scholarships for many of his students. By 1871 Gallaudet College had truly become a national institution, with deaf students from 23 states and the District of Columbia. One of Gallaudet's goals was to train deaf students to become teachers of the deaf. By 1867 there were 3,000 deaf students enrolled in 28 elementary schools across the United States; many of the schools were in desperate need of professionally trained teachers.

Gallaudet retired in 1887 and built a home in Hartford, Connecticut, 30 years after he came to Washington. However, his love of the college and commitment to furthering its interests kept him there for another 23 years. He rented out the Hartford house until he finally moved there in 1910. The former president's last project was to write a history of the college. After 46 years directing the school's affairs, Gallaudet died in Hartford in 1917 at the age of 80. A statue of him presides over the grounds where most of the Victorian buildings he helped construct, including House One, have been carefully preserved.

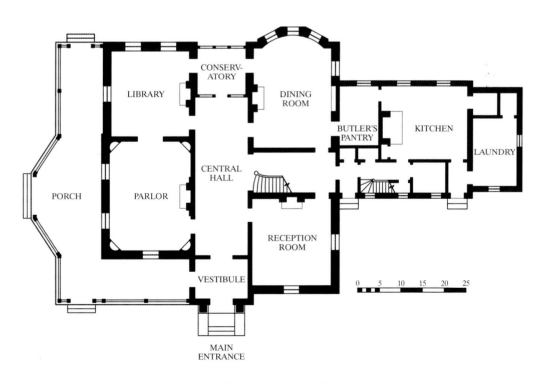

FIRST-FLOOR PLAN

COOKE'S ROW

3007–3029 Q STREET, N.W.
WASHINGTON, D.C.

1868–70

Architect: Starkweather & Plowman
Neighborhood: Georgetown
Status: Private Residences

FACADES OF VILLAS I AND 2

PORCH IN SECOND EMPIRE STYLE

THE PICTURESQUE ROW OF SEMIDETACHED houses on the north side of Q Street between 30th and 31st Streets in Georgetown is known as Cooke's Row. Henry D. Cooke (1825–1881), a Columbus, Ohio, journalist who came to Washington to cover the inauguration of Abraham Lincoln in 1861, built the four pairs of residences in 1868. He stayed on at the request of his brother, Jay Cooke, well-known owner of the Philadelphia bank Jay Cooke & Company. Henry established the Washington branch of Jay Cooke & Company in February 1862,

and his financial assets began to soar. Henry secured the sale of U.S. Treasury bonds through Jay Cooke & Company by means of his friendship with Secretary of the Treasury Salmon P. Chase. In 1862 he founded the Washington & Georgetown Railroad Company and served as its first president. He also persuaded Chase to become a fellow investor.

In 1871 President Grant appointed Henry D. Cooke the first governor of the District of Columbia as a reward for financially supporting his presidential campaign in 1868. Congress had just changed the

SPIRAL STAIRCASE IN ENTRANCE HALL

government of Washington from the traditional form of an elected mayor to a territorial government with a governor appointed by the president and an elected legislature. Cooke's position did not last long, however, because of his brother's business failure, which was a major cause of the Panic of 1873.

Jay Cooke's bankruptcy also toppled his brother. Henry lost his Georgetown mansion, designed by the partnership of Andrew Jackson Downing and Calvert Vaux, which still stands at 30th and Q Streets. It was remodeled in 1903 and expanded with two large wings into the Hammond Court Apartments, then converted to condominium status with 26 units in 1982 and renamed the Downing & Vaux House.

During more prosperous times Henry D. Cooke had embarked on a major building program in Georgetown. Both as an investment and as the future home of some of his 12 children, Cooke bought the southern half of the block across the street from his mansion, bounded by Q, R, 30th, and 31st Streets, and began construction in 1868 of the row that bears his name. The two pairs of houses at each end of the row were designed in the Second Empire mode with mansard roofs, while the two pairs in the middle were

Right: STAIR DETAIL

DOUBLE PARLOR

in more of an Italianate vein, with low-slung roofs and towers. The houses were originally named Cooke's Park No. I, beginning at 30th Street, through Cooke's Park No. 8, near 31st.

Norris G. Starkweather, principal partner of the prominent architectural firm Starkweather & Plowman, designed Cooke's Park. The firm began in Philadelphia in 1854 but had moved to Baltimore by 1856. Some of its notable projects include the First Presbyterian Church in Baltimore (1855), an Italianate mansion named Camden near Port Royal, Virginia (1857), and the Virginia Theological Seminary for the Episcopal Church near Alexandria, Virginia (1860). Starkweather designed another important Washington building, the Georgetown Academy of the Visitation, before his death in 1882.

The houses that comprise Cooke's Row are set back 25 feet from Q Street, and each has a spacious side lawn and large rear yard. The floor plans vary slightly among the houses, but all have basically the same arrangement—a long side hall, a large front drawing room, usually 29 by 15 feet, followed by a library, dining room, pantry, and kitchen. The kitchens were originally located in the basement and contained a dumbwaiter to help transport the food. The second and third floors had six or seven bedrooms. Two of the most impressive features of the houses are the front spiral staircases and the doors with high-relief moldings. The spaces are unusually tall—12 feet on the first floor and 11 feet on the second. The houses were insulated with 3-inch open-air spaces in the outer walls, which results in greater warmth in the winter and coolness in the summer.

After his financial setback Henry D. Cooke kept two of the houses on Cooke's Row and sold the remaining six. He and his wife moved into House No. I, at 3007 Q Street, where he died from Bright's disease in 1881. His widow lived in the house until her death in 1904.

Over the years a number of prominent residents have lived in Cooke's Row. Dr. Walter Reed lived in House No. 5 when he was director of the U.S. Army Medical Museum and professor of bacteriology and clinical microscopy at the Army Medical School. In 1900 he was sent to Cuba to investigate the cause of yellow fever, and his findings confirmed that mosquitoes transmitted the disease. During World War II, Field Marshall Sir John and Lady Dill lived in House No. 6, at 3023 Q Street. Dill was the leading British military representative to the United States and a close friend of both President Franklin D. Roosevelt and General George C. Marshall. After Dill died there in 1944, friends erected a bronze equestrian portrait statue in his honor at his grave in Arlington National Cemetery. Today, Bob Woodward, well-known *Washington Post* reporter who exposed the Watergate scandal, occupies House No. 7.

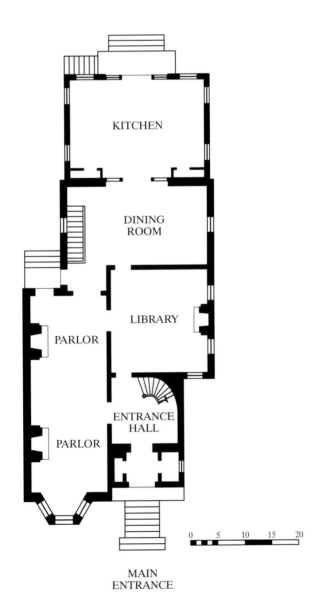

FIRST-FLOOR PLAN OF VILLA NO 7

COOKE'S ROW,
VILLAS 3, 2, AND I,
(LEFT TO RIGHT)

BREIDING HOUSE

1523 31ST STREET, N.W.
WASHINGTON, D.C.

1885

Architect: Harvey L. Page, 1885
Alterations: Henry Simpson, 1899
Neighborhood: Georgetown
Status: Private Residence

FACADE

DETAIL OF QUEEN ANNE FACADE

ONE OF ARCHITECT HARVEY L. PAGE'S BEST Queen Anne houses in Washington with its array of picturesque roof angles and textures, Page designed this small house for Lt. and Mrs. Harrie Webster. It was named Breiding House by the Historic America Building Survey, which entered it into their list of historic buildings in the 1990s when it was owned by Bruce and Hope Breiding. The prominent entrance porch has four cast-iron columns supporting a balustraded cornice. The dark-orange pressed brick was laid with tight mortar joints of the same color, while a shingled second floor adds variety and texture. Under the front gabled roof is a range of three windows whose upper sashes feature a large central pane surrounded on four sides by small panes. The upper sashes of the two first-floor windows have this same arrangement.

The basement door on the far right of the facade originally led to the kitchen, located below the first-floor dining room. A dumbwaiter located in the pantry between the dining room and the foyer brought food to the dining room. In modern times the kitchen was moved to the sunroom in the left rear of the house, and the pantry became a wet bar. In 1999 the current owner cleverly converted part of the rear porch into a family room that opens to the modern kitchen.

Most of the original interior details remain intact. The foyer opens onto a narrow but richly designed staircase with turned balusters. The square newel post is decorated with circles of graduating sizes, with recessed panels below. The living room in the front and the dining room in the rear have fireplaces with glazed terra-cotta tiles featuring birds and vines.

FRONT PARLOR

DINING ROOM

CERAMIC TILE FLOOR IN THE FOYER

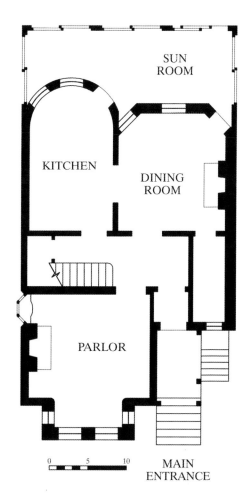

FIRST-FLOOR PLAN

DENMAN–WERLICH HOUSE

1623 16TH STREET, N.W.
WASHINGTON, D.C.

———————

1886
ADDITION 1906

Architect: Fuller & Wheeler.
Addition: Frank H. Jackson, 1906
Neighborhood: Dupont Circle
Status: Office Building

CORNER ELEVATIONS

DORMER WINDOW DETAIL

B ORN IN OHIO, HAMPTON B. DENMAN (1829–1895) served as mayor of Leavenworth, Kansas, in 1858 and was elected to the first state senate in 1859. In his later years his appointment as the Indian agent for Nebraska and Kansas proved very lucrative, and he was able to build a house in Washington, on the northeast corner of 16th and Corcoran Streets, N.W.

It is not known why Denman moved to Washington in 1876 or why he waited a decade to commission the architectural firm Fuller & Wheeler of Albany, New York. Fuller & Wheeler maintained a practice in Albany from 1883 to 1897. Albert W. Fuller (1854–1934), a native of Clinton, New York, founded the firm in 1880. He learned his profession as a draftsman in Albany. In 1883 he and William Arthur Wheeler formed a partnership and made a name for themselves in the 1880s designing Queen Anne houses, several of which were published in architectural periodicals. From 1897 to 1924 Fuller practiced

with other partners in Albany, designing schools, hospitals, office buildings, banks, clubs, libraries, and many noteworthy houses. His 1882 book, *Artistic Houses*, went through a number of editions and helped further his career. On his death in 1934, the *New York Times* listed him as the dean of Albany architects.

The first-floor plan and perspective of the house on fashionable 16th Street, N.W., were featured in the respected *American Architect and Building News* magazine on June 19, 1886. Its fine construction work and the myriad shapes and angles on the side street elevation make it one of the city's most significant Romanesque Revival houses. The many intricate and free-spirited details make the elevations all the more interesting. The first-floor exterior is built of rough granite, with red brick on the upper stories. Decorative cast-iron grilles are set into the basement windows. The massive corner tower anchors the house to its site and provides transition to the side elevation.

ENTRANCE HALL DETAIL

Left: CARVED PANELING ON THE
ENTRANCE HALL AND STAIRCASE

The impressive entrance and stair halls are paneled in walnut, with elaborately carved decoration; even the ceilings are paneled in wood. The pocket doors (which slide into the walls to conserve space), decorative fireplace mantels, and lighting fixtures are original to the space.

After Denman's death his widow continued to live in the house; she died there in 1898. Their son, Hampton Y. Denman, inherited the house; he died soon afterward at age 30 in 1902. He left his estate entirely to charities, prompting his next of kin to contest the will. The heirs won the case and sold the house to Eleanora Hinckley, the estranged wife of prominent Washington portrait painter, Robert Hinckley (1853–1941).

Soon after purchasing the house in 1906 Hinckley added a conservatory and large dining room-ballroom at the rear. It was here that her daughter Gladys had her coming-out party. Gladys made the headlines in 1911 when she became the first woman in Washington to fly in an airplane.

While traveling in Europe with her mother, Gladys met McCeney Werlich, a native of Cleveland, graduate of M. I. T., and American diplomat. She married him shortly afterward in 1923. They traveled to a number of diplomatic assignments—the last being France, where he died in 1926 from complications of malaria, which he had contracted in Monrovia, Liberia. She and her son, Robert, then moved back from Paris to the 16th Street house. While living alone there in 1976, she died tragically—struck down and robbed by three teenagers while walking back from the grocery store three blocks away. The teens were apprehended and sentenced the following year. Her son sold the house in 1977 to Arthur Auerbach, who leased it in 1980 to the Green Door, a nonprofit organization that educates and trains low-income, mentally challenged people to become self-supporting. The Green Door remained a tenant for several years. When Auerbach decided to sell the house in 1987, the Green Door's directors voted to buy it for $800,000, and then raised another $2 million to renovate it and restore the exterior and the elaborate woodwork on the first floor.

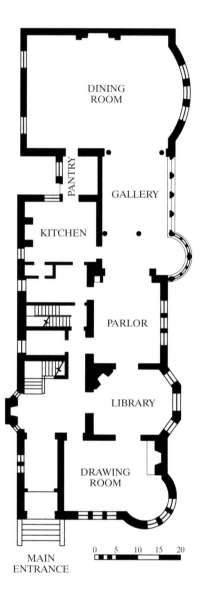

FIRST-FLOOR PLAN

BROWN–TOUTORSKY HOUSE

1720 16TH STREET, N.W.
WASHINGTON, D.C.

1892–94

Architect: William H. Miller
Neighborhood: Dupont Circle
Status: Embassy of the Democratic Republic of the Congo

FACADE

ONE OF THE MOST EXUBERANT LATE VICTO-rian houses in Washington is the 32-room Brown-Toutorsky House, designed in a Flemish Renaissance vein. Its most prominent exterior features are the stepped gables, one on the facade on 16th Street, two slightly smaller ones facing south on Riggs Place, and a fourth on the rear elevation facing west. The windows on the facade of the three-story house are uniform on each story and are set in rows, separated by pilasters. The tops of the windows are lintels on all three levels. The windows on the Riggs Place elevation are asymmetrical, especially on the octagonal staircase tower. The Brown-Toutorsky House is one of the few surviving Victorian mansions in Washington with an intact rear service wing, carriage house, and courtyard.

The first-floor interior is just as impressive as the facade, with paneled walls and floors laid in chevron patterns. The wide entrance hall features a dramatic oak staircase with dozens of turned balusters rising to a landing and then sweeping upward on the right. Two intricately carved wooden griffins flank the newel posts. The spacious front hall was originally used as a reception room. The large fireplace, set at an angle to the side of the staircase, is built of brick and stone. The dining room opens beyond the entrance hall, while double parlors lie to the right of the entrance.

The house was built for Henry Billings Brown (1836–1913), a native of Lee, Massachusetts. After graduating from Harvard, Brown toured Europe, where he became familiar with Renaissance architecture. Subsequently he studied law at both Harvard and Yale and then established a legal practice in Detroit in 1860. While serving as a judge of the U.S. District Court in Detroit, he was appointed to the U.S. Supreme Court in 1890. Brown retired in 1906 and continued to live in the 16th Street house until his death there in 1913.

Previous pages: SOUTH FACADE WITH CARRIAGE HOUSE ON THE LEFT

Right: RECEPTION ROOM MANTEL AND STAIRCASE

PARLOR FIREPLACE

Henry Billings Brown's most prominent Supreme Court case, *Plessy v. Ferguson* (1896), cast a long shadow. It endorsed the "separate but equal" doctrine, specifically upholding the separation of whites from blacks in public transportation facilities. Brown wrote the majority opinion that upheld the Jim Crow laws until the Supreme Court reversed its stance in 1954.

After Brown's death, the mansion changed hands a number of times before prominent Russian pianist Basil P. Toutorsky and his wife, Maria Howard, bought it in 1947. Howard spent her youth in Mexico, where her English father worked as a mining engineer. Toutorsky was born into a noble Russian family in 1896. After completing his music studies in Moscow in 1916, he served as a lieutenant in the Imperial Russian Navy in World War I, and on the staff of the White Army and Navy during the Russian Civil War.

After escaping Russia in 1920, he spent two years in Turkey and then moved to the United States, where he toured as a concert pianist, as well as in Mexico and Canada. While on tour in Mexico City he met Maria Howard and married her there. In the 1930s he established the Toutorsky Academy of Music in Los Angeles, but Maria's fear of earthquakes forced the couple to relocate to Washington, where they bought the Brown house. Both Toutorskys gave piano lessons on six pianos scattered around the first and second floors of the house. Among their best friends were Sergei Rachmaninoff and Ignace Paderewski. The Toutorskys offered the house to the National Trust for Historic Preservation in the 1970s for permanent use as the residence of its president, but the offer was declined due to the high estimated cost of maintaining it.

The architect of Brown-Toutorsky House, William Henry Miller (1848–1922), a native of Trenton, New York, was the first graduate of the architectural school at Cornell University in Ithaca in 1872. Miller became the most prominent architect in Ithaca, designing many public buildings in the city, more than a dozen large estates, and a similar number of buildings for the university, including the president's house. While touring Europe in 1874, he was introduced to the Queen Anne style in England and became one of the first New York architects to design houses in that vein. Miller designed his other prominent Washington mansion, at 1701 Connecticut Avenue, in 1888 in the Romanesque Revival style for Senator Philetus Sawyer. Unfortunately, it was razed in the early 20th century for commercial development.

Among the house's owners after the Toutorskys died was Bruce Johnson, who restored it and lived there a number of years before selling it to another owner, who added several bathrooms upstairs in anticipation of running it as a bed-and-breakfast. Neighborhood opposition to the proposed number of guest rooms, which exceeded the zoning limit, put that plan to rest. The landmark was then sold to the Democratic Republic of the Congo for an embassy in 2011. Neighbors in the Dupont Circle area became outraged when the new owners cut down the trees in front of the house and paved over the front lawn. The Dupont Circle Conservancy was successful in December 2011 in convincing the U.S. Department of State to require the Congolese government to remove the concrete pavement.

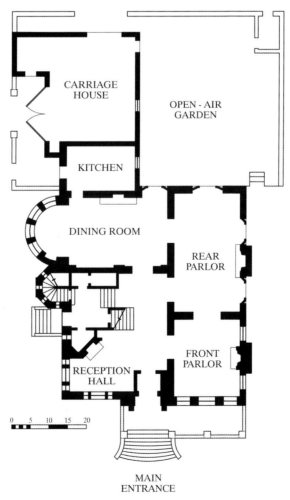

FIRST-FLOOR PLAN

CLARA BARTON HOUSE

5801 OXFORD ROAD

GLEN ECHO, MARYLAND

———————————

1891

REMODELED 1897

Designer: Julian Hubbell

Status: Historic House Museum

FACADE

SIDE ELEVATION

CLARA BARTON (1821–1912), BEST KNOWN FOR her work with Union soldiers in the Civil War and as founder of the American Red Cross, devoted her life to public service. She spent her first 12 working years as a teacher near her native North Oxford, Massachusetts, then founded a public school in Bordentown, New Jersey. Before the Civil War broke out, with the help of her congressman, she secured the position of clerk in the U.S. Patent Office in Washington—she was one of the first women to hold a job in the federal government.

Early in the war Barton went to the U.S. Capitol to tend soldiers suffering from wounds received in the Baltimore riots. Soon her ailing father in Massachusetts encouraged her to volunteer helping wounded Union soldiers. Barton's major contribution to the war effort involved collecting medical supplies for wounded soldiers, beginning with the Battle of First Manassas.

In 1869 an exhausted Barton sailed for Europe to recuperate. While in Switzerland, she learned of the establishment of the Red Cross there and, a decade later, in 1881, founded the American Association of the Red Cross in Washington. Assisted by Julian Hubbell, she brought relief in the 1880s to those displaced by forest fires in Michigan and Texas and by floods of the Mississippi and Ohio rivers, as well as those afflicted by a typhoid fever epidemic in New York, a drought in Texas, a yellow fever epidemic in Florida, and a tornado in Illinois. Her most successful post–Civil War relief project was in response to the infamous Johnstown, Pennsylvania, flood in 1889, when 2,000 people died and thousands more had their houses swept away. Through the Red Cross, Barton raised $200,000 to bring medical supplies and build three large temporary shelters for the homeless, designed by Julian Hubbell. The State of Iowa

donated the thousands of feet of pine the Red Cross used in the Johnstown construction.

At the end of the Johnstown project, Barton was offered the gift of a lot on which to build her own house in the new suburb of Glen Echo, Maryland, 7 miles from Washington. Two brothers, Edwin and Edward Baltzley, were planning an upper-middle-class residential development there, with large houses facing the Potomac. They promoted the area's rural nature and distance from the city. The Baltzleys organized a Chautauqua assembly there each summer that provided a hotel and lectures. They even urged the American Red Cross in 1890 to locate its headquarters there. Barton decided to leave Washington for a more restful and healthy environment in Glen Echo and abandoned plans to build on the lots she had bought in the Kalorama Heights section of the city.

The Baltzley brothers also provided the labor to build her headquarters free of charge. Clara Barton's became one of the most eccentric houses in the Washington area. Barton's assistant, Julian Hubbell, suggested they use his plan for the Johnstown hotels for the new Glen Echo building. The three pine-board hotels in Johnstown were dismantled in 1890, some of the wood was used for the Red Cross headquarters. The atypical, long rectangular plan featured a three-story open interior hall with balconies; it also held 78 closets and rooms at all levels to store Barton's substantial emergency supplies, including blankets, medicine, bandages, and lanterns. Her office, bedrooms for staff and visitors, and dining room were located on the second floor. Parlors and storerooms were on the first floor, with additional bedrooms and storerooms on the third floor. Stained-glass windows displayed the Red Cross design, and linen was stretched to cover the walls and ceilings to prevent drafts.

After she moved into the house in 1890, Barton found the half-day commute to Washington by carriage or wagon inconvenient. Consequently, she moved to a hotel in Washington and, in 1892, rented a house

SECOND FLOOR, LOOKING FROM THE
LIVING ROOM TOWARD THE DINING ROOM

FRONT PARLOR

for Red Cross activities at the corner of 17th and F Streets, N.W. that General Grant had used as his headquarters. In 1897 a streetcar line opened between Georgetown and Glen Echo, which prompted Barton and her staff to move back to her wooden house, which was modernized with improved heating, plumbing, and electricity. She also added refinements to the exterior: stone towers on the sides of the facade, as well as a gable roof and front porch. Barton raised eyebrows when she assigned the Red Cross treasurer, George Pullman, a bedroom next to her own. She was infatuated with him, even though he was nearly 50 years her junior and a chronic alcoholic. The Barton House was always full of ill and homeless friends and relatives. She performed much of the household work

herself—cooking, raking leaves, and tending the vegetable garden. At the end of the 19th century, Barton traveled widely for the American Red Cross, delivering aid to Turkey and Cuba, as well as to victims of the Galveston hurricane in 1900.

In 1904, at the age of 83, Barton resigned from the Red Cross, more than 20 years after she founded it. The Glen Echo neighborhood never became the elite enclave the developers had envisioned. Their company went bankrupt in the 1890s and the lots intended for mansions were quickly filled with modest cottages. An amusement park was built on the Chautauqua site near her house. Barton became a Christian Scientist and experimented with the occult spiritualism that was fashionable at the time. While working

Right: CORNER OF OFFICE

LOOKING FROM THE SECOND FLOOR TO THE OPEN GALLERY

on her autobiography, she died of tuberculosis in 1912 at the age of 90.

Barton left the house and her furnishings to her longtime aide, Julian Hubbell, also a spiritualist. Hubbell established the Clara Barton Memorial Association and devoted his life to her memory. Upon Hubbell's death in 1929, the landmark went to his two nieces, who had known Clara for many years. One of them, Rena Hubbell, moved into the house and rented rooms, using the proceeds for repairs. The nieces not only facilitated publication of the first Clara Barton biography—*Clara Barton, Daughter of Destiny* by Blanche Colton Williams, in 1941—they donated her extensive papers to the Library of Congress, where they are preserved.

When the Hubbell sisters could no longer care for the Clara Barton House, they sold it to the Franks sisters, who also tended to its preservation. The Franks sold it to a group called the Friends of Clara Barton in 1963 for $35,000. In 1975 the Friends donated the house and its contents to the National Park Service, which maintains it as a historic house museum.

Left: ENTRANCE HALL LOOKING
BACK THROUGH OPEN GALLERY

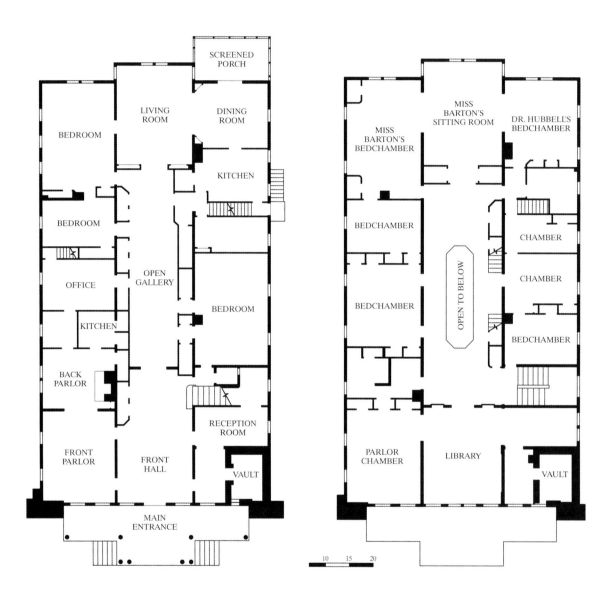

SCREENED
PORCH

LIVING
ROOM

DINING
ROOM

BEDROOM

KITCHEN

BEDROOM

OPEN
GALLERY

OFFICE

BEDROOM

KITCHEN

BACK
PARLOR

RECEPTION
ROOM

FRONT
PARLOR

FRONT
HALL

VAULT

MAIN
ENTRANCE

FIRST-FLOOR PLAN

MISS
BARTON'S
SITTING ROOM

DR. HUBBELL'S
BEDCHAMBER

MISS
BARTON'S
BEDCHAMBER

BEDCHAMBER

CHAMBER

OPEN TO BELOW

CHAMBER

BEDCHAMBER

BEDCHAMBER

PARLOR
CHAMBER

LIBRARY

VAULT

10   15   20

SECOND-FLOOR PLAN

HEURICH HOUSE

1307 NEW HAMPSHIRE AVE, N.W.
WASHINGTON, D.C.

1892–94

Architect: John Granville Meyers
Architect: Appleton P. Clark Jr., North Garden Wall 1901,
Carriage House 1902, North Wing 1914, Conservatory Roof 1923
Neighborhood: Dupont Circle
Status: Historic House Museum

FACADE

REAR LAWN AND CARRIAGE HOUSE

Heurich house is not only the most important late Victorian house in Washington; it is considered one of the best-preserved examples in the country. Located one block south of Dupont Circle, it is now open to the public for tours, public events, and private event rentals. The house was built for Christian Heurich, a German immigrant who made a fortune in Washington as a brewer and real estate investor.

Heurich was born in Germany in 1842, and, at the age of 14, began serving a two-year apprenticeship as a brewer; he immigrated in 1866 to Baltimore. Heurich and another young German brewer there formed a partnership, moved to Washington in 1872, and acquired the failing Schnell Brewery located south of Dupont Circle. After a year in business together, Heurich bought out his partner's interest and

rapidly expanded the brewery. In 1873 he married Amelia Mueller Schnell, widow of the brewery's former owner.

The Christian Heurich Brewing Company continued to expand and, between 1894 and 1895, Heurich built a far larger brewery on an entire block in Foggy Bottom. Production grew to a capacity of 500,000 barrels of beer a year and his adjacent ice plant produced 120 tons of ice daily. The brewing company manufactured 13 types of beer under 47 different labels. His lager won many international awards for its purity and fine flavor. When Congress in 1917 imposed prohibition on the District through the Volstead Act, Heurich closed the brewery and continued to operate the ice company. At the age of 91, when prohibition was repealed in 1933, he reopened the brewery.

ELEVATION OF THE CONSERVATORY FACING SUNDERLAND PLACE

Three years after his first wife died, in 1884, Heurich married Matilde Daetz, an immigrant from Bremen, Germany, and sister of his brewery's treasurer. She died in 1895, only a year after Heurich completed his mansion. He had no children with either wife. However, in 1899, at 57, Heurich married his third wife, Amelia Louise Keyser, the 33-year-old niece and namesake of his first wife. They eventually had four children (one died in infancy), and she presided over Heurich House for the following 57 years.

The neighborhood near Dupont Circle in which Heurich first bought the brewery rapidly evolved from a blue-collar area with small businesses and even smaller frame houses to the city's most fashionable residential district. Realizing that Governor Alexander R. Shepherd's plan to grade and pave the streets and install curbs and streetlights would transform the nation's capital, a number of successful western miners with surplus capital began in 1871 to buy vacant land around Pacific Circle (subsequently renamed Dupont

STAIRCASE DETAIL

Circle), at 10 cents per square foot. Grand Victorian mansions filled the area over the next two decades. When finished in 1894, the Heurich House would prove to be the last great residence in Washington to be built in the Richardsonian Romanesque vein.

The exterior of Heurich House has an impressive facade of dark-red Seneca sandstone facing New Hampshire Avenue and more subdued brick on its south side facing Sunderland Place. In the rear is a long, rectangular garden and carriage house. The facade has a complex design of double and triple window openings. The prominent stone corner tower looms above the steep roof, which housed the servants' quarters. The tower's circular copper roof is crowned by a bronze salamander, symbol of survival through both fire and flood. Columns decorated with carved grotesques support the massive stone porte cochere.

Left: ENTRANCE HALL, STAIRCASE,
AND MUSICIANS' BALCONY

FRONT PARLOR

The unusual wedge-shaped lot dictated the floor plan; it has an entrance opening into a spacious central hallway. On the left is the reception room, with an impressive brass, onyx, and white marble staircase beyond. Beneath the staircase, guarded by a knight in iron armor, is the entrance to the two-story north wing, which was added in 1914. Heurich used the first-floor room of the wing for his home office; the second-floor room was a library and playroom for the Heurich children. On the right side of the central hallway are double parlors, with a music room, dining room, and conservatory beyond. Sliding pocket doors provide an open plan allowing free circulation among all these public spaces. A musician's balcony opens onto the central passage below, as well as into the music and dining rooms.

The mansion's most ornate room is the white oak–paneled dining room, which features elaborate

Left: VIEW FROM THE MUSIC ROOM
TO THE DRAWING ROOM AND FRONT PARLOR

Following Pages: THE *BIERSTUBE*

DINING ROOM

carvings by August Grass, a local cabinetmaker. Carvings of fruit, vegetables, and game adorn the woodwork and furniture. This rich interior decoration is found throughout the first- and second-floor rooms. Portraits of historical figures and emblems relating to the liberal arts embellish the first-floor reception room walls and ceiling. The *bierstube*, or tavern room, in the basement has walls painted with German drinking idioms; paintings of beer steins and happy beer-drinkers decorate the ceiling.

Heurich installed the most modern mechanical systems of the time. It was the first totally fireproof house in Washington, with wrought-iron beams and extensive poured concrete interior walls and subflooring. Chandeliers and wall fixtures were fitted with electroliers, a combination of electric bulbs and gas burners. Indoor plumbing supplied hot and cold water, and a large coal-fired furnace fed steam to radiators throughout the house. Speaking tubes connected the second and third floors and the tower to the basement kitchen, and pneumatic call bells summoned household staff from the kitchen to six stations in the house. Installed later, an electric burglar alarm sounded if the outside doors were opened during the night. There was a hand-operated dumbwaiter between the basement kitchen and the first-floor pantry.

Also installed later was a central vacuum system that most likely serviced the whole house.

Following Heurich's death in 1945, his widow continued to live in the house. After the brewery closed, the federal government exercised eminent domain and razed the plant to make way for the Theodore Roosevelt Bridge and the Kennedy Center. At 88, Amelia Heurich gave the landmark Heurich House to the Columbia Historical Society (now the Historical Society of Washington, D.C.) but retained a life tenancy. After her death in 1956, the Heurich children donated most of the original furnishings as well.

After ongoing restoration and conservation efforts by the Society in the 1970s and 1980s, they reopened the mansion and the rear garden to the public for tours in 1982. Desiring a larger building, the society sold the Heurich House to the Heurich House Foundation in 2003 and relocated to the former Carnegie Public Library building on Mount Vernon Square. The foundation, formed by two of Heurich's grandchildren, Jan Evans Houser and Gary Heurich, open the landmark for public tours several days a week; it ensures that the building and its contents are preserved for future generations to enjoy.

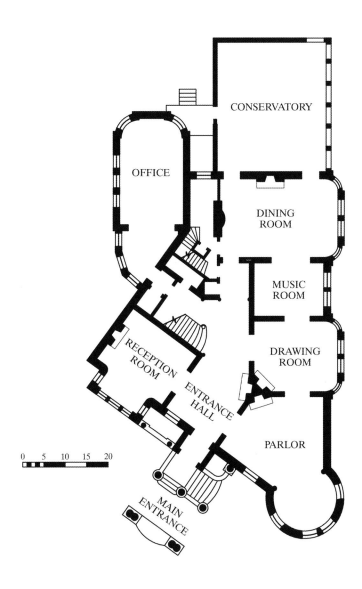

FIRST-FLOOR PLAN

ARTS AND CRAFTS HOUSES

THE OWL'S NEST

3031 GATES ROAD, N.W.
WASHINGTON, D.C.

———————————

1897
ADDITIONS 1912; 2007

Architect: Appleton P. Clark Jr. Addition: George Myers, 2007
Neighborhood: Forest Hills
Status: Private Residence

FACADE

STAINED-GLASS WINDOW AT STAIR LANDING

THE OWL'S NEST WAS BUILT IN 1897 ON A promontory in Forest Hills for journalist and trade representative William L. Crouse at a time when this neighborhood was still semirural. The first houses built in Forest Hills had large lots, in this case, two acres. Those constructed between 1925 and 1950 had lots of less than half an acre. The extension of Connecticut Avenue between downtown and Chevy Chase, Maryland, by the Chevy Chase Land Company in 1891 spurred the development of houses such as The Owl's Nest, just off the Connecticut Avenue corridor.

Architect Appleton P. Clark Jr. (1865–1955), who later became municipal architect for Washington,

designed the 2½-story Shingle-style house with wide wood shingles, rough stones, and a slate roof with wide eaves. The rich surface textures and diversity of shapes—intersecting roof lines, wide eaves, dormers, oriels, stone pillars and arches, and a stone porte co-chere—make for an unusually interesting design.

The Owl's Nest is one of only a few houses Clark designed. He specialized in commercial and office buildings, apartment houses, and churches. After graduating from Central High School in Washington in 1883, Clark worked as an apprentice in the Washington office of Alfred B. Mullett for three years. Clark is best known for his Romanesque Revival Washington Post Building (built in 1893 and razed

Following Pages: ELEVATIONS FROM SOUTHWEST

ENTRANCE HALL AND STAIRS

in 1957), his Gothic-Revival Foundry (United) Methodist Church (1903), the Beaux-Arts Presidential Apartments (1922), and the Renaissance-Revival Roosevelt Hotel (1919).

The Owl's Nest, his only Shingle-style design, is one of the best examples of that genre in Washington. A stone turret, entrance arch, and hip-roof dormers define the main, or west, elevation. The broad curve of the entrance arch is repeated in the curve of the roof immediately above it. Crowning the entrance is an unusually large dormer with two windows. The house was enlarged in 1912 with a one-story wing on the rear, or east, face, which included three bedrooms for household staff.

Left: LOOKING FROM THE ENTRANCE HALL
INTO THE DINING ROOM

The interior of the original house is well preserved. A central hallway with parquet flooring terminates in a segmented staircase with paneled walls and a stained-glass window that features an owl, a book, and candle. An inglenook sits at the foot of the stairs—a built-in bench that faces an Arts and Crafts concrete fireplace mantel. A large parlor opens to the left of the hallway; the dining room with pocket doors that slide into the walls to save space opens on the right. Both rooms have their original hardware and beamed ceilings.

In 2001, the house's fourth owner, Alvin Brown, sold the Owl's Nest to the Jewish Primary Day School. The school's board of directors planned to demolish the landmark and build a three-story brick schoolhouse on the site. However, the Forest Hills Neighborhood Alliance quickly and successfully applied for a D.C. Historic Landmark designation for the Owl's Nest based on its superior design, craftsmanship, and age. The school consequently sold the landmark to Gibson Builders, a developer who subdivided half of the lot for new construction. Jim Gibson then offered it to a second developer, Chris Donatelli, who became captivated with the design. Donatelli and his wife decided in 2006 to sell their Potomac, Maryland, house and make the Owl's Nest their residence. They commissioned architect George Myers of GTM to design a large north addition to the left of the main entrance and contracted Gibson Builders to restore the original house and build the addition. The sensitive three-story addition now looks as if it were part of the original house.

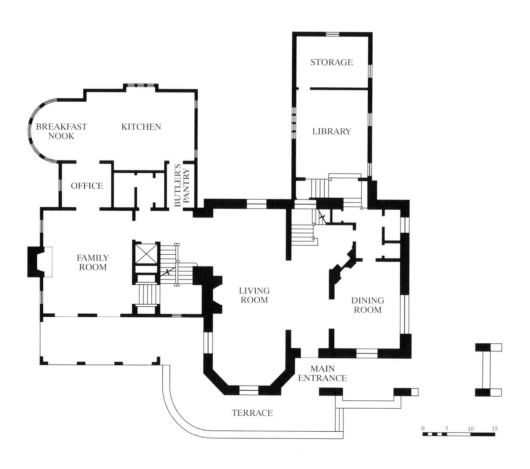

FIRST-FLOOR PLAN

BARNEY STUDIO HOUSE

2306 MASSACHUSETTS AVENUE, N.W.
WASHINGTON, D.C.

1902
GARAGE ADDED 1911

Architect: Waddy B. Wood
Neighborhood: Sheridan-Kalorama
Status: Embassy of Latvia

FACADE

STAIRS

BARNEY STUDIO HOUSE IS ONE OF THE BEST surviving examples of Arts and Crafts architecture in Washington. The four-story stucco building has a curvilinear gable and two terra-cotta tile roofs vaguely alluding to Spanish Colonial missions of California. The main portal contains an archway, which leads to two large oak doors that retain their original hardware: On the left is the entrance to the house, while the double doors on the right lead to a garage that accommodated Barney's small electric car. Located on the southwestern side of Sheridan Circle, the house is surrounded by Beaux-Arts mansions largely constructed between 1905 and 1920. The stuccoed garage was added in 1911 on the adjacent north lot.

Alice Pike Barney (1857–1931) built the house purely for entertaining and to house her painting studio. Her father, Samuel Pike, was a wealthy and artistic whiskey distiller from Cincinnati who played the flute and wrote poetry. He took Alice to the opera, plays, and exhibitions at an early age, instilling in her a love of the arts. A major philanthropist, Pike built a large opera house in Cincinnati in 1857—reputedly the largest west of Philadelphia. The Pike household

DINING ROOM DETAIL

was filled with artistic people—musicians, actors, painters, and singers. After a brief period living in New York City and then traveling in Europe, Alice returned to Ohio and in 1876 married Albert Clifford Barney, heir to a Dayton, Ohio, railroad car manufacturing company. The couple spent the next decade in Cincinnati with their two daughters, Natalie and Laura. In 1886 Alice began to study painting, first in Cincinnati, and then in Paris. Unlike Alice, her husband was indifferent to the arts. The family moved to Washington in 1889 to build a Renaissance-inspired mansion at 1626 Rhode Island Avenue, N.W., adjacent to Scott Circle.

In order to provide space for her painting studio and to produce her frequent plays, Alice Barney asked Washington architect Waddy B. Wood (1869–1944) in 1902 to design a building on the Sheridan Circle lot. She planned to emulate the ambiance of Parisian studios, where artists and society met. Alice believed that Washington would become the center for the nation's artistic life. She worked closely with Wood to design the interior details—an eclectic combination of carved woodwork and plasterwork that utilized the Renaissance, Medieval, Aesthetic, and Arts and Crafts motifs. She also commissioned a number of pieces of dark oak, carved Renaissance Revival furniture for the house. Shortly after her husband's death in 1902, Alice left the mansion on Scott Circle and made the Barney Studio House her principal residence.

Most of the house's interior woodwork is dark-stained oak. Brick and red clay tiles are used extensively throughout the first two floors, which were designed for entertaining. Most of the original iron light fixtures with decorative opaque and green glass are intact. The foyer opens onto a salon with exposed ceiling beams and a stone hearth. The first floor also contains a dining room and library. The second floor,

the principal level, features a large studio-theater with a high ceiling and carved wooden beams. It also acted as a reception area for parties and a stage for performing plays. Above the massive fireplace is a long balcony that serves as a focal point for the room; twisted columns carved with vines, leaves, and cupids support the balcony. The third and fourth floors have small sitting rooms and bedrooms.

By 1906 Alice Barney was actively engaged in lobbying for a national art museum. In 1917 she founded the National Sylvan Theatre for outdoor plays and tableaux, many of which she wrote, on the grounds of the Washington Monument. Barney Studio House became an important arts center for Washington—a venue for plays, concerts, and painting exhibitions. Her own pastel portraits were shown here as well as in New York, London, and Paris, where they often won awards. Alice's philanthropic interests were also centered on founding and endowing the Barney Settlement House, which aided the poor in Southwest Washington.

In 1909 Barney met 22-year-old Christian Hemmick at the studio house, where he played a small part in one of her plays, *The Man on the Moon*. She fell in love with Hemmick, whom she referred to as a Greek god. Even though Alice was 30 years older than Christian, they married two years later in Paris. Alice's Bohemian lifestyle extended to her two daughters, Laura, a sculptor, and Natalie, a painter and acknowledged lesbian. In 1910 Alice shocked Washington by installing a life-size cast-stone statue of a nude recumbent Natalie, sculpted by Laura in her Paris studio, on the front lawn of Barney Studio House. After police covered it with a cloth, Alice's Hindu butler stood guard and accepted gratuities from visitors for lifting the cover. The piece survives today; it reclines on the rear lawn of the house.

After her divorce from Christian, Alice moved to Los Angeles to be near her sister. She founded a small playhouse there, which became popular with young actors and emerging playwrights. When Alice died in Los Angeles in 1931, she left Barney Studio House to

Left: STUDIO AND LARGE THEATER

BALCONY SUPPORT COLUMN

her two daughters, who leased it out until 1960. The following year Laura and Natalie donated the house and its contents to the Smithsonian Institution as a memorial to their mother, with the intent that it be used for educational and cultural purposes.

From 1960 to 1979, the Smithsonian used Barney Studio House for institutional offices and apartments for Smithsonian scholars in residence. In 1979 many of the original Barney furnishings were restored, and Joshua Taylor, director of the National Collection of Fine Arts (now the Smithsonian American Art Museum), and his curator, Jean Kling, who oversaw much of the restoration, opened the two main floors to the public for tours and for special music programs and art exhibitions.

In 1987 it was discovered that the foundation at the rear of the house, built on infilled land, was settling. Smithsonian officials, including Tom Freudenheim and Secretary Robert McCormick Adams, decided not to spend the funds needed to strengthen the structure. While the Smithsonian debated what to do with the house, a group of concerned preservationists and art historians formed the Friends of the Alice Pike Barney Studio House to safeguard the landmark. Despite these efforts, the Smithsonian finally sold the house and selected furnishings in 1999 to the owner of a large music store in northern Virginia, who planned to turn the house into a music school. Concerned about the potential for traffic congestion, neighbors blocked his zoning change request, which would have permitted a business in the midst of this residential enclave. The remaining furnishings were auctioned, and the house was sold in 2001 to the Latvian government. At a fraction of the cost originally estimated by the Smithsonian, the Latvians shored up the foundation and made the house its embassy; it has carefully preserved the surviving original interior features.

THE CONTROVERSIAL RECLINING STATUE OF NATALIE BARNEY

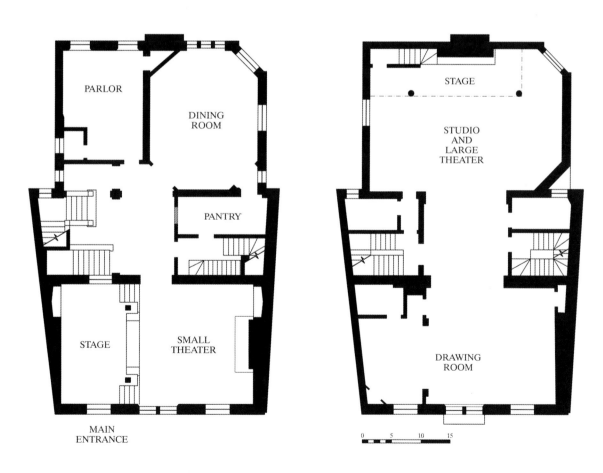

FIRST-FLOOR PLAN

SECOND-FLOOR PLAN

MORSE STUDIO HOUSE

2133 R STREET, N.W.
WASHINGTON, D.C.

―――――――――――

1902

Architect: Hornblower & Marshall
Neighborhood: Sheridan-Kalorama
Status: Private Residence

FACADE

This small, four-room, freestanding brick house, two blocks from Sheridan Circle, was built on a lot only 25 by 101 feet. Yet it is one of Washington's prime examples of Arts and Crafts–movement architecture, both on the exterior and the interior. The simplicity—the starkness of the red-brick facade—is characteristic of the best work of architects Hornblower & Marshall. The plain, stepped roofline is vaguely reminiscent of 17th-century Dutch urban houses. In keeping with the spirit of Arts and Crafts, the current owner has painted blue the massive, diagonal bead board front door. The door's hardware is unique to Washington: Its heavy iron hinges bear the original owner's initials, "E. L. M.," for artist Edward Lind Morse. The door was built extra-wide to permit easy entry of large stone blocks into the studio for Morse's sculpture. The iron door pull is in the shape of a salamander, which according to mythology, could survive fire. Leading to the front door from the sidewalk is the original chain handrail, which is attached to an iron post, cast in the shape of a stump with intertwining leaves. Flat brick arches set in the facade emphasize the door and the flanking paired windows, as well as the central, three-part window on the second floor.

The house was designed in 1902 as a combination art studio and residence for Edward Lind Morse (1857–1923), an artist who had studied in Paris and Germany. Morse exhibited his paintings in New York, St. Louis, and Chicago, as well as at the Paris Salon of 1893. His chief literary work was *Samuel F.B. Morse, His Life and Letters*, a biography of his father, the famous inventor and artist. Not only did the senior Morse invent the telegraph and patent it in 1849, he also devised the Morse Code system that uses light flashes, short and long sounds, or dots and dashes to convey messages.

The basement of the house originally held the kitchen and a one-bedroom housekeeper's apartment. The first-floor plan has a small office, with a bedroom and bath in the front, and a large two-story studio with a 20-foot ceiling in the rear. Within the studio is an open dining area and a narrow new

FRONT DOOR

kitchen. The second floor comprises the master bedroom, which opens onto a balcony overlooking the two-story studio, with a massive fireplace and a bathroom. Maximum light is provided by a range of windows on the rear, or north, wall of the room and a large skylight. Allen Raywid, the house's fourth owner, remodeled parts of the interior in 1982. The front part of the studio area, a total of 24 by 36 feet, became a living room. Raywid installed a new open kitchen on the left rear, or west, side of the space, enclosed by a low counter. The area to the right rear of the studio became an open dining area, raised on a low platform accessed by two steps. In the process, Washington architect Robert Schwartz replaced the original simple balustrade with a streamlined low plaster wall that ran along the edge of the balcony and around the chimney.

INTRICATE CARVING AROUND
STAIRCASE AND BALCONY

The fifth and current owner, Richard Squires, a filmmaker and former exhibition designer at the Smithsonian's National Portrait Gallery, purchased the house in 1993. He promptly removed the streamlined balcony walls and commissioned a talented craftsman, Harrison Minor, to restore the simple, square wooden balusters and hand carve a new base for the balcony out of golden oak. The design is in the spirit of the Arts and Crafts style and features mistletoe and clouds. Minor also carved and installed a wood screen with decorative cattails to partition the staircase leading from the studio level to the balcony. Minor's painting, *The Hidden Language of the Vegetable Oracle,* commands the fireplace mantel. The designs of William Morris, called the soul of the English Arts and Crafts movement, have inspired much of Minor's work. Squires also had the chimney restored to its original condition. A second craftsman, Joan Gardner,

Right: LOOKING FROM THE DINING
AREA TOWARD THE FRONT

created a rectangular panel of green ceramic tiles—also in an Arts and Crafts vein—that sits on the fireplace mantel behind the painting. MUD pi Tiles provided the handmade Arts and Crafts–style green ceramic tiles mounted on the outer side of the kitchen counter.

Hornblower & Marshall was one of the most prominent architectural firms in Washington between 1883 and World War I. Joseph Hornblower (1848–1908) was educated at Yale University and the Ecole des Beaux Arts in Paris, while James Rush Marshall (1851–1927) studied architecture at Rutgers University and on a grand tour of Europe. Marshall joined the Office of the Supervisory Architect of the Treasury, where he met Hornblower. They both left government service in 1883 to start their own firm.

Among their principal public buildings were the National Museum of Natural History at the Smithsonian Institution, the Marine Corps Barracks in Washington, and the Baltimore Custom House. They were also responsible for many important mansions in Washington's Dupont Circle neighborhood, including the Fraser House, 1701 20th Street, N.W.; the Lothrop House, 2001 Connecticut Avenue, N.W. (now part of the Russian Embassy); the Boardman House, 1801 P Street, N.W. (now the Iraqi Embassy); and the Phillips House, 1600 21st Street, N.W. (now the Phillips Collection). Although Marshall continued to practice after Hornblower's death in 1908, the firm received fewer commissions. One of Marshall's last notable buildings was the Army-Navy Club on Farragut Square, built in 1911.

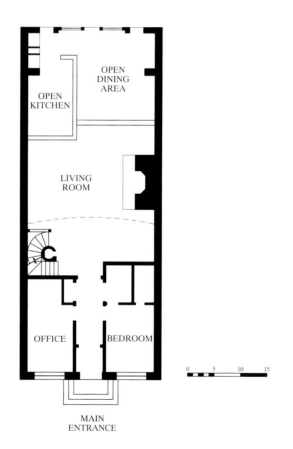

FIRST-FLOOR PLAN

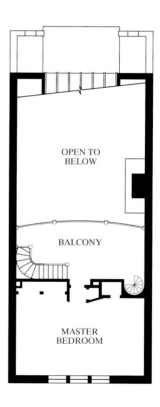

SECOND-FLOOR PLAN

GRANGER COTTAGE

3615 MACOMB STREET, N.W.
WASHINGTON, D.C.

1911

Architect: W. Granville Guss
Neighborhood: Cleveland Park
Status: Private Residence

FRONT GATE

GRANGER COTTAGE IS ONE OF WASHINGTON'S most charming and least-known small houses from the Arts and Crafts period before World War I. Ralph W. Kirkham, an employee of the Interior Department who commuted to work downtown by streetcar, built it in 1911 and then sold it to a Presbyterian minister, who lived there for 20 years. The third owner was William Howell, who loved the house and loved to garden. Neighbors remember that he had a sign advertising his New Zealand spinach for sale.

The fourth owners were Dr. and Mrs. Stephen Granger; they lived in a house one block away and had waited a decade for the house at 3615 to go up for sale. When that finally happened in 1983, they immediately bought it.

As part of a plan to restore the house, Eleanor and Stephen Granger attended an adult evening class, "Landscape Architectural Improvements for Your House," taught by Matthew Evans at the nearby National Cathedral School for Girls. When the class was

FACADE

completed, they commissioned him to restore their spacious grounds, which cover two city lots. Evans recalls that an asphalt driveway spoiled the appearance of the house, which was then dilapidated; he replaced the front paved driveway with a narrow gravel one on the left side of the lot that leads to a free-standing garage in the back. Here, the Grangers stored two of their Checker cabs; Stephen Granger was especially fond of the cars' high ceilings and spacious rear seats. The family had three cabs at one time: one for the parents and

one each for their two daughters. During the two years that Evans worked on the project, he restored the front lawn, including the terrace, fishpond, and wisteria vine over the front porch. Evans also installed new footpaths and even an old 4-foot-tall Japanese stone lantern. The Grangers added a wooden fence and gate, with a pergola facing the Macomb Street sidewalk.

The Grangers also lovingly restored the house's interior. They stripped the paint from the chestnut-paneled walls and ceiling and had the surfaces hand-rubbed

STAIR DETAIL

LIVING ROOM

FRENCH DOORS TO FAMILY ROOM WITH WROUGHT IRON GATES

with oil. They also restored the staircase to its 1911 appearance, featuring a design of vertical rails. The Craftsman ornament in the spacious living room continued on the doors, with wide, exposed, wrought-iron strap hinges. The wrought-ironwork continues on the window and door guards, which have images of birds, both standing and in flight.

The low-slung, standing-seam metal roof and a long group of dormer windows on the facade belie the house's spaciousness. As seen in the floor plan below, the house is very deep. It has five bedrooms— one on the first floor and four on the second. The square posts on the front porch and exterior walls are faced with an especially rough stucco, known as "pillow stucco"—wavy, puffy, and full of exposed stones. It sets the mood for the wonderfully pre-served rustic feel of both Granger Cottage's exterior and interior.

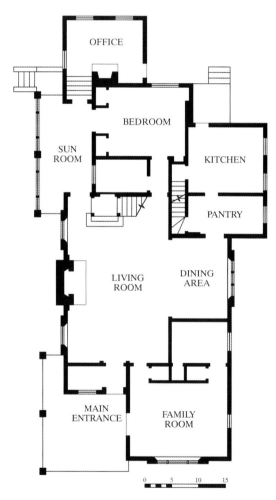

FIRST-FLOOR PLAN

DUMBLANE

4120 WARREN STREET, N.W.
WASHINGTON, D.C.

1911

Architect: Gustav Stickley and his Craftsman Architects
Neighborhood: American University Park–Tenleytown
Status: Private Residence

FACADE

ENTRANCE HALL, WITH INGLENOOK, LOOKING TOWARD THE DINING ROOM

A LARGE FIVE-BEDROOM BRICK HOUSE LOCATED three blocks from Tenley Circle on Wisconsin Avenue, Dumblane is a fine example of Arts and Crafts construction in Washington. Attorney Samuel Hazen Bond and his wife, physician Mabel Cornish Bond, built this landmark on a 15-acre site in 1911. They met with Gustav Stickley in New York to select a 1904 design published as "Craftsman House Plan X," in Stickley's magazine, *The Craftsman.*

A low-lying, gabled, green tile roof, with three wide shed-dormer windows, crowns the rectangular three-story house, built of tapestry brick in colors ranging from salmon to brown to dark blue. A pergola wraps around three sides of the house, which faces a circular drive entered through an iron gate supported by original stone piers. At the time it was built, the area was semirural with curved dirt roads, a pattern that did not conform to the city's modern

Right: FIREPLACE WITH COPPER HOOD IN ENTRANCE HALL

Following Pages: DINING ROOM

Each man's chimney is his golden mile-stone.

grid system. Over the years, the land belonging to Dumblane has been gradually subdivided, leaving the house on a one-acre lot, which includes the original garage and a modern swimming pool. The design features a wide, tapered chimney on the south elevation and an additional interior chimney, which rises from the center of the roof. Both have short stacks, following a favored Arts and Crafts practice.

The house takes its name from a work by Scottish poet Robert Tannahill that celebrates the pleasure of rural living. The original owners had great affection for the Arts and Crafts movement. Mabel Bond made the curtains and pillows for the rooms from Craftsman designs. Hazen Bond supervised the daily construction and even designed much of the built-in furniture, fixtures, and woodwork. The Craftsman Workshop of Syracuse, New York, fabricated and installed the furniture; it even supplied the Bonds their china and silver. The fully paneled dining room, painted in earth-toned colors, retains the original built-in sideboard and china cabinets, stained glass window (featuring swallows in flight), beamed ceiling, window seat, and light fixtures. Remarkably, the inglenook in the entrance hall, with its copper fireplace hood, remains in place as well.

The Bonds altered the original floor plans to their taste. The first floor comprises capacious living and dining rooms connected in the center by the entrance hall, with fireplace, inglenook, and side stairs. The second floor contains five bedrooms with plenty of closets. The attic floor holds a billiard room and a large playroom connected by a wide well-lighted open hall on which the maid's room and bath connect.

During the first three decades of the 20th century, the Arts and Crafts movement exercised a major influence on house design, from Prairie School dwellings to the California houses of Greene & Greene to simple bungalows that became dominant in middle-class housing for some two decades. Conceptually, the movement drew much of its inspiration from the work of William Morris, which celebrated "honest" construction and natural materials, and shunned excessive or needless detail.

The principal spokesman for the Arts and Crafts in the United States was Gustav Stickley (1858–1942), who grew up in Minnesota, the son of German immigrants. He and his brothers began business as makers of reproduction furniture. After three trips to England, he left his partners and established the Stickley Company in order to create furniture that looked handmade, free of "cheap ornament," based on the honest principles of joinery, structural lines, and finish. Stickley was influenced by Irene Sargent, who taught art at Syracuse University. Stickley founded a magazine, *The Craftsman*, which began to feature Arts and Crafts houses as early as 1902. Many people who built houses from his designs purchased their furniture and fittings from his company after their houses were constructed.

Stickley felt that Dumblane was one of the largest and most successful of his designs, and he devoted a major article to it in *The Craftsman* in 1913. Dumblane was successful in integrating the house with its site, as well as featuring open interiors, simplicity of detail, and exposed natural materials. The R. Kendall Nottingham family has carefully maintained Dumblane since they purchased it in 1999.

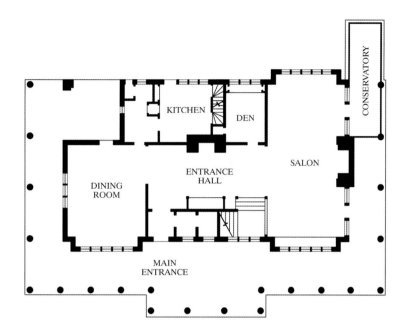

FIRST-FLOOR PLAN

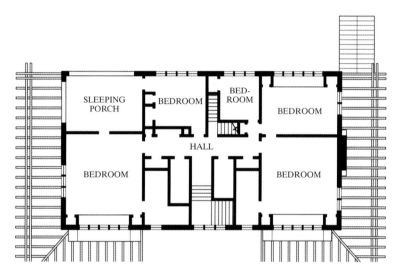

SECOND-FLOOR PLAN

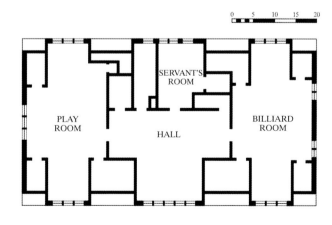

THIRD-FLOOR PLAN

BEAUX–ARTS HOUSES

Patterson House

Townsend House

Anderson House

Beale House

Everett House

Marly

Marwood

PATTERSON HOUSE

15 DUPONT CIRCLE, N.W.
WASHINGTON, D.C.

1901

Architect: McKim, Mead & White
Neighborhood: Dupont Circle
Status: Luxury Rental Apartments

FACADE

ENTRANCE HALL AND MAIN STAIRS TO MAIN FLOOR

NOTED ARCHITECT STANFORD WHITE OF McKim, Mead & White designed the four-story, Beaux-Arts Patterson House at the corner of Dupont Circle and P Street in 1901 for Robert Mc-Cormick Patterson, editor in chief of the *Chicago Tribune.* White marble sheathes the impressive multi-faceted facade with glazed terra-cotta classical details. At the far left on the ground floor are the original doors to the city's first built-in automobile garage. The ground floor contains a large foyer with an Italian Renaissance–inspired mantel and a formal white marble staircase whose elaborate iron railing has a red velvet handrail; a fountain is located on the landing. The major space on the second, principal floor is an expansive ballroom with a distinctive musicians'

balcony. The Pattersons' daughter, Cissy, married Count Josef Gizycki of Poland in the house in 1904.

Cissy divorced the count six years later and returned to Washington. She spent 1925–29 with her second husband, attorney Elmer Schlesinger, in New York City, and upon his death, moved back to Washington to live in Patterson House permanently. While living in New York, she rented Patterson House to President and Mrs. Coolidge as their temporary quarters from March to September 1927, while the third floor of the White House was being reconstructed. It was here that the Coolidges entertained Col. Charles Lindbergh and his mother after his famous solo flight to Paris. During their stay at Patterson House, Mrs. Coolidge gave a spring tea and invited

BALLROOM DETAIL

famed Russian pianist Sergei Rachmaninoff (who had performed three times at the White House for the Coolidges) to play for her guests.

It was natural for Cissy Patterson, having been raised in a family of journalists, to take over publishing *The Washington Herald* for her friend William Randolph Hearst in 1930. She was so successful at the job that Hearst sold her both *The Washington Herald* and *The Washington Times* in 1939. Cissy combined the two papers into *The Washington Times–Herald* and made it competitive with other local newspapers. Following Cissy's death, the Washington Club, a women's social

DRAWING ROOM

organization, purchased the mansion in 1951. The group entertained and held concerts and lectures there until it disbanded in 2013.

The Washington Club's Preservation Committee restored the third-floor bedroom occupied by Charles Lindbergh, including the bed in which he slept. An enlarged photograph over the fireplace showed Lindbergh and prominent government officials on the platform erected adjacent to the Washington Monument in 1927, where, having received the Distinguished Flying Cross from President Coolidge, he is pictured speaking to a record-breaking crowd of 200,000 that filled the Mall for blocks. Loudspeakers installed along the length of the Mall carried his address.

A banquet was held in the ballroom every year to raise funds for the continuing restoration of this last great house facing Dupont Circle. Concerned members of the Washington Club, headed by Maribelle Moore, organized the club's Preservation Committee as a private foundation in 1983 "to preserve and memorialize the history and architecture of the District of Columbia with particular reference to the Washington Club and the Dupont Circle area." Over the past 25 years, they raised more than $400,000 to replace the roof and to restore the Lindbergh bedroom, the terra-cotta facade, the entrance doors, interior of the 1909 elevator, marble mantels and fireplaces, marble staircase and rails, and the ballroom and dining room floors.

After the club's membership fell from 500 women to 45, it was determined to sell the building and close the club. In 2014 a local real estate firm purchased Patterson House for conversion to small luxury apartments.

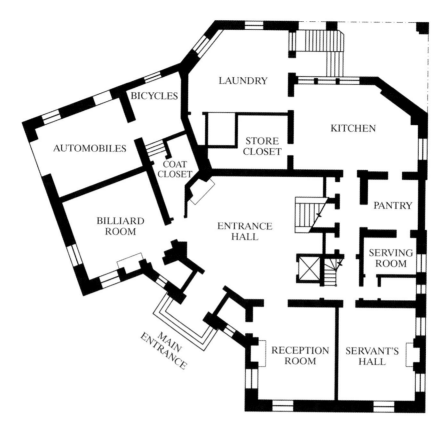

FIRST-FLOOR PLAN

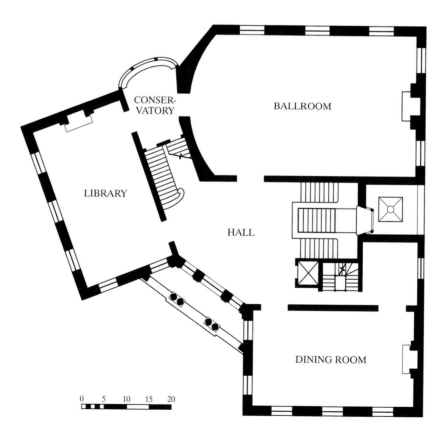

SECOND-FLOOR PLAN

TOWNSEND HOUSE

2121 MASSACHUSETTS AVENUE, N.W.
WASHINGTON. D.C.

———————————

1872
REBUILT 1899–1901

Architect: Unknown. Remodel: Carrère & Hastings, 1899
Neighborhood: Dupont Circle
Status: Private Club

DETAIL OF CARVED STONE ON FACADE

Following Pages: FACADE

ENTRANCE HALL

R ICHARD H. AND MARY SCOTT TOWNSEND were the builders of Townsend House. Married in 1879, she was the daughter of William Lawrence Scott and Mary Matilda Tracey Scott of Pennsylvania. William Scott had a wide variety of business concerns, and Richard Townsend was an ambitious young Philadelphian who managed a brokerage company for him. Townsend became involved in his father-in-law's railroad concerns and took over as president of Scott's Erie & Pittsburgh Railroad when the former congressman died in 1891. After Mary Townsend inherited her father's estate of more than $15 million, the young couple decided to move to Washington permanently.

In 1899 the Townsends commissioned the New York City firm Carrère & Hastings to design their residence. Their railroad interests may have influenced this decision because their friend, Henry Flagler, another railroad magnate, had recently commissioned the firm to design two hotels and two churches in St. Augustine, Florida, which Flagler was promoting as a tourist attraction. The firm also designed Flagler's own Palm Beach mansion, Whitehall. The ballroom designs at Whitehall and the Townsend House are very similar.

In 1898 Mary Scott Townsend had purchased a house at the corner of Massachusetts and Florida Avenues that had been built in 1872 by Curtis J.

LIBRARY

Hillyer, a western lawyer who prospered from investments in California and Colorado mines. The Townsends instructed Carrère & Hastings to design their new house around the existing Hillyer residence, which, in the more than 25 years since it had been built, had become unfashionable, and was too small for their needs.

The dimensions of the existing tall narrow structure in good part determined those of the four-story central section of the new limestone-clad house. Symmetrical two-story wings were added on each side of the central section. French work in the Louis XVI manner inspired the general architectural character chosen for the new house. A rusticated granite veneer visually unifies the ground floor of the new house and its wings. Massive stone quoins (corner blocks) define the sides of both 34-foot-wide wings. An elegant cast-iron marquee projects over the entrance. The second floor of the central block has three floor-length windows, with shorter windows on the third floor. Four massive fluted composite pilasters that extend two stories unite these elements. A stone balustrade crowns the third floor, and three large dormer windows punctuate the slate mansard roof.

The entry is a spacious hall laid in white marble with a green border, the principal staircase sitting at the far right. Half of the ground floor, behind the lobby, was devoted to service rooms. The staircase,

which was modified slightly in the 1950s to comply with the fire code, sweeps up to the second (main) floor, where the public rooms are located. The two principal spaces here are the ballroom to the west and the library to the east, connected in the front by two salons decorated with antique landscape paintings installed in the wall paneling. A poor copy of John Singer Sargent's portrait of Mathilde Townsend, the couple's daughter, hangs over the fireplace in the larger salon. The original is in the National Gallery of Art.

The most important space in the house is the splendid ballroom. Its painted and gilded walls are in the Louis XV Rococo style. The elaborate ceiling painting shows Aurora, the goddess of dawn, in her sea chariot pulled by a pair of dolphins. As she raises her arm, the first light of dawn appears in the distance—an appropriate theme for a ballroom where dancing went on into early morning. The architect employed the expert firm on French period interiors, Jules Allard et Fils, with offices in New York and Paris, for the Townsend House. The original records show that the architects turned over the house's unfinished interior walls for Allard to decorate; the firm was responsible for the interiors of many prominent American mansions of the day, including two of the Vanderbilt houses on Fifth Avenue in Manhattan and three great houses in Newport.

The rear of the second floor contains a long gallery that originally terminated in a large open terrace with steps down to the east garden. Architect Horace Peaslee, a member of the Cosmos Club, who had principal responsibility for renovation of the house in 1950–54, after the club purchased it, enclosed this space. It was named the National Geographic Society

Room in honor of that organization, which was founded in 1888 by Cosmos Club members at the old clubhouse on Lafayette Park. John Wesley Powell and other scientists founded it chiefly as a social club that also welcomed artists and literary figures. The long gallery also opens onto the spacious Georgian Revival paneled dining room, whose ceiling is decorated with three painted panels portraying celestial skies and frolicsome putti.

The handsome original, cast-iron fence that surrounded the west and east gardens of Townsend House remains in place. Unfortunately the west garden was lost when the Cosmos Club converted most of it for parking in the early 1950s. Its small marble fountain and most of the adjacent decorative Byzantine columns were saved and used in the club's new first-floor dining room.

Richard H. Townsend died in 1902 from a skull fracture after being thrown from a horse less than a year after the house was finished. After a suitable period of mourning, Mrs. Townsend began entertaining on a grand scale in her 44-room mansion with a staff of 35 in full livery.

Mathilde, her only child, was pampered from birth. Educated by tutors, she spent summers in Europe, and Mrs. Townsend was determined to marry Mathilde to European royalty. Mrs. Townsend focused her efforts on the Spanish Duke of Alba. The duke agreed to the proposed arrangement, provided he receive an annual stipend of $250,000. But Mathilde, who was by then of age, had a mind of her own and placed no value on having a title. Later, at 26, Mathilde married Peter Goelet Gerry of New York City and Rhode Island, who was 10 years her senior. Her mother arranged a spectacular wedding in the mansion's ballroom, attended by President William Howard Taft and his entire cabinet in 1910. Gerry was elected to the U.S. Senate from Rhode Island in 1916.

The saga of Mathilde Townsend reached a turning point at a Washington dinner party on January 10, 1921, when she met and immediately fell in love with Sumner Welles, a good-looking young American diplomat from New York City. She was 37 and Welles was 29. Both were married. Welles was not rich but was from a well-connected New York City family—one of his aunts was Edith Wharton, the novelist and author on interior decoration; another aunt, Mrs. William Astor, ruled New York Society. He had been a ring bearer in Franklin Roosevelt's wedding and was close to the president. Welles became a highly respected diplomat, and as under secretary of state in the Roosevelt administration, helped promote the Good Neighbor Policy in Latin America.

When they met, Mathilde and Sumner were bored with their spouses. Although friends and family tried to stop their romance, it continued for four years. They would take separate ocean liners to Europe and then rendezvous to travel together to remote places. Finally they divorced their spouses in Paris and married in 1925 at Mount Vernon, New York. Senator Gerry then married Edith Stuyvesant Dresser, widow of George Washington Vanderbilt, who built the Biltmore estate.

At that time divorce was scandalous. The notoriety almost caused Mary Scott Townsend's endless parties and musical evenings to cease. Upon their return to Washington in 1925, the new couple rented a 25-room unit at the McCormick Apartments at 1776 Massachusetts Avenue, N.W. In 1927 Mathilde and Sumner purchased 250 acres in Prince George's County, Maryland. Here they commissioned prominent Washington architect Jules H. de Sibour to design a handsome 40-room Georgian Revival country house named Oxon Hill Manor, where they lived for the rest of their married life. Mathilde inherited her mother's vast wealth when Mary Scott Townsend died in March 1931, still heartbroken over the scandal of her daughter's divorce. Within months, the French government, eager to move from 16th Street to the more fashionable Dupont-Kalorama neighborhood, offered Mathilde $1 million (about $10 million

Following Pages: BALLROOM JUST BEFORE A CONCERT

BRONZE FOUNTAIN ON EAST LAWN

today) for the Townsend House, which she refused because of fond memories of growing up there. With the added wealth from Mary Scott Townsend's bequest, the Welleses maintained other estates in Bar Harbor, Maine, and Palm Beach, Florida.

During the 1930s, the Welleses spent little time at the Townsend House, owing to increased urban congestion, noise from streetcars, and the decline of Dupont Circle from commercial encroachment. Mathilde died from a sudden attack of peritonitis in July 1949, while they were on vacation in Switzerland. In 1950, increased living costs prompted Welles to

sell Townsend House, then in a state of neglect, to the Cosmos Club for $365,000. In 1952 he sold Oxon Hill Manor with all its furniture, as well as the original Townsend House furnishings stored there. The following year he married Harriette Post, a lifelong friend, and spent the rest of his life in a much smaller house at 1840 24th Street, N.W., summering at his Bar Harbor retreat. Following his death in 1961 at age 68, a Scott cousin, Mrs. Thora Ronalds McElroy, inherited the Townsend-Welles fortune. When she died in 1990, she left her considerable estate, including the famous Townsend jewels, to charity.

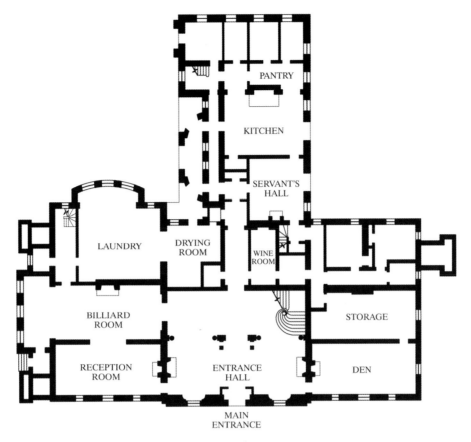

FIRST-FLOOR PLAN

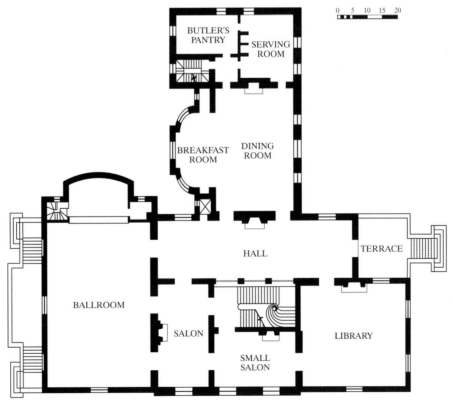

0   5   10   15   20

SECOND-FLOOR PLAN

ANDERSON HOUSE

2118 MASSACHUSETTS AVENUE, N.W.
WASHINGTON, D.C.

1902—05

Architect: Little & Browne

Neighborhood: Dupont Circle

Status: Historic House Museum, Headquarters of The Society of The Cincinnati

FACADE

FRONT COURTYARD OF FACADE

L
ARZ AND ISABEL ANDERSON WERE A REMARK-
able couple at the center of Washington's social
scene in the early 1900s. They loved to entertain,
travel, and collect European and Asian antiques. They
were popular in Washington, where they maintained
a winter home, and in Brookline, Massachusetts, at
their "permanent" home, and in cities they knew
well—London, Paris, and Rome. Both came from
wealthy, long-established families.

Larz Anderson (1866–1937), who grew up in
Cincinnati, Ohio, enjoyed a cosmopolitan youth. He
was born in Paris, graduated from Phillips Exeter in
1884, and from Harvard in 1888. The Foreign Service
(and foreign travel) soon became Anderson's career.
In 1891, through his father's friendship with Robert
Todd Lincoln, son of President Abraham Lincoln, and
minister to Great Britain, President Benjamin Harrison appointed Larz second secretary of the American Embassy in London. It was by means of his next
appointment, by President Grover Cleveland, in 1894,
as first secretary of the American Embassy in Rome,
that he met his future wife.

CONSERVATORY

After their much-publicized Boston wedding in 1897, Larz Anderson and Isabel Weld Perkins made two wedding trips, the first to Hawaii and Japan in 1897–98, the second to Europe and India, in 1898–99. Between these trips, Larz served briefly as a captain in the U.S. Volunteer Army during the Spanish-American War, at Camp Alger near Falls Church, Virginia. Larz resumed his diplomatic career when President William Howard Taft, a family friend, appointed him American minister to Belgium in 1911. After losing the 1912 election, Taft appointed Anderson ambassador to Japan, where he served for the first few months of 1913.

Isabel Perkins Anderson (1876–1948) was born in Boston, the daughter of Commodore George H. Perkins (1836–1899), a graduate of the Naval Academy who had achieved fame by helping take New Orleans from Confederate forces during the Civil War. Her grandfather, William Fletcher Weld (1800–1881), owned the Boston-based William F. Weld Company, which then had the largest fleet of merchant ships in the United States—51 clipper ships and 10 steam vessels. When Weld died, Isabel was a beneficiary of his estate, a legacy that afforded the Andersons a life of luxury and comfort. Isabel was a prolific writer, credited with more than three dozen works, including short stories, novels, children's and travel books, plays, poems, and memoirs. During World War I, she helped the Allies, serving as a volunteer nurse and canteen worker behind the front lines in both Belgium and France.

Left: CARRIAGE DRIVEWAY ARCH

BALLROOM

GRAND STAIRCASE FROM SECOND FLOOR

The Andersons' life revolved around three residences: First, they purchased the 62-acre country estate built by Isabel's cousin, William Fletcher Weld II, at Brookline, Massachusetts. Her cousin had commissioned distinguished Boston architect Edmund M. Wheelwright (1854–1912) to design a large Shingle-style country house (1887) and a carriage house said to be modeled after the Château de Chaumont, a 15th-century Renaissance castle in the Loire Valley. Second, they spent part of each summer at another country house in New Hampshire.

Third, they acquired two adjacent vacant lots in Washington, at 2118 Massachusetts Avenue, N.W., from the Patten sisters, who lived next door to the property. The couple commissioned Boston architects Arthur Little and Herbert W.C. Browne to design a 50,000-square-foot Beaux-Arts mansion. This crown jewel of Washington domestic architecture was planned for entertaining on a grand scale during the social season. Even though the Andersons moved into the house in 1905, work continued on the elaborate murals, ceiling panels, and trompe-l'oeil walls until 1912. The total cost of the house came to $800,000. Only the Edward Everett House at Sheridan Circle (now the Turkish ambassador's residence) cost more to build than did its contemporary, the Anderson House.

The classical design is based on early-18th century houses in both England and France. Larz Anderson was very familiar with such examples from his extensive time spent there in the Foreign Service. The

founders of Little & Browne had both studied architecture in France and were also familiar with many classical mansions. The facade's most prominent feature is an enclosed courtyard with a central wall pierced by two massive stone arches—a configuration inspired by the great houses of 18th-century Paris. The imposing two-story semicircular portico within the courtyard serves as a porte cochere, with four fluted composite columns and a pair of pilasters set on pedestals at acute angles from the plane of the house. At the center of the pediment above the portico is the seal of the Society of the Cincinnati, with a scroll bearing "Anderson" clutched in an eagle's claws.

The house's rear faces a small walled garden. Here the flat roof of the first-floor conservatory provides a terrace above with a balustrade, which allows outside access between the second-floor drawing rooms on the west end of the house and the dining room on the east end. Four Ionic columns partially built into the wall of the house extend from the second to the third floors on the rear elevation.

Under the front portico is an entrance to a central hall. Family and friends proceeded left into the family quarters, while other visitors proceeded right through a small room that holds 16th-century Italian walnut choir stalls with carved angels and animal forms. Murals by W. Siddons Mowbray document the Andersons' memberships in patriotic organizations such as the Society of the Cincinnati, Sons of the American Revolution, Colonial Dames, and Daughters of the American Revolution, as well as honors and ranks accorded Larz during his diplomatic service. Through the choir-stall room was the great stair hall, where servants took guests' coats before escorting them to the *piano nobile* above.

From the grand stair hall, guests continued up the wide marble staircase to pass below the monumental 1882 painting by Spanish artist Jose Villegas Cordero, *The Triumph of the Dogaressa*, showing a scene from the 1424 coronation of the new ruler of Venice. At the top of the staircase lies a formal reception room. More

CINCINNATI ROOM

elegant murals by H. Siddons Mowbray adorn all four walls. The most noteworthy of them shows George Washington presenting the Marquis de Lafayette a certificate of membership in the Society of the Cincinnati. Other officers of the Continental Army stand in groups in the background, including Col. Richard Clough Anderson, former aide-de-camp to Lafayette and ancestor of Larz. The Andersons referred to this space as the Cincinnati Room in honor of the murals depicting Lafayette and an early-19th century view of the city of Cincinnati, Ohio, which was named for the Society.

On the west end of the second floor are the French and English drawing rooms. The French drawing room is decorated with four silk tapestries originally woven for a palace in Venice, while the English drawing room has eight English paintings, including a portrait of the Duke of Wellington. After cocktails guests would proceed to the dining room at the east end of the second floor by the open-air rear terrace in mild weather or by the gallery, 77 by 16 feet, on the front side of the house. Displayed in the long gallery are 17th-century Brussels tapestries, antique European chests, and the diplomatic uniform Larz Anderson wore in Europe, consisting of his custom-designed gold-embroidered coat, hat, and sword.

Entering the grand dining room from the long gallery, the marble floor pattern and the door frame slant to direct the visitor forward. The Andersons could seat 20 at the 65-foot-long table, which was made to order for the room. Full-length portraits of Larz and Isabel Anderson grace the walls, as well as additional Brussels tapestries. The 1901 painting of Isabel by Cecilia Beaux, one of the most beautiful in the house, portrays her in a simple but elegant white silk dress.

After dinner, guests would descend a floating staircase mounted on the ballroom's north wall. At Anderson's suggestion the architects based the proportions of this space on the great room at Wilton House in England. At the east end of the room are four striking Verona marble spiral-turned columns that support the musicians' balcony above. The beamed ceiling has carved and gilded panels, and the floor is set with a walnut strap-work design. The southeast corner of the ballroom connects to the family library, where additional Anderson family portraits hang on the walnut-paneled walls.

The great hall connects on the south, or rear, of the house to the long glass-enclosed conservatory, or winter garden. In the Andersons' time it held plants, wicker furniture, and Southwestern Native American pottery. The Andersons used the east end as a breakfast room, and the west end as a card room. Mowbray wall murals decorate both spaces. For the breakfast room, Mowbray painted a mural of the Anderson's elaborate Italian garden at Weld, their summer estate in Brookline, Massachusetts. Two of the artist's most charming murals are in the card room—maps showing the Anderson's favorite driving routes in the Virginia and Maryland suburbs.

After Larz's death in 1937, Isabel gave Anderson House and most of its original furniture and interior decoration to the Society of the Cincinnati for its national headquarters. In 1939, at the formal transfer of the property, she also gave the Society $100,000 as an endowment for the property's upkeep. Since then, the society has been a conscientious steward of the mansion, and has initiated a number of projects to protect the Andersons' legacy, including the restoration and conservation of the tapestries, and most recently, the Mowbray murals in the Cincinnati Room.

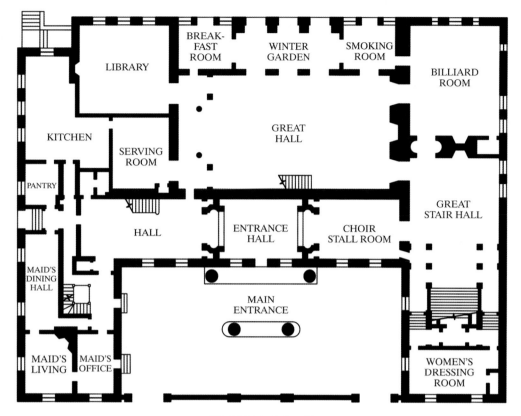

FIRST-FLOOR PLAN

0   5   10   15   20   25

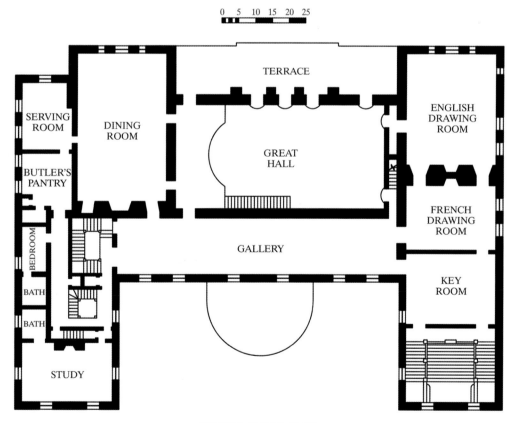

SECOND-FLOOR PLAN

BEALE HOUSE

2301 MASSACHUSETTS AVENUE, N.W.
WASHINGTON, D.C.

————————————

1907–09
Architect: Glenn Brown
Neighborhood: Sheridan-Kalorama
Status: Residence of the Ambassador of Egypt

FACADE

ENTRANCE HALL DOORS

JOSEPH BEALE, A SUCCESSFUL WASHINGTON realtor, built this imposing neoclassical house on Sheridan Circle between 1907 and 1909; he and his wife, Margaret, lived there from 1909 to 1917. After World War I it remained vacant for more than a decade before it was first rented by the Egyptian Embassy in 1928 and then purchased for the ambassador's residence. The chancery, or embassy offices, are now located at 3521 International Court, N.W., near the intersection of Van Ness Street and Reno Road.

The wedge-shaped lot on which the Beale House was built accounts for the curved facade; it features a prominent Venetian loggia, or deeply recessed second-story porch, directly above the entrance. Two pairs of stone columns frame the opening. The wall surfaces are stucco with limestone rustication.

DINING ROOM

Beale House is noted for its neoclassical-inspired interior plasterwork, perhaps the best of any house in the city. The most important rooms are on the second or principal floor. An elegant, round sitting room adjoins the loggia. Here the entire 14-foot-high walls and domed ceiling are richly decorated with plaster ornamentation. Corinthian pilasters flank the four openings; eight radiating ribs divide the low dome.

At the center of each panel is a rosette and acanthus-leaf medallion surrounded by palmettes. The rich plasterwork in the circular room was all originally painted stark white. Now it is highlighted in gold leaf. Even though the lily has ben guilded somewhat, the beauty of the room remains. The first floor includes one room devoted to a museum of ancient Egyptian artifacts

Left: ENTRANCE HALL TO MAIN STAIRCASE

CIRCULAR SITTING ROOM

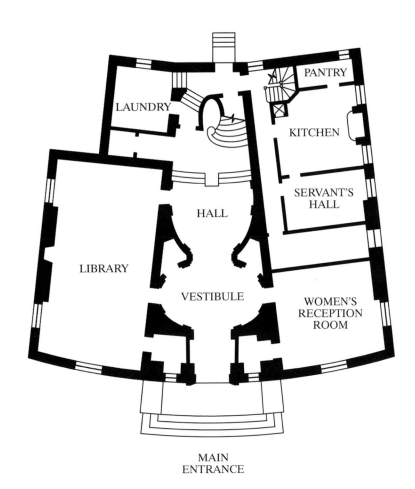

LAUNDRY

PANTRY

KITCHEN

SERVANT'S
HALL

HALL

LIBRARY

VESTIBULE

WOMEN'S
RECEPTION
ROOM

MAIN
ENTRANCE

FIRST-FLOOR PLAN

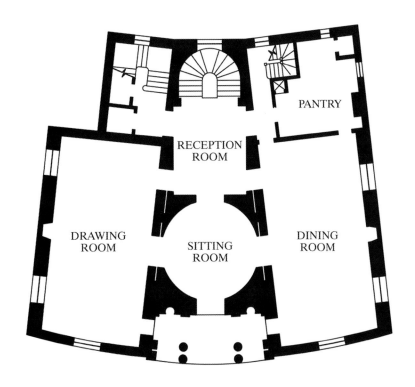

PANTRY

RECEPTION
ROOM

DRAWING
ROOM

SITTING
ROOM

DINING
ROOM

SECOND-FLOOR PLAN

EVERETT HOUSE

1606 23RD STREET, N.W.
WASHINGTON, D.C.

1910–15

Architect: George Oakley Totten Jr.
Neighborhood: Sheridan-Kalorama
Status: Residence of the Ambassador of Turkey

FACADE

SOUTH ELEVATION WITH ROOFTOP PERGOLA

EDWARD HAMLIN EVERETT (1851–1929) BUILT one of the largest and most eclectic Beaux-Arts houses in Washington, on the southwest side of Sheridan Circle at 23rd Street, N.W., just before World War I. A native of Cleveland, Ohio, Everett became a millionaire during the nation's post–Civil War economic boom. His secret to success in manufacturing was, like that of Howard Hughes, to purchase and operate supporting industries, such as a sand company and gas and oil wells, to provide power for making glass bottles–then all blown by hand.

Everett absorbed several other Ohio glass companies during the 1890s to earn the nickname Bottle King in 1903, when he purchased the rights to a new bottle-making machine from its inventor, Michael J. Owens, of Toledo. He retained Owens' 900 glassblowers and

Following Pages: SOUTH AND WEST ELEVATIONS

taught them how to operate the new automated machines. His popularity soared when he gave his workers health insurance, which was almost unheard-of at the time. Although he retained his original bottle business, the Edward H. Everett Glass Company of Newark, Ohio, Everett started a second, larger operation, the American Bottle Company, by buying and merging a number of competing firms.

Rumors persisted for decades in Washington that Everett's fortune came from the invention of the crimped bottle cap, but Everett had nothing to do with it: William Painter of Baltimore, Maryland, took out a patent for the cap in 1891. No doubt Everett's customers paid Painter's royalties indirectly.

Everett and his first wife, Amy Webster King, married in Ohio in 1886 and had three daughters over the following decade. In 1907 the Everett family began to spend winters in Washington and travel extensively in Europe at other times of the year. In 1909 Everett decided to build a major residence on Massachusetts Avenue, and acquired two adjoining lots on Sheridan Circle. He commissioned George Oakley Totten Jr., one of the most prominent architects in Washington, to design it. At the same time, he engaged Totten to design an impressive mansion, The Orchards, as a summer retreat in Bennington, Vermont, in the English Norman Revival style. Both Everett House and the Orchards are in much their original condition today and are splendid examples of early-20th century domestic architecture.

George Oakley Totten Jr. (1866–1939) was born in New York City. After taking his M.A. from Columbia University in 1892, he studied architecture in Paris from 1893 to 1895. For the next three years he served as chief engineer in the office of the supervising architect of the U.S. Department of the Treasury. He left government service in 1898 to start his own architecture practice in Washington.

The facade of Everett House faces 23rd Street, with a narrow semicircular drive that leads to an entrance sheltered by an elegant iron-and-glass marquee.

ENTRANCE HALL

CONSERVATORY

DINING ROOM

The three-story residence is clad in limestone with a rusticated first floor. Unusual features of the house include the facade's impressive bowed central section, with a massive curved porch supported by four fluted columns with composite capitals, a frieze, and a stone balustrade. The west elevation of the house is also impressive. Here, an open pergola crowns the third floor that overlooks the Q Street (Buffalo) Bridge.

The entrance hall features a large expanse of white marble with a screen of columns flanking each side. The grand staircase has a landing that leads to a musicians' niche adorned with an extravagantly painted ceiling. Two monumental 16th-century Italian paintings by

Alessandro Allori, *Narcissus at the Pool* and *Aeneas Fleeing the Burning of Troy*, dominate the double staircase walls. The elaborately carved balustrade terminates at the spacious reception hall on the second (main) floor. The elegant drawing room has impressive views of Sheridan Circle, while the corridor on the other side of the reception hall leads to a comfortable sitting room, a large dining room with a sumptuously paneled ceiling, a conservatory, and a ballroom. Tiffany Studios stained-glass windows and signature favrile glass mosaics adorn the conservatory, the only complete Tiffany interior in Washington. One enters the ballroom through a pair of double doors whose upper

STAIRHALL CEILING DETAIL

halves are defined by semicircular openings with intricately carved fretwork. Here, the walls are upholstered. The hardware on the doors and windows in the ballroom and other public rooms is gold-plated.

Everett's first wife, Amy, died in the house in 1917, shortly after the family moved in. Several years later Everett attended a dinner given by Mrs. John B. Henderson in Henderson's Castle on 16th Street, where he met Grace Burnap (1879–1969), a music teacher 28 years his junior. They were married in March 1920 in Chicago and soon had two daughters: Grace, born in 1921, and Sarah, born in 1922. During their nine-year marriage, Edward and Grace traveled frequently and entertained lavishly in the Sheridan Circle mansion. The second Mrs. Everett loved having guests, often engaging opera stars and entire orchestras from New York City for evening concerts.

Edward Everett died in Boston in April 1929 at age 77, following complications from prostate cancer. Shortly after his death, the three daughters from his first marriage contested his will, which had been rewritten in 1928 and substantially reduced their interest in the estate in favor of Grace and her two daughters. A trial ensued, and the court ultimately invalidated the 1928 will. The estate was probated as if Everett had died intestate: All five daughters inherited equally.

Right: STAIRCASE AND LANDING LOOKING DOWN FROM THE SECOND-FLOOR RECEPTION HALL

BALLROOM DOORS

Having lost the case, Grace rented Everett House in 1932 to the Republic of Turkey for use as an embassy and moved to the Orchards in Vermont. The Turkish government purchased the house in 1936 with nearly all the original furnishings.

Mehmet Münir Ertegün, chief legal adviser to the government of Kemal Atatürk, the founder of modern Turkey, served as ambassador to the U.S. from 1933, the start of Franklin D. Roosevelt's administration, to his death in the embassy in 1944. Both of Ertegün's sons were enthralled by American jazz. The older son, Nesuhi, introduced his nine-year-old brother, Ahmet, to the Duke Ellington and Cab Calloway orchestras at the Palladium when their father was posted to London. After they moved to Washington in the early 1930s, the boys invited local black jazz musicians to play in the spacious embassy. Ahmet (1923–2006) frequented the Howard Theater in Washington and met the leading black musicians and singers of the day: Duke Ellington, Ella Fitzgerald, Count Basie, Billie Holliday, Louis Armstrong, and Lionel Hampton. After his father's death, he remained in Washington, became an American citizen, and made a career in music. He founded the legendary Atlantic Records in 1947 with a loan of $10,000. Ahmet's jazz and rock-and-roll records made him a fortune; he sold the company 25 years later for $17 million.

Everett House became the Turkish ambassador's exclusive residence in 1999, when a new chancery opened a short distance north on Massachusetts Avenue. The house underwent a multiyear, $20 million restoration that was completed in 2007. Washington architect Belinda Reeder directed the installation of new lighting, cooling, and heating systems, and oversaw a team of experts who restored the valuable artwork and architectural detailing. The project remains a model for other embassies that are housed in some of Washington's grandest historic buildings.

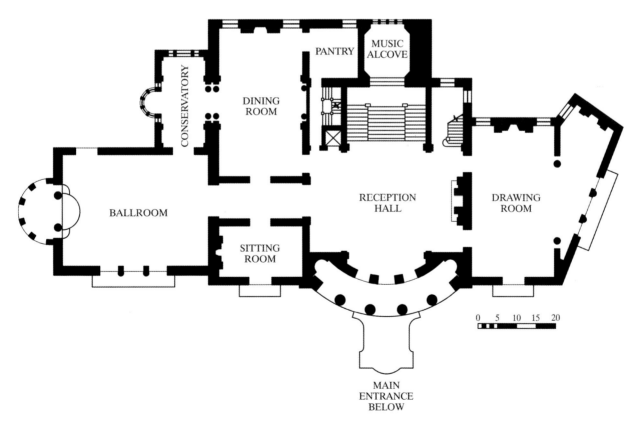

SECOND-FLOOR PLAN

MARLY

2300 FOXHALL ROAD, N.W.
WASHINGTON, D.C.

1931–32

Architect: Horace Trumbauer

Neighborhood: Berkley

Status: Residence of the Ambassador of Belgium

FACADE

VESTIBULE

ANNA DODGE DILLMAN, WIDOW OF DETROIT car manufacturer Horace Dodge and heiress to his fortune, commissioned Marly, one of the finest houses in Washington and one of its most nearly correct interpretations of an 18th-century French classic. Anna Dillman built the house as a wedding present for her daughter, Delphine Dodge, a concert pianist, on her marriage to Raymond Baker, former director of the U.S. Mint under President Wilson. The Bakers named the house Marly, but lived there for only three years. After Raymond Baker's death in 1935, Delphine moved out. The house was rented to several residents between 1935 and 1945, including Dwight F. Davis, the former secretary of war and governor of the Philippines, and Eva Stotesbury of Philadelphia. Stotesbury,

a good friend of Anna Dillman, had originally recommended Horace Trumbauer as the architect for Marly. Delphine's first husband was James H.R. Cromwell, Eva Stotesbury's son.

Trumbauer had designed Whitemarsh Hall for Stotesbury, a 147-room classical mansion, built outside Philadelphia between 1916 and 1920. Mrs. Dillman named her house Marly at the suggestion of Stotesbury, after one of Louis XVI's favorite châteaux, located just west of Paris. The Dodge heirs sold the house in 1945 for $325,000 to the Kingdom of Belgium for its ambassador's residence. The first Belgian ambassador to live there was Baron Silvercruys, who added to the collection of French antique furnishings.

Following Pages: DRAWING ROOM

Horace Trumbauer (1868–1938) became well-known for his Beaux-Arts designs. A native of Philadelphia, he left public school at the age of 14 to work as an errand boy for the architecture firm G.W. & W.D. Hewitt. After honing his skills as a draftsman, Trumbauer opened his own office in 1890. Marly, one of his best houses, lies on a spacious 9.6-acre site that was used during the Civil War for Battery Parrott, one of the many Union fortifications protecting Washington from Confederate attack. The model for the house is the early-18th century French mansion, the Hôtel de Rothelin-Charolais on the rue de Grenelle in Paris. It was commissioned by the Marquis of Rothelin and later occupied by the granddaughter of Louis XIV, the Countess of Charolais. Trumbauer's architectural assistant, Julian Abele, is credited with much of the design for Marly. Abele, the first African American graduate of the University of Pennsylvania School of Architecture and the Ecole des Beaux-Arts, joined Trumbauer's staff in 1906.

The 142-by-59-foot house has 30 rooms on the first and second floors, while the attic level originally provided 14 rooms for the staff. The interior detailing reflects the style of the French regency when France was governed by Philippe d'Orléans, uncle to Louis XV. The focal point of the first floor is the grand salon, which opens onto the entrance hall in the front and overlooks the rear terrace and lawn. The paneled walls are accented in gold. The dining room, designed in the French Rococo style of Louis XV, is lighter in feeling than the more formal grand salon. It was inspired by the 18th-century Château de Villarceaux.

The front and rear elevations of Marly are identical. Each side has nine pairs of windows, designed as French doors. A shallow stone portico crowned by an iron balustrade defines the central three sets of windows. The second-floor windows are framed by pilasters and crowned by a low sculptured pediment that depicts Flora, the Roman goddess of flowers and spring.

DINING ROOM

BEDROOM

MRS. DODGE'S BATHROOM

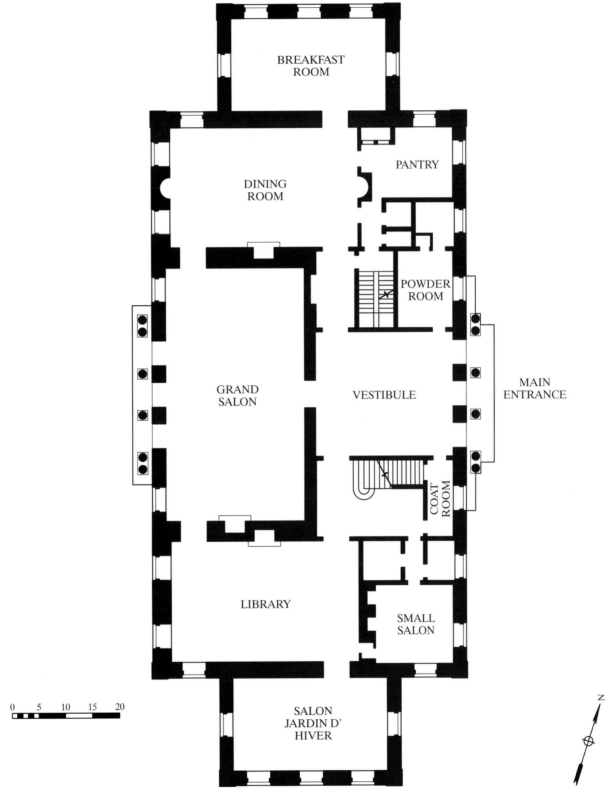

BREAKFAST
ROOM

PANTRY

DINING
ROOM

POWDER
ROOM

GRAND
SALON

VESTIBULE

MAIN
ENTRANCE

COAT
ROOM

LIBRARY

SMALL
SALON

0   5   10   15   20

SALON
JARDIN D'
HIVER

N

FIRST-FLOOR PLAN

MARWOOD

11300 RIVER VIEW DRIVE
POTOMAC, MARYLAND

1931
Architect: John J. Whelan
Status: Private Residence

FACADE

Right: SOUTHEAST ELEVATION

ART DECO STATUE ADJACENT TO THE MAIN STAIRCASE

ONE OF THE MOST DRAMATIC RESIDENCES included in this study is Marwood, a Beaux-Arts country house built on a grand scale in Potomac, Maryland, and now owned by Ted Leonsis. Marwood—Old English for "forest near the river"—sits on tall cliffs overlooking the former Chesapeake & Ohio Canal and the Potomac River, 15 miles from Washington. John J. Whelan, a Washington architect, designed the three-story, 33-room stucco mansion.

In 1930 Samuel K. Martin II, a young socialite from New York City, purchased a 192-acre farm in Montgomery County from Jesse H. Magruder for the site of Marwood. Martin was the grandson and heir of wealthy Chicago real estate entrepreneur and merchant Otto Young. Orphaned as a young boy, Martin was raised by an aunt in New York City. He was educated at Lawrenceville School and Princeton University. After he received his $7 million inheritance at age 20, he left college and went to New York City to live a life of leisure during the Roaring Twenties. Martin was smitten with a young actress with the stage name "Mary Jane" while attending Flo Ziegfeld's hit

Left: MAIN STAIRCASE

FAMILY ROOM

Broadway musical *Whoopee!* After a whirlwind courtship, 19-year-old stage star Jane Catherine Young married the 21-year-old millionaire. They entertained in their Manhattan town house and traveled extensively in Europe.

After visiting the Château du Malmaison near Paris, with its associations with Empress Josephine, the Martins determined to use it as a model for their American residence. They moved from New York City to Washington and began searching the suburbs for the right site on which to build. The Martins found their ideal location early in 1930. Construction of the house began in the spring of 1931 and was largely complete by late 1932. Both Martins loved French Renaissance architecture, and Samuel wanted his own house to match the scale of his grandfather's Beaux-Arts summerhouse, Younglands, on the shores of Lake Geneva, Wisconsin.

Whelan, the Martins' architect, was a native of Atlantic City, New Jersey. Educated at Princeton, he studied architecture in Europe before beginning his practice in Washington in the early 1930s. Two of his most prominent buildings are the current Norwegian and South African embassies, both on Massachusetts Avenue. Whelan closely followed the design of the central core of Malmaison, with adaptations.

Right: FIREPLACE IN THE FAMILY ROOM

MOVIE THEATER

Marwood's symmetrical facade focuses on a slightly projecting central pavilion at the entrance. The rear elevation, which overlooks the Potomac, is identical to the front, and is similar in many ways to Marly, now the Belgian ambassador's residence. Four tall stucco chimneys punctuate the low-pitched, red-tile roof. Acanthus leaf brackets surmount the first-floor windows, while head ornaments adorn the areas above the second-floor windows. Limestone string-courses between the second and third floors heighten the classical effect. Large rectangular stucco quoins emphasize the house's corners; they also decorate the 6-inch-deep central pavilions containing both the front and rear entrances. A series of nine French doors on both the front and rear elevations further enhance the design. The second-floor windows are embellished with shallow wrought-iron grilles that simulate balconies.

After living in Marwood for two years, the Martins separated in January 1934, Samuel having become a chronic alcoholic and a womanizer. He leased Marwood later that year to Joseph P. Kennedy, chairman of the Securities and Exchange Commission, and father of the future president John F. Kennedy. During Joseph P. Kennedy's residence there, President Franklin D. Roosevelt visited Marwood at least three times to attend dinner parties and watch films. With Marwood leased, Jane and their three-year-old son, Samuel K. Martin III, moved to southern France, while Samuel II traveled in the United States. He died in 1935 from a heart attack caused primarily by chronic alcoholism, at the DeSoto Hotel in Savannah, Georgia, just before his 27th birthday. Jane, still legally married to him, inherited his considerable fortune.

When the Kennedy lease expired in 1937, Jane Martin returned to live at Marwood. Shortly afterward, on a trip to New York City, she met 25-year-old Seward Pulitzer, grandson of newspaper magnate Joseph Pulitzer and great-grandson of William H. Vanderbilt; she soon married him in Palm Beach. They lived in Old Westbury, Long Island, while Marwood remained vacant. Jane Pulitzer sold Marwood in 1943 to H. Grady Gore of Tennessee, who

GARDEN AND POOL HOUSE

had made a fortune in Washington real estate; he managed Marwood as a working farm, raising crops and cattle. After Gore's death in 1980, his widow and their three children, James Grafton Gore, Mary Gore Dean, and Louise Gore, continued to live at Marwood. The Gore family are cousins of Vice President Albert Gore.

After subdividing most of the farm, the Gores sold the mansion and 13 remaining acres in 1995 to Dr. Yonas Zegeye and his wife. They in turn sold it in 2005 to Christopher Rogers, a founder of Nextel Communications, and his wife, Nalini, who renovated the house over a three-year period.

Rogers had portions of the interior redesigned as well. He retained the large marble-floored elliptical front foyer that extends from the front door to the rear, facing the river. The long central corridor that runs the length of the house and crosses the foyer was also kept intact. The 40-foot room on the far left of the plan was originally the dining room but was changed to a family room. The former library facing the right became a small dining room. The second and third floors contain 10 bedrooms and a second library, while the basement level includes a large movie theater, six servants' bedrooms, and a servants' hall.

Following Pages: REAR ELEVATION
FACING POTOMAC RIVER

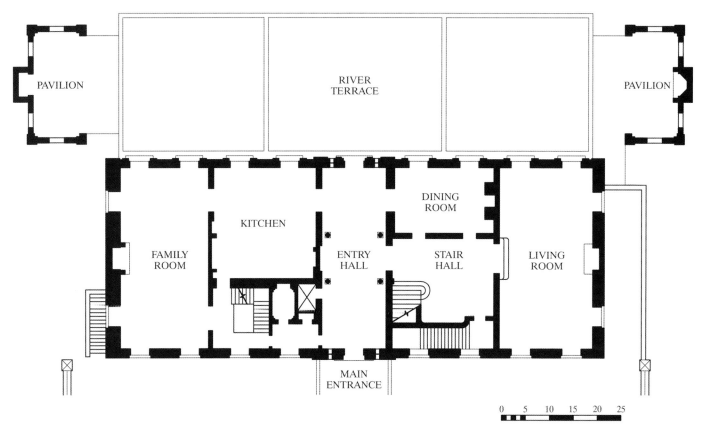

PAVILION

RIVER
TERRACE

PAVILION

KITCHEN

DINING
ROOM

FAMILY
ROOM

ENTRY
HALL

STAIR
HALL

LIVING
ROOM

MAIN
ENTRANCE

0   5   10   15   20   25

FIRST-FLOOR PLAN

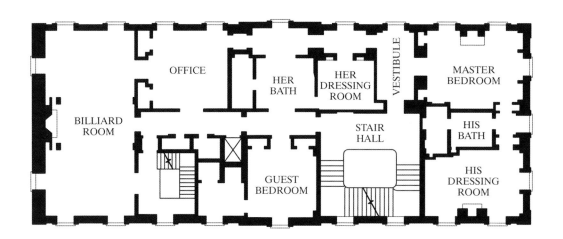

OFFICE

HER
BATH

HER
DRESSING
ROOM

VESTIBULE

MASTER
BEDROOM

BILLIARD
ROOM

HIS
BATH

GUEST
BEDROOM

STAIR
HALL

HIS
DRESSING
ROOM

SECOND-FLOOR PLAN

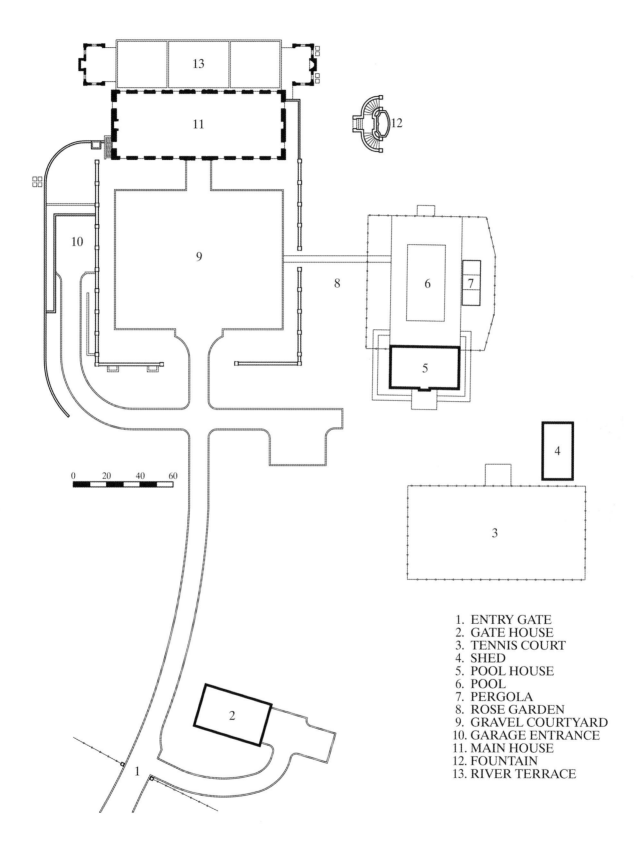

1. ENTRY GATE
2. GATE HOUSE
3. TENNIS COURT
4. SHED
5. POOL HOUSE
6. POOL
7. PERGOLA
8. ROSE GARDEN
9. GRAVEL COURTYARD
10. GARAGE ENTRANCE
11. MAIN HOUSE
12. FOUNTAIN
13. RIVER TERRACE

0   20   40   60

SITE PLAN

GEORGIAN REVIVAL HOUSES

Dudlea

Woodrow Wilson House

Dumbarton Oaks

British Ambassador's Residence

Woodend

Hillwood

DUDLEA

1 QUINCY STREET
CHEVY CHASE, MARYLAND

———————————

1908

Architect: Ellicott & Emmart

Status: Private Residence

FACADE FROM ENTRY DRIVE

DUDLEA STANDS AS ONE OF THE EARLIEST grand residences built in Chevy Chase, Maryland. The suburb is a model for excellence among communities developed in the United States during the late-19th and early-20th centuries. Behind its genesis is William Sharon, who controlled much of the Comstock silver and gold mines in Nevada and parlayed that into ownership of the Bank of California, the San Francisco Waterworks, the Palace Hotel in San Francisco, and vast tracts of land in Nevada. Both Sharon and his son-in-law, Francis G. Newlands (*see also* Woodley), became U.S. senators from the young state of Nevada. In 1890 Newlands arrived in Washington with $5 million in gold bullion. He founded the Chevy Chase Land Company the following year, and to service the new community, promoted the extension of Connecticut Avenue from Calvert Street in the District, together with a streetcar line that terminated at Chevy Chase Lake in Maryland.

This large three-story Georgian Revival house, noted for its pebble-dash exterior and wide wraparound porch, is prominently situated on the southeast corner of Connecticut Avenue and Bradley Lane, directly across from the Chevy Chase Club. The property occupies 2½ acres, on which the house is set back considerably from Connecticut Avenue. The unusually large entrance hall was designed both for entertaining and to provide air circulation during the hot summer months. The hall opens to a large living room and sunroom (originally an open-air porch on the north side); to the right are a parlor and dining room. The main staircase, pantry, kitchen, and breakfast room are in the rear. The second and third floors have eight bedrooms.

Only two families—the Morgans and the Sauls—have owned Dudlea since its completion in 1909. The house was built by Dr. James Dudley Morgan (1861–1919) and his wife, Mary Abell. Morgan was descended from two of Maryland's founding families—the Diggeses and the Carrolls. Edward Digges, an early colonial governor of Virginia, emigrated from Kent, England, where he lived in Chilham Castle. His son, Col. William Digges, moved to

Maryland and founded a tobacco plantation, Warburton, on the Potomac River at Piscataway Creek in the early-18th century. The Digges family were close friends with George and Martha Washington, who lived across the Potomac from Warburton. Through marriage the Digges family was related to Daniel Carroll of Duddington, the largest landowner in what would become the Federal City in 1791. Because of its strategic location on a high bluff, the federal government purchased part of Warburton and built Fort Washington there in the early-19th century. One member of the family, William Dudley Digges, became a good friend of Peter Charles L'Enfant and allowed him to live at Green Hill, his plantation near Hyattsville. It was here that L'Enfant died in poverty and was buried in 1825; not until 1911 was L'Enfant's body exhumed and moved from Green Hill to Arlington National Cemetery amid great ceremony.

Nora, a member of the next generation of the Digges family, married Dr. James Ethelbert Morgan, a Washington doctor who helped tend President Lincoln after he was shot. Their son, Dr. James Dudley Morgan, built Dudlea. The term is a play on the owner's middle name, which had been used consistently in the family as a first or middle name for more than 300 years. Morgan changed the spelling to Dudlea—*lea* meaning "field" in Old English. With the house in Chevy Chase they gained a large front lawn and more space for entertaining. Dudlea was built with part of Mrs. Morgan's considerable inheritance—her grandfather, Arunah Shepherdson Abell, founded *The Baltimore Sun* in 1837; she came into a fortune when her father died of a heart attack after witnessing his newspaper building burn to the ground in the Great Baltimore Fire of 1904. Although the family sold the newspaper in 1910, they continued to own a large body of stock in it until the 1990s.

A noteworthy object on the grounds of Dudlea when the Morgans lived there was a lead sundial set on a limestone pedestal. It was brought from England by Virginia governor Edward Digges to remind him of his birthplace, the sundial originally having sat in the garden at Chilham Castle. The 17th-century inscription on the sundial's top reads: "Chilham Castle Manor. Time is golden—it passes by like a shadow." On the base is the 18th-century inscription: "Warburton—the Grist Stone—1717—Digges." It has stood at the residence of the Digges family and their descendants in America for nine generations. When Dudlea was sold, the sundial was moved to the home of Charles C. Morgan's son, Leroy Morgan, at the foot of Sugarloaf Mountain in Montgomery County.

James Dudley Morgan's son, Carroll Morgan (1899–1970), inherited the house and lived there until he sold it to close family friends B.F. Saul II and his wife, Elizabeth Patricia English, in 1968. The house was ideal for the Sauls (known as Frank and Trish) and their five children. The grounds include a cottage for household staff, a pool, pool house, and a three-car garage.

Bernard Francis Saul II remains the owner of Dudlea today; he is chairman of the board of the B. F. Saul Company, one of the oldest real estate firms in Washington—established in 1892 by his grandfather. B. F. Saul II founded the Chevy Chase Bank in 1969 and sold it to Capital One Bank in 2009. After the sale, Saul expanded Chevy Chase Trust into the largest trust company in the Washington metropolitan area.

Saul's great-grandparents, John Hennessy Saul (1819–1897) and Rosina M. Lawley, immigrated to Washington in 1851 from Bristol, England, where Saul managed a large nursery. Andrew Jackson Downing, the "father of American landscape architecture," brought the elder Saul to the United States. President Millard Fillmore commissioned Downing to landscape the Mall in Washington in 1850, and Saul supervised the early stages of Downing's landscape plan for the project, as Downing was too busy to leave his business in Newburgh, New York. The Saul family had been gardeners for generations: John H. Saul's father and grandfather had been head supervisors of the estates of the Boyle family, the Earls of Shannon and Cork. The Boyles in Ireland acquired their vast

ENTRANCE HALL

landholdings from Sir Walter Raleigh in the early-17th century, Queen Elizabeth having originally granted them to Raleigh. All of John H. Saul's four brothers were gardeners: Two others also came to the United States and prospered—Andrew managed Downing's nursery in Newburgh, and James established his own in Davis, California.

After Downing died in a steamboat explosion on the Hudson River in 1852, John Saul continued to work on landscaping plans for the Smithsonian Institution grounds and for Lafayette Park until Congress greatly reduced the funding in 1853. He then went into private practice in Washington. With the help of his patron, William Wilson Corcoran, Saul began a small nursery and seed store on 7th and G Streets, N.W., opposite the Patent Office; he eventually bought an 80-acre farm near the present-day intersection of Georgia Avenue and Emerson Street, N.W., which he named Maple Grove. Saul built greenhouses that supplied the Buchanan and Lincoln administrations with fresh vegetables and fruit. By 1880 he had built 20 greenhouses and was shipping plants across the United States to fill orders from his eight annual catalogs. One of his greatest joys before he died in 1897 was serving without pay on the three-member District of Columbia parking commission, which planted thousands of trees on the narrow medians between Washington's sidewalks and streets.

DINING ROOM

PANTRY

Of John H. Saul's nine children, perhaps the most distinguished was B. F. Saul I (1872–1931), who started a real estate company in 1892, immediately after graduating from the Georgetown Prep School at the age of 18. His natural instinct for business led him to establish the Home Savings Bank at 7th Street and New York Avenue, N.W., only five years later. At the time his bank merged in 1919 into the Security and Savings Bank, Saul became chairman of the executive committee. When the 14th Street electric streetcar line was extended in 1895 from Florida Avenue northward through the center of Maple Grove, his father's former nursery, Saul laid out streets, sold hundreds of building lots to developers, and made a fortune in the neighborhood now known as Brightwood. After the death of B. F. Saul I in 1931, his son John A. Saul managed the company until the end of World War II, when a younger son of B. F. Saul I, Andrew Saul, took it over. B. F. Saul II joined the company at the age of 25 in 1957 and became president in 1969.

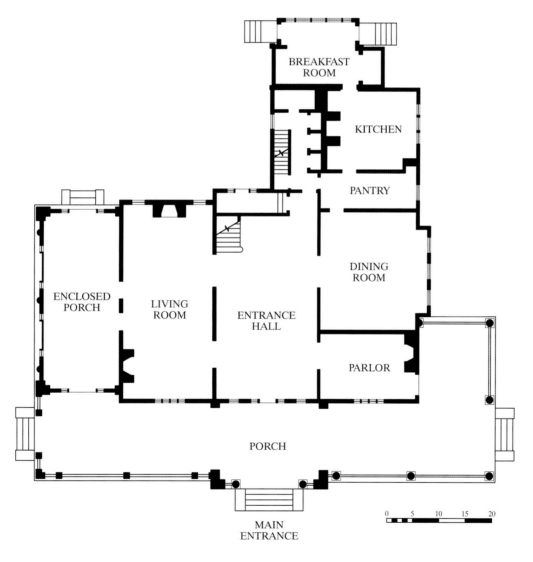

FIRST-FLOOR PLAN

WOODROW WILSON HOUSE

2340 S STREET, N.W.
WASHINGTON, D.C.

_____

1915

Architect: Waddy B. Wood
Neighborhood: Sheridan-Kalorama
Status: Historic House Museum

FACADE

REAR ELEVATION

THE DESIGN IN 1915 OF NOTED LOCAL ARCHI-tect Waddy B. Wood, who was responsible for a number of buildings in the area, this handsome Georgian Revival, four-story brick town house lies in the Sheridan-Kalorama neighborhood, two blocks northwest of Sheridan Circle. Henry Park Fairbanks (1871–1946), a Boston businessman who was part owner of the Bigelow Carpet Company, commissioned the residence. He moved to Washington in 1914 and served as director of a federal agency during World War I. After returning to Boston in 1920, Fairbanks sold the house to President and Mrs. Wilson as a retirement home.

The house was built at a cost of $58,000 and included state-of-the-art technology throughout. The exterior walls are steel-reinforced concrete faced with brick. The house fronts a short semicircular driveway, while the rear opens onto a terraced garden with a central fountain. The arched, north-facing entrance is sheltered by a small, elegant classical porch with a pair of columns supporting an entablature and a wrought-iron railing. Two limestone belt courses provide a base for the second floor, which features three Palladian windows with distinctive scalloped spandrels. Ornamental rondelles separate two pairs of small rectangular windows and flanking single windows to provide interest and symmetry to the third floor.

The low-ceilinged first floor contains a long rectangular entrance hall, office, small reception

DINING ROOM

room, and service rooms. The central hall plan has a large staircase leading to the second, or principal, floor. On the second floor, the living room faces the front, while the library and dining room, separated by a small bowed solarium, face the rear garden. The third floor features two guest bedrooms in the front and two master bedrooms and a sleeping porch (over the solarium) in the rear. The fourth floor, which is concealed by a brick parapet, has five servants' bedrooms, a bathroom, and a large laundry. The rest of this floor is occupied by a flat roof, which was used as a drying area for laundry.

The Woodrow Wilson House is one of only two presidential house museums in Washington—the other is the Lincoln Cottage. Wilson (1856–1924)

decided to retire in the nation's capital when he left the White House in March 1921 in order to have ready access to the Library of Congress to research the books he planned to write. Wilson had no hometown. He was raised in the household of a Presbyterian minister father, who served churches in Virginia, Georgia, South Carolina, and North Carolina during the Civil War era.

Wilson's national reputation as a reform governor of New Jersey between 1910 and 1912 culminated in his nomination for president on the Democratic ticket in 1912. He won the election because the Republican vote was split between Theodore Roosevelt and William Howard Taft. Wilson was inaugurated in 1913 and served two terms. He favored a reduction

Left: LIBRARY

in import tariffs that Congress enacted, but then had to propose an increase in income taxes to replace the lost revenue; he witnessed the establishment of the Federal Reserve system, which was created to bring stability to the nation's banking industry. Wilson led the nation to victory in World War I and helped negotiate the Treaty of Versailles in 1919. Unfortunately, the U.S. Senate refused to ratify the treaty because it contained a provision for establishing a League of Nations, an international association for which isolationist-leaning senators had no use. Members of the Republican-controlled Senate were also affronted that Wilson had not included any of them in the U.S. delegation to the peace conference. During a nationwide railroad tour to promote ratification of the treaty, President Wilson suffered a paralyzing stroke, which left him an invalid for the remainder of his life.

Edith Bolling Galt, whom the widower President Wilson married in December 1915, found the Fairbanks house for sale in late 1920 for $150,000, a price greatly increased by wartime inflation. Ten of Wilson's friends donated most of the funds for the purchase. The Wilsons made several important modifications to the house in early 1921. They installed a driveway with iron gates and added a garage on the right side of the house, converted a vacant shaft to an electric elevator, and built bookcases for Wilson's 8,000-volume library. Mrs. Wilson moved in some of the furniture from her former home at 1308 20th Street, N.W., near Dupont Circle, to help furnish the spacious new residence. She adapted old curtains from the White House to the windows.

Wilson lived in the house for almost three years, until his death in early 1924. Mrs. Wilson maintained the house exactly as he had left it until her own death in 1961. She bequeathed it and the original furnishings to the National Trust for Historic Preservation, which has kept it open to the public since 1963. It was the Trust that unfortunately approved construction of the house next door on a lot that had been purchased to preserve the Wilsons' privacy.

KITCHEN

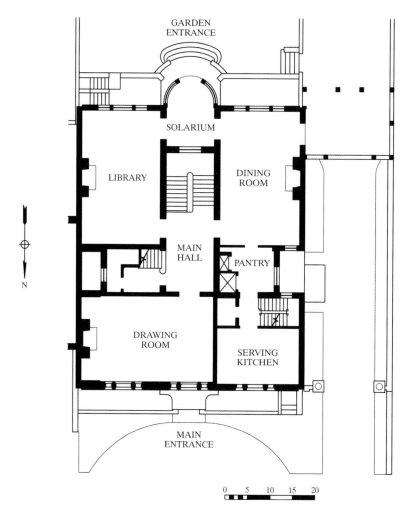

GARDEN
ENTRANCE

SOLARIUM

LIBRARY

DINING
ROOM

MAIN
HALL

PANTRY

DRAWING
ROOM

SERVING
KITCHEN

N

MAIN
ENTRANCE

0 5 10 15 20

SECOND OR PRINCIPAL-FLOOR PLAN

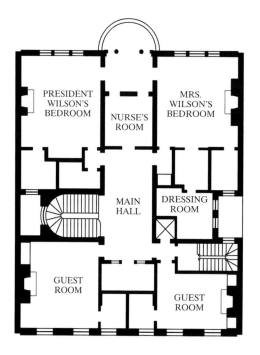

PRESIDENT
WILSON'S
BEDROOM

NURSE'S
ROOM

MRS.
WILSON'S
BEDROOM

MAIN
HALL

DRESSING
ROOM

GUEST
ROOM

GUEST
ROOM

THIRD-FLOOR PLAN

DUMBARTON OAKS

3101 R STREET, N.W.
WASHINGTON, D.C.

1801
REMODELED 1846; 1865
REMODELED AND ENLARGED 1921–24

Architects for the Blisses, 1921–24 onward: McKim, Mead & White,
Frederick H. Brooke, Beatrix Farrand, and Thomas T. Waterman.
Architects for recent additions to the house and grounds include Philip Johnson,
George Hartman, and Venturi, Scott Brown Associates
Neighborhood: Georgetown
Status: Offices of the Dumbarton Oaks Foundation

FACADE

R STREET GATES

FEW LARGE WASHINGTON, D.C., HOUSES HAVE undergone more major remodeling and expansion than Dumbarton Oaks. The original 22-acre site was purchased in 1800 by real estate investor William Hammond Dorsey (1764–1818) from Thomas Beall. The Bealls had owned most of what became the eastern half of Georgetown—a tract of 795 acres that extended north to the present Washington National Cathedral. Thomas Beall's grandfather, Ninian Beall, had acquired the tract in 1703 by a grant from the English crown, and named it the Rock of Dumbarton after a landmark on the Clyde River near his native Glasgow, Scotland.

Dorsey built a two-story, brick, Federal-style house there in 1801. Indebtedness forced him to sell it four years later. There were three other owners before Edward M. Linthicum, a wealthy Georgetown hardware merchant, purchased the house in 1846. He called it Monterrey after the hard-won American victory in the Mexican–American War and remodeled it in the Greek Revival style. After Linthicum's death in 1869, Henry F. Blount, a successful plough manufacturer from Indiana, bought the house and remodeled it in the Second Empire style and renamed it The Oaks. He added a third floor with a mansard roof crowned by iron cresting, two new wings with bay windows, cast-iron porches, and a porte cochere.

The last private owners, Ambassador Robert Woods Bliss (1875–1962) and his wife, Mildred Barnes Bliss (1879–1969), purchased the estate in 1920 and began laying out 16 acres of terraced gardens under the direction of landscape architect Beatrix Farrand. While traveling in the foreign service, they had acquired the property for their retirement home. Over the next two decades they increased the estate to more than 40 acres. The Blisses then changed the

CONSERVATORY

name of the house to Dumbarton Oaks and began remodeling and enlarging it in a project that continued from 1921 to 1924, embellishing it in a late Georgian–Federal vein. Lawrence Grant White of the New York firm McKim, Mead & White (and son of Stanford White) remodeled the exterior, while Frederick H. Brooke took charge of the interior. Brooke had just finished construction of a group of Georgian Revival buildings at the Virginia Episcopal School campus in Lynchburg. By the end of the decade he

would also design Georgian Revival interiors for Sir Edwin Lutyens' new British ambassador's residence on Massachusetts Avenue.

Mildred Bliss contributed a number of design elements to the house's exterior. She commissioned a student from the Parsons School of Design in New York to illustrate the effects she wanted, which were influenced in large part by the Nathaniel Russell House in Charleston, South Carolina, an 1808 Federal masterpiece. Dumbarton Oaks' prominent central

Following Pages: REAR ELEVATION

PEBBLE FOUNTAIN

entrance, projecting from the central block, features a shallow limestone portico and dramatic flared limestone steps and balustrades. It was Mildred Bliss' decision to extend the first-floor windows to the floor in the central part of the house. The windows are embellished with lunette-shaped wrought-iron guards similar to those on The Octagon in Washington. She also had the dormer windows on the third floor accented with alternating curvilinear and triangular pediments to add variety and interest and to help integrate the design of the lengthy facade. The center of the rear elevation features a two-story bow front with a limestone door surround, crowned by a stately broken

pediment. The two projecting rear wings extend at 90-degree angles to create a rear courtyard. The first-floor plan is one-room deep, with a central hall surviving from the 1801 plan, and a long gallery in the rear. The long gallery is embellished with a pair of elegant wrought iron staircases featuring birds made by Samuel Yellin of Philadelphia.

While the Blisses were living in the U.S. ambassador's house in Sweden in 1929, they installed a large music room for concerts on the west side of Dumbarton Oaks. They commissioned Paris architect and decorator Armand-Albert Rateau to design it with a mixture of Georgian Revival and Renaissance elements.

Left: POOL LOGGIA

MUSIC ROOM

The major wall features a massive Palladian window and a pair of rondelles. Rateau carefully reproduced an elaborately painted beamed Renaissance ceiling, the original of which is still in place at the Château de Cheverny in France. He then shipped two authentic French Renaissance embellishments for the music room—a parquet floor and a stone mantelpiece. In 1930 Rateau designed the interiors of the oval salon and the living room.

As the renovation of the main house was nearing completion, the Blisses decided to add four Georgian Revival service buildings to the estate: an elegant double house for the head gardener and butler, located at the corner of 32nd and S Streets, N.W.; a garage with rooms above for male staff members; a greenhouse; and an orangery. Rateau worked with Beatrix

Farrand to create the iron gates, vases, benches, statues, finials, and stone baskets for the grounds. In 1933 Farrand designed the Fellows Lodge on nearby S Street and its enclosed courtyard. Construction of other buildings on the estate continued in 1938, when Mildred Bliss commissioned architect Thomas T. Waterman, who had worked on the restoration at Colonial Williamsburg, to design two separate pavilions west of the main house for the library and museum for their collection of Byzantine art. In 1963 Philip Johnson was hired to design a new museum to house the Robert Woods Bliss Collection of Pre-Columbian Art. In her final major building effort at Dumbarton Oaks, Mildred Bliss and her new landscape architect, Ruth Harvey, designed the elegant pebble fountain in the space that had been the tennis

Right: PAIR OF GALLERY STAIRCASES

court. In 1987 George Hartman roofed over the open area between the library and collections pavilions to create a courtyard gallery.

Mildred Bliss began her garden library with the assistance of Beatrix Farrand in 1940. When Farrand retired that same year, her assistant, Ruth Harvey, took her place, collecting garden books and continuing designs for the garden itself. Bliss and Harvey created "garden rooms," each of which had its own individual character.

In 1940 the Blisses deeded the 16½-acre core of the estate and its buildings to Harvard University as a scholars' center, with the provision of their life occupancy. The remaining 27 acres were given to the National Park Service for parklands. The Blisses' gift to Harvard came with an endowment of $10 million. Through careful management the endowment had grown to more than $1 billion by 2014.

Harvard University has continued to enhance the grounds with additional buildings over the years, adding a large modern library building designed by Venturi, Scott Brown Associates, near the Fellows Lodge in 2005. In 2013 Harvard bought an existing brick building on the northwest corner of Wisconsin Avenue and R Street, N.W., and converted it into a new, larger residence for the fellows.

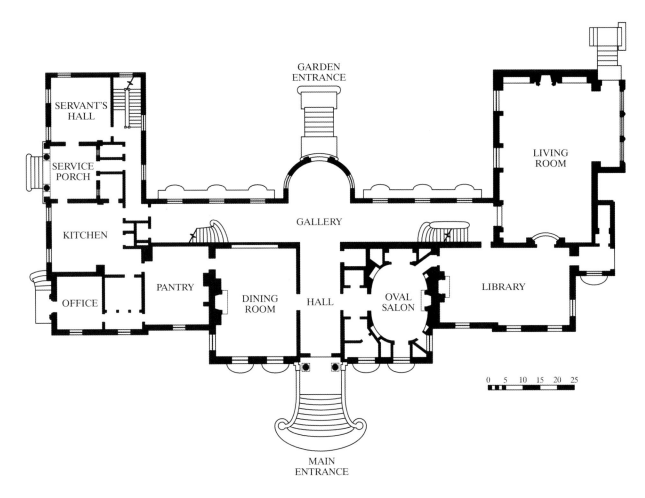

FIRST-FLOOR PLAN

BRITISH AMBASSADOR'S RESIDENCE

3100 MASSACHUSETTS AVENUE, N.W.
WASHINGTON, D.C.

1927–31

Architect: Sir Edwin Lutyens
Associate Architect: Frederick H. Brooke
Neighborhood: Cathedral Heights
Status: Residence of the Ambassador of the United Kingdom

GARDEN FACADE

IONIC CAPITAL ON AN ENGAGED PILASTER

G REAT BRITAIN WAS THE FIRST FOREIGN ministry in Washington to build its embassy as two separate but adjoining buildings. The original chancery, or office, faces east onto Massachusetts Avenue, and the residence, located behind the chancery, faces south onto a large, hilltop terraced lawn that is hidden from the street. Washington real estate developer Harry Wardman, an American citizen who emigrated from England as a youth, exchanged the 4-acre site for the old British Embassy property on the northwest corner of Connecticut Avenue and N Street,

N.W., and agreed to pay an additional $300,000 when the new embassy was completed. The site was protected from future development by the U.S. Naval Observatory on the north and a federal park to the east. The south side of the embassy backs up to White-haven Street, on which imposing houses were built in the 1920s and 1930s; philanthropist Paul Mellon was an early resident, and today Bill and Hillary Clinton own one of the houses.

Shortly after his appointment as architect of the new embassy, Sir Edwin Lutyens (1869–1944) visited

Left: DRIVEWAY TO PRINCIPAL ENTRANCE

CENTRAL HALL

DRAWING ROOM

Washington in April 1925 to study the site. After construction began, he returned three times between 1927 and 1930 to check on progress. During his first visit the American Institute of Architects presented him their gold medal at its annual meeting in New York. It was at this same meeting that Frank Lloyd Wright praised Lutyens for his unusual heating system for the embassy. During his early career, Lutyens designed more than a dozen country houses in England and, often, the gardens that accompanied them, usually working with landscape architect Gertrude Jekyll. He planned the British embassy as he was finishing the monumental Viceroy's House in Delhi, India (1912–30)—also a combination of chancery and residence. This important architectural work earned Lutyens a knighthood.

Since Lutyens could not be on-site regularly, Washington architect Frederick H. Brooke, who had worked on the remodeling of Dumbarton Oaks, supervised the construction. Completion of the embassy was delayed repeatedly for several reasons. One was the lack of funding by the British Office of Works. When funds were not available to finish landscaping and build the swimming pool and tennis court, eight

Following Pages: PAIR OF STAIRCASES RISE FROM THE DRIVEWAY ENTRANCE ON THE GROUND FLOOR TO THE FIRST FLOOR

British citizens who were New York City residents donated $50,000. Another delay resulted from the bankruptcy of the builder, Harry Wardman, owing to the stock market crash in 1929. The first occupants of the embassy, Sir Ronald Lindsay and Lady Lindsay, stayed at the Mayflower Hotel for three months before they could move into the new residence on June 11, 1930. Even then, work continued on both the exterior and interior.

Lady Elizabeth Sherman Hoyt Lindsay (an American by birth and great-niece of General William T. Sherman), an experienced landscape architect who managed Eastover, her large family estate on Long Island, after her mother's death, devoted a decade to establishing the embassy gardens. She began the popular annual spring and summer garden parties at the embassy, to which invitations were as sought-after as those to the White House. The British government extended the Lindsays' stay in Washington from 5 to 10 years. Their last grand entertainment was a garden party for King George VI and Queen Elizabeth on June 8, 1939. Because the 1,400 guests were so crowded, the next ambassador, Philip Kerr, 11th Marquis of Lothian, purchased an acre of adjacent land bordering Massachusetts Avenue with his own funds to enlarge the garden space.

Between 1941 and 1953 the British government purchased vacant lots to the north of the embassy. This space was used for a new and much larger chancery, designed by Eric Bedford, and built between 1957 and 1960. Today it is considered architecturally incompatible with the old embassy.

The British Embassy complex is now composed of four basic parts—the original stately U-shaped chancery that faces Massachusetts Avenue; the residence, which is hidden behind the original chancery; the extensive gardens forming the terraced south lawn of the residence; and the mid-century modern chancery to the northwest. The original access to both chancery and residence was on Massachusetts Avenue through two massive iron gates with flanking stone

DINING ROOM

TERRACED GARDEN STEPS

pillars surmounted by lions. Visitors to the chancery would take the circular drive to the front door. Those visiting the residence would drive around the chancery to a porte cochere in the rear to enter the residence at ground level. An elegant double marble staircase ascends to the first floor of the embassy, which is set at right angles to the chancery. Located above the porte cochere is the ambassador's unusual paneled study, nearly a perfect cube, with fluted Corinthian pilasters encircling the walls. A central hallway, beginning at the study, runs the full length of the house, and leads to the west door, which connects to a westward path to the swimming pool and tennis court. The house's facade fronts the extensive lawn and gardens to the south.

The central section of the house is composed of a portico of Ionic columns crowned with a pediment containing the sculptured royal coat of arms. Behind the portico are the ballroom and service rooms, and the kitchen courtyard beyond. On the left, or west, wing are the drawing and dining rooms. The library

Left: WEST DOORWAY DETAIL

is located in the right, or east, wing. Bedrooms and sitting rooms occupy the second and third floors.

Visitors to the British Embassy would do well to explore and study the elevations of the complex to discover Lutyens' hidden architectural surprises. The architect added a certain tension to the building by making the windows taller than normal. The massive, tall chimneys on both the chancery and the embassy are also unusual. Lutyens disdained rainwater drains on the exterior of buildings, so he hid them inside the walls. However, reality trumped his aesthetics: The pipes leak in many places, yet no one would think of changing his original scheme. He designed atypical Ionic pilasters by installing carved capitals with no supporting shafts. Unusual circular windows punctuate the garden wall near the porte cochere; most have

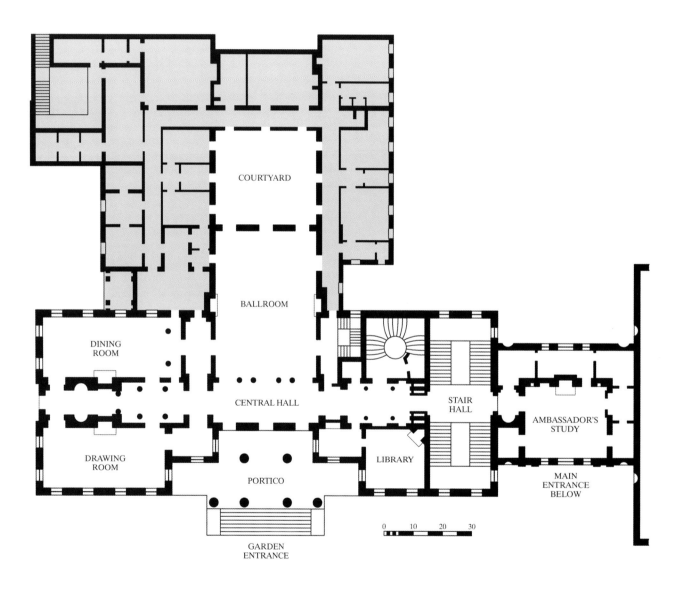

COURTYARD

BALLROOM

DINING ROOM

CENTRAL HALL

DRAWING ROOM

STAIR HALL

AMBASSADOR'S STUDY

LIBRARY

PORTICO

MAIN ENTRANCE BELOW

0   10   20   30

GARDEN ENTRANCE

FIRST-FLOOR PLAN

grilles but the several that do not allow children on the grounds to watch guests entering through the port cochere below. Another surprise is the two massive Egyptian-style lions on the walls flanking the ambassador's study—a feature that cannot be seen from the street. Patterned dark slate defines the principal terrace in front of the main portico: The slate is not laid flat but in tight vertical rows. Lutyens also repeated this pattern on the path to the swimming pool. Surprisingly, the rows are not uncomfortable to walk on. Finally, Lutyens emphasizes the edges of walls, and door and window surrounds, by using hand-rubbed brick that has a smooth texture and brighter red color than the body of the brickwork. These unusual features make his architecture a delight to residents and visitors alike.

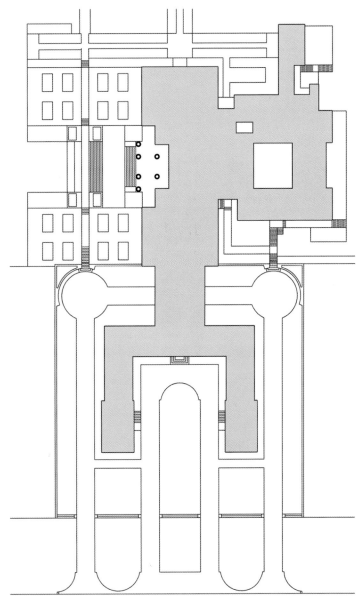

MASSACHUSETTS AVENUE SITE PLAN

WOODEND

———————

1928

Architect: John Russell Pope

Status: Offices of the Audubon Naturalist Society

ROUNDED PORCH

MAIN ENTRANCE

WOODEND, A SYMMETRICAL, I-SHAPED, red brick Georgian Revival house, is the design of celebrated architect John Russell Pope (1874–1937). Pope's imposing public buildings in Washington include the Scottish Rite Temple, Constitution Hall, the National Archives, the National Gallery of Art, and the Jefferson Memorial. Woodend is one of a group—including Strathmore and Stoneridge—of surviving country houses built in the early-20th century in suburban Maryland, along the Wisconsin Avenue–Rockville Pike corridor.

Captain Chester Wells and his wife, Marion Leigh Dixon Wells, built Woodend in 1928. Wells retired from the U.S. Navy the year after the house was completed. He became a bank director and was active in civic affairs, serving on the boards of the George Washington University Hospital and the Columbia Hospital for Women, and as president of the Washington Council for the Boy Scouts.

Wells (1870–1948) was a native of Wyalusing, Pennsylvania, and a graduate of the U.S. Naval Academy. He was posted to Cuba, the Philippines, and China, and served in World War I. While in Sydney in 1905, serving as a lieutenant commander on the world tour of the Great White Fleet, Wells met his future wife, Marion Dixon (formerly Dixson). They became engaged at a mountain resort in Australia named Woodend and were married in England in 1907.

Marion Wells came from a distinguished family in Australia. She was born in 1884 in Sydney, the

RECEPTION HALL FIREPLACE

youngest child of Sir Hugh Dixson and Lady Emma Shaw Dixson. Her father owned the British-Australasia Tobacco Company, which had been founded by his father, who had immigrated to Australia from Scotland in 1839. The family lived at Abergeldie, a large estate near Sydney, and frequently traveled to Europe.

In 1910, three years after they were married, the Wellses purchased 10 acres of farmland in Montgomery County as the site of their future home when Wells retired from naval service. By the time Woodend was built in 1928, their landholding had grown to 80 acres. The land had originally been part of a large tobacco plantation known as Clean Drinking Manor; the Charles Jones family who owned it had also built a flour mill nearby on Rock Creek.

The grand house the Wellses built has a hipped roof with a balustrade on its outer perimeter that conceals the third story. The roof cornice is decorated with an egg-and-dart molding. The walls are laid in Flemish bond with brick quoins at the corners. Woodend has three entrances; the main one is set in the center of the west face, which has a curved terrace connecting the north and south wings. Fluted limestone pilasters with

MAIN STAIRCASE

acanthus capitals flank the double doors, an eclectic classical touch Pope often used; they are crowned with a massive broken pediment. A semicircular portico shelters the south wing entrance, which is also embellished with a stone balustrade. The sight is spectacular when approaching from the long, curving driveway. The north entrance consists of a small stone porch with a pair of Ionic columns and a rounded pediment.

Through the main door is a large central hall connecting the north (left) and south (right) wings. The principal staircase, with a large Palladian window at the landing, is straight ahead. An elaborate

Georgian Revival fireplace is on the immediate right. The billiard room, a replica of the one from Marion Wells' childhood home in Australia, is through a door on the right, while the dining room is to the far left.

The Wellses maintained a large staff at Woodend: a butler, a cook, three maids, a chauffeur, several groundsmen, and one or two governesses for their two adopted daughters. The staff lived either on the third floor or above the three-car garage located down the hill from the house next to the front driveway. Family bedrooms were on the second floor, while the first floor served as living and entertaining space. The large central hall was ideal for receptions or dances.

Financial reversals brought on by the Great Depression, World War II financial restrictions (funds could not be moved from Australia during the war), and estate taxes resulting from Captain Wells' death in 1948 forced the sale of half the land at Woodend—40 acres. Marion Wells, an avid bird-watcher, decided in 1959 to bequeath the house, together with 33 acres and one-quarter of her residual estate, to the Audubon Naturalist Society (ANS) of the District of Columbia for its headquarters and a bird sanctuary.

She died in 1967 and the ANS relocated to Woodend in 1969. The Audubon Naturalist Society is not part of the national Audubon Society; it is a separate organization that predates the national group. Since it was established in 1897 to protect birds from overhunting, the ANS has included eminent scientists and naturalists among its leaders and members. These include Theodore Roosevelt, John Burroughs, Roger Tory Peterson, and Pulitzer Prize–winners Rachel Carson and William Warner. Today the society offers a wide range of educational programs and plays a major role in regional environmental issues.

FIRST-FLOOR PLAN

HILLWOOD

4155 LINNEAN AVENUE, N.W.
WASHINGTON, D.C.

1926
REMODELED 1955

Architect: John Deibert; Renovation: Alexander McIlvaine, 1955
Neighborhood: Forest Hills
Status: Historic House and Decorative Arts Museum

FACADE

HILLWOOD, THE FORMER HOME OF CEREAL heiress Marjorie Merriweather Post, is the most significant estate in Washington that is open to the public as both a historic house and European decorative arts museum. Post purchased the property in 1955 to showcase her important collection of French and Russian decorative arts. Today the Hillwood Museum and Garden Foundation owns and operates the impressive estate, welcoming visitors to the house and extensive gardens and woodlands in a secluded upper northwest Washington neighborhood. The original Georgian Revival mansion and outbuildings, including a garage, stable, and greenhouse, as well as a swimming pool and formal garden, were built in 1926. Washington social and civic leader Mrs. Delos A. Blodgett, whose husband accumulated a fortune from lumber mills in Michigan, built the house for her daughter and son-in-law, Col. and Mrs. Henry Parsons Erwin. The mansion, which the Erwins named Arbremont or "wooded hill," occupies a 24-acre site on a high bluff overlooking Rock Creek Park; it remains the largest private estate in the city.

Little is known about the architect, John Deibert; he designed the house with two stories and a small third floor over the central section behind the portico. Most of the roof was flat and therefore concealed by the parapet. The south facade, with a four-columned portico, opens onto a spacious lawn that offers a good view of the Washington Monument 6 miles away. The house was constructed of fireproof steel beams and brick, a factor that appealed to Mrs. Post, to safeguard her extensive collection of paintings and decorative arts.

Mrs. Post greatly enjoyed entertaining at the estate, which she renamed Hillwood. She held a place alongside Gwendolyn Cafritz and Perle Mesta as one of the capital's leading hostesses in the Cold War years. At the time of her death in 1973, Post's assets had reached $250 million ($5 billion today), making her the wealthiest woman in the United States. Her

Right: RECEPTION HALL AND STAIRCASE

Following Pages: LIBRARY; PORTRAIT OF MARJORIE MERRIWEATHER POST AT RIGHT BY FRANK O. SALISBURY, 1934

FRENCH DRAWING ROOM

fondness for and skill in entertaining as well as her love of collecting decorative arts is a remarkable story in itself.

Marjorie Merriweather Post (1887–1973) was born in Illinois but grew up in Battle Creek, Michigan, the only child of Charles W. Post. Her father developed a very successful business manufacturing Postum, a healthy substitute for coffee, and Grape-Nuts and Post Toasties cereals. Marjorie Post became a keen businesswoman, thanks to her father's training: she attended his board meetings seated behind a screen and traveled with him on business trips.

After attending Mount Vernon Seminary in Washington, Marjorie in 1905 married Edward B. Close, a young investment banker and member of an old New England family in Greenwich, Connecticut. Her father built them a stone mansion, the Boulders, in Greenwich, reserving one wing for himself. He taught Marjorie how to manage the large staff and finances associated with the Boulders—valuable lessons from which she benefited for the rest of her life. During her marriage to Close she had two daughters, Adelaide and Eleanor. The sudden death of C.W. Post in 1914 left Marjorie heir to the Postum Cereal Company.

FOUNTAIN SEEN FROM THE BOXWOOD GARDEN

Differences between Marjorie and Edward's views on religion (Marjorie was a Christian Scientist), business management, and entertaining resulted in their divorce in 1919. Within months she fell in love with and married E.F. Hutton, a successful New York stockbroker. In contrast to her first husband's less-than-satisfactory business performance, Hutton skillfully managed the Postum Cereal Company, and at Marjorie's insistence he added the Birdseye Frosted Foods Company to its holdings. When the value of the corporation's stock skyrocketed, Hutton changed its name to General Foods in 1929 and moved the headquarters to New York City. During the 1920s Marjorie's vastly increased income allowed her to acquire a 54-room triplex apartment at Fifth Avenue and 92nd Street in Manhattan, a 176-acre country estate on Long Island called Hillwood, a 207-acre camp in the Adirondacks that was ultimately named Topridge, and a spectacular Mediterranean Moorish–style mansion in Palm Beach called Mar-a-Lago.

In addition to Adelaide and Eleanor, the daughters from her first marriage, Marjorie's marriage to Hutton resulted in the birth of a third daughter, Nedenia, better known as actress Dina Merrill.

During the Depression Marjorie curtailed her entertaining and contributed in many ways to helping the poor, including establishing food stations and canteens in New York City. Even so, she could not resist commissioning a new yacht in Kiel, Germany, in 1931. The 316-foot-long yacht, which she named *Sea Cloud*, had a staff of 71 and was the largest privately owned yacht in the world. During the 1930s she and her family sailed for four- to six-month periods to Europe or the Caribbean.

Her second marriage ended in divorce in 1935—largely due to the couple's political differences (she supported FDR; he did not) and extramarital affairs. While planning the divorce, she met and fell in love with Joseph E. Davies, a well-established Washington lawyer and fellow Democrat, whom she met at a Palm

Beach dinner party. They were married in New York in December 1935, and enjoyed a wedding trip to the West Indies on the *Sea Cloud.* In late 1936 President Roosevelt rewarded Davies for his political support by appointing him ambassador to the Soviet Union. With her natural ability to entertain—using fine china and linen and even frozen foods for dinner parties—Marjorie wowed the diplomatic community in Moscow and became a popular figure with the Soviets. The couple, especially Marjorie, took the opportunity to buy fine china, paintings, and silver that had been seized by the Soviets from the imperial and various noble Russian families. The Soviets sold these decorative arts at reduced prices to help support their industrial revolution and military buildup. After a year and a half in Moscow, Davies was appointed ambassador to Belgium, where he served from 1938 to 1939. Marjorie joined him there but became ill and had to return to the United States.

Davies resigned from the State Department in December 1939 and the couple settled in Washington, renting a house on Foxhall Road until 1940, when they purchased the Parmelee estate, a Georgian Revival mansion designed by Charles Platt and set on 20 acres on Macomb Street in Cleveland Park. Renovations took two years. Marjorie had rooms built to display her Russian decorative arts, including the famed Fabergé Easter eggs, chalices, icons, silver, and French furniture and tapestries that she had originally collected for her New York apartment. They named the estate Tregaron after a Welsh place name that relates to Davies family history. It is now home to the International School.

When World War II began Marjorie loaned the *Sea Cloud* to the federal government for military convoy use in Europe. In late 1941 Joseph Davies published his memoirs of service in the Soviet Union, *Mission to Moscow,* which cast the Soviets as loyal allies against Hitler. The best-seller became a motion picture.

The increasingly belligerent behavior of Joseph Davies toward Marjorie in front of her children,

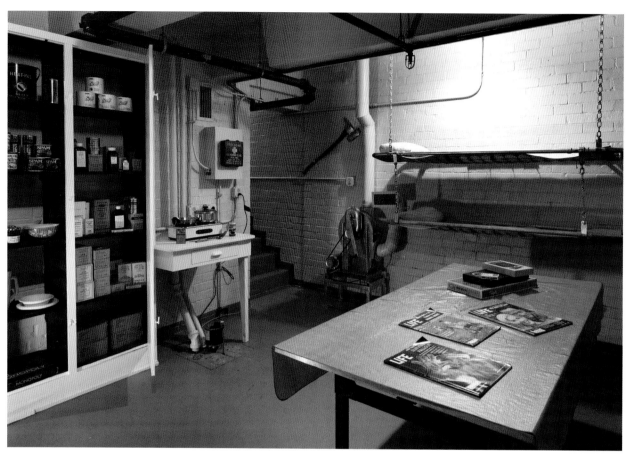

COLD WAR ERA FALLOUT SHELTER IN THE BASEMENT

friends, and staff—perhaps from dementia—strained their marriage during the 1940s and 1950s and resulted in their divorce in March 1955. Marjorie purchased Arbremont the same year and renamed it Hillwood after her former Long Island country house (now C.W. Post University). She commissioned New York architect Alexander McIlvaine to remodel and double the size of the house and add a number of ancillary buildings. She had the ceilings raised, the dining room doubled in size, the entrance hall enlarged, and the main staircase moved from the east end of the house to the west. She added the pavilion, a large room for showing first-run movies and staging events, including square dancing, to the west end of the house. An impressive curved porte cochere was designed for the entrance. Marjorie had a breakfast room built on the south side of the dining room adjacent to the portico, extending slightly onto the south lawn. Here, too, she added a number of rooms to display her Russian decorative arts, highlighted by the Fabergé collection.

After two years of construction Marjorie moved into Hillwood in 1957. The following year she quietly married one of her frequent social companions, Herbert A. May, a successful businessman and widower from Pittsburgh. Their life was uneventful until 1963, when she learned that May was attracted to men. After their divorce, May moved to an apartment in Fort Lauderdale, where he died several years later. Marjorie reclaimed her maiden name and was thereafter known as Mrs. Post.

In her will Marjorie Merriweather Post left Hillwood to the Smithsonian Institution, which held it for three years after her death there in 1973. The secretary of the Smithsonian found it difficult to maintain the estate with the many restrictions the will imposed, including prohibiting the use of the dining room to entertain guests. Since the Smithsonian could not charge admission to the public to fund the upkeep of the estate, it returned the property to the Post Foundation in 1977. The foundation has successfully managed the estate and made a number of improvements, including the construction of a new visitors' center, opening a popular café, and creating many changing exhibitions. Unusual features on the estate include Marjorie's Russian cottage, or dacha, the circular cemetery for her pet poodles, the large greenhouse with hundreds of orchids, and a Japanese garden with a pool and bridge. In 2013 a special behind-the-scenes tour was added to the regular tour offerings. Visitors can view Mrs. Post's private beauty parlor on the second floor, the projection booth and balcony in the pavilion, and the restored fallout shelter in the basement, one of five built on the estate during the Cold War.

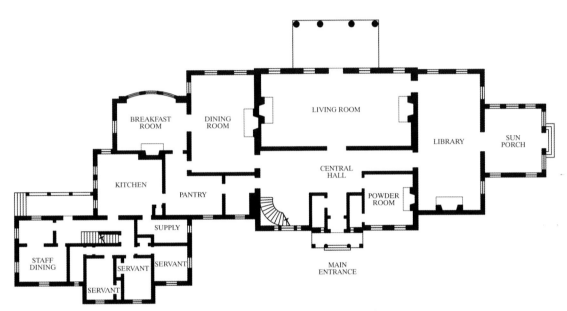

ORIGINAL 1926 FIRST-FLOOR PLAN

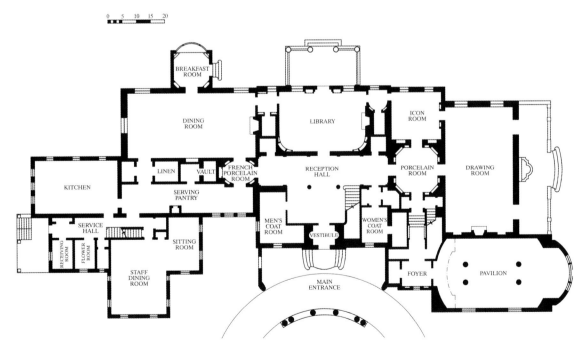

MRS POST'S REVISED 1955 FIRST-FLOOR PLAN

TUDOR REVIVAL HOUSES

Lawrence House

Firenze House

Stirling House

LAWRENCE HOUSE

2221 KALORAMA ROAD, N.W.
WASHINGTON, D.C.

───────────────

1910

Architect: Jules H. de Sibour
Neighborhood: Sheridan-Kalorama
Status: Residence of the Ambassador of France

FACADE

PICKLED-WOOD PANELED LIBRARY

THE ELEGANT TUDOR–JACOBEAN REVIVAL house at 2221 Kalorama Road, N.W., was built in 1910 for William Watson Lawrence (1859–1916), an important Pittsburgh industrialist. Lawrence commissioned one of Washington's most talented architects, Jules H. de Sibour, to design it after his marriage that year to Jane Yuille of Montreal. The following year he purchased two adjoining lots to increase the grounds to 2.4 acres. In 1914 Lawrence persuaded his sister, Annie M. Lawrence, to hire de Sibour to design a house for herself adjacent to his, at 2125 Kalorama Road—now the Portuguese embassy.

W.W. Lawrence's father, John Jacob Lawrence (1827–1903), established a paint and lead manufacturing business in Pittsburgh just after the Civil War. In 1884 William started his own firm, the William W. Lawrence Paint Company in Pittsburgh. His success allowed him to build a massive six-story brick factory on the south side of Pittsburgh at the Duquesne Incline in 1902. The paint factory was closed in 1973, and the landmark razed in 2001.

On his death in 1916 at his principal residence, 9 E. 89th Street in New York City, William Watson Lawrence left an estate valued at $1 million, then an enormous sum. One-fourth was set aside for his

LANDING ON MAIN STAIRCASE

widow and unmarried sisters. His alma mater, Princeton University, received the bulk of the estate, $750,000. Lawrence's two sisters received the Kalorama Road house in Washington. Upon the death of the second Lawrence sister, the house was sold to John Hays Hammond (1855–1936), a mining engineer and San Francisco native. Hammond grew rich from locating gold mines in California, Mexico, and especially South Africa, and made a second fortune drilling for oil for the Burnham Exploration Company. His son, John Hays Hammond Jr. (1888–1965), inherited his acumen: He created more than 400 inventions relating to radio control and naval weaponry. Called the Father of Radio Control, Hammond Jr. made a fortune equal to his father's. His development of radio remote controls pioneered the way to modern missile guidance systems, including the first radio-guided torpedoes.

PANELLED DRAWING ROOM

After Mrs. John Hays Hammond died in 1932, the house on Kalorama Road was closed, and after the death of John Hays Hammond Sr., the house was sold in 1936 to the French government. It has served as the French ambassador's elegant residence ever since. Before moving to Kalorama Road, the French ambassadors resided (from 1907 to 1935) in a Beaux-Arts mansion rented from Mrs. Mary Henderson at 2460 16th Street, N.W., opposite Meridian Hill Park.

Architect de Sibour drew on postmedieval English precedents for the design of Lawrence House, incorporating medieval detailing and asymmetrical window placement in an otherwise symmetrical composition, with a central gabled pavilion flanked by a series of receding sections. Limestone door and window surrounds and quoins complement the subtly toned brown brick walls. Carved salamanders and large quatrefoils adorn the impressive arched entry.

Following Pages: THE RED EMPIRE
DRAWING ROOM HONORS NAPOLEON

Square, three-story towers with balustrades step back from the central entrance pavilion, flanked by paired-window gabled dormers surmounted by multiple-stack chimneys. The architect's playful nod to the spirit of Gothic architecture materializes in the carved limestone grotesques located near the tops of the chimneys on both sides of the house. The symmetrical rear elevation overlooks a valley of Rock Creek and features a spacious bowed slate terrace that is ideal for receptions.

Since World War II, various ambassadors have altered the interior to make it reflect French decor. In the Salon des Boiseries, the paneled drawing room, a Louis XV mantel replaced a Gothic one, and the wood wall panels were lightened. The Grand Salon underwent the most dramatic change, transformed into a drawing room decorated in the style of Napoleon I.

Red silk walls with the emperor's signature gold bees, a grand rug with the initial N in the center, a striking period crystal chandelier, Empire white-and-red-painted armchairs, and period wall sconces now enhance the room. Eighteenth and early-19th century French pieces gradually replaced the American and English furniture left by the Hammonds. Several of the primary rooms hold important Gobelins tapestries and Aubusson carpets. The elegant paneled walls in the dining room are painted antique green with gold trim in the French manner.

Adjacent to the 18th-century oil portrait of General George Washington are portraits of French officers who aided the American cause: the Marquis de Lafayette, the Duc de Rochambeau, and Admiral François-Joseph de Grasse—a fitting tribute to French–American friendship.

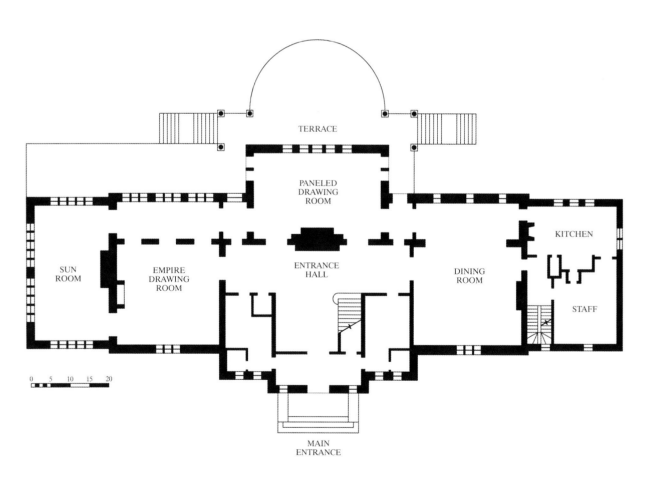

FIRST-FLOOR PLAN

FIRENZE HOUSE

2800 ALBEMARLE STREET, N.W.,
and 4400 BROAD BRANCH ROAD, N.W.
WASHINGTON, D.C.

———————————

1925–27

Architect: Russell O. Kluge
Neighborhood: Forest Hills
Status: Residence of the Ambassador of Italy

FACADE

F IRENZE HOUSE IS NOT ONLY THE LARGEST
Tudor Revival house in Washington; at 22 acres,
it also occupies one of the city's largest residential sites.
Built for Col. and Mrs. Arthur O'Brien, the sprawling
house is 200 feet by 49 feet and contains more than
50 rooms. Mrs. O'Brien—Blanche Estabrook Roebling O'Brien (1881–1953)—inherited a fortune
following the death in 1921 of her first husband, Karl
G. Roebling, a grandson and heir of John Augustus
Roebling, pioneer of American iron-suspension bridges
known for designing the Brooklyn Bridge. She married
Col. Arthur O'Brien (1884–1942) in 1923.

Blanche, whose family controlled a large block
of stock in the Western Union Telegraph Company,
gave the new house her maiden name, Estabrook.
Col. O'Brien, assistant secretary of war under President Woodrow Wilson, was an early political sup-
porter of Franklin D. Roosevelt in the presidential
campaign of 1932. When the O'Briens became disil-
lusioned over Roosevelt's policies they decided to
leave the capital, in 1935, and build a new house in
Seattle, Washington.

They rented Estabrook to the Hungarian legation
in 1935 and, in 1941, sold the estate to M. Robert

REAR ELEVATION

Guggenheim (1885–1959) and his wife, Polly Pollard Guggenheim. He was the grandson of Meyer Guggenheim, who founded the nation's most important mining and silver corporation in the early-20th century. Robert Guggenheim served as a director of the American Smelting and Security Company of Colorado, one of the family business holdings, until 1929. Major philanthropists, the Guggenheims in 1939 founded the museum in New York City that bears their name, for the study and preservation of modern art.

In the 1930s Guggenheim devoted much of his time to yachting. After he married Polly Pollard in 1937—his fourth wife—they lived on his yacht, *The Firenze*, named for his mother, Florence. It was frequently docked on Washington's southwest waterfront. Guggenheim was active in the Republican Party and served as ambassador to Portugal under President Eisenhower. The Guggenheims found the house, which they renamed Firenze House, ideal for entertaining, especially after living on the yacht for four years. The estate had a six-car garage with overhead apartments for the staff, a tennis court, large swimming pool, bowling alley, and gardener's cottage; a staff of 12 maintained it. Polly became a leading

FOYER

THE THREE-STORY-HIGH GREAT HALL

Following Pages: DRAWING ROOM DETAIL

DINING ROOM

OCTAGONAL EAST PORCH

hostess at Firenze House during her marriage to Guggenheim.

Washington architect Russell O. Kluge designed the house in a Tudor vein, with variegated brick and half-timber work at the main entrance. The low-ceilinged foyer opens to a richly paneled small library on the left that, according to family legend, is the study removed from architect Sir Christopher Wren's house in Oxford, England. Down a short flight of steps from the foyer, guests enter the spectacular great hall, with a 30-foot ceiling and grand staircase to the right leading to a landing and second-floor balcony housing a 300-year-old pipe organ. The great hall has enormous arched windows and an elaborate beamed ceiling.

Firenze House suffered a major fire in February 1946 while the Guggenheims were en route to a vacation in California. The great hall, living room, and dining room were badly damaged. Many pieces of antique furniture were lost, as well as 18th-century tapestries and a number of Renaissance oil paintings, including two by Titian. The Guggenheims returned immediately, thankful to find their large rare-glass collection unharmed. They rebuilt the house to its original design.

Two years after Robert Guggenheim died, Polly married John Logan, in 1961, and continued to live at Firenze House. She remained a leading Washington hostess. Because Polly and John Logan began spending more than six months each year away at their estates in St. Mary's County, Maryland, and St. Croix in the Virgin Islands, they sold the house in 1976 to the Italian government for the ambassador's residence.

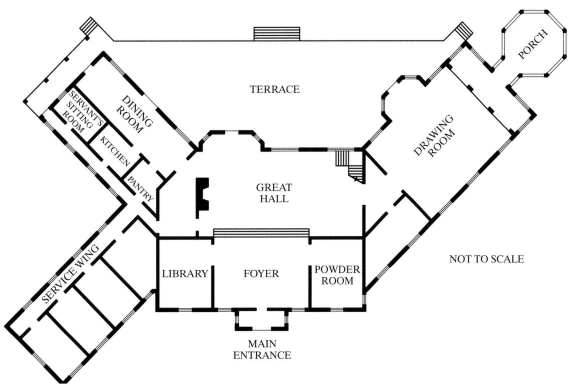

FIRST-FLOOR PLAN

STIRLING HOUSE

2618 31ST STREET, N.W.
WASHINGTON, D.C.

———————————

1927

Architect: Horace W. Peaslee
Neighborhood: Massachusetts Avenue Heights
Status: Private Residence

FACADE

WASHINGTON ARCHITECT HORACE W. Peaslee designed the picturesque 2618 31st Street, N.W. in 1927 for the William C. Stirling family, who apparently welcomed his "recycling" the prominent features of a historic Washington house for their new one. Peaslee, a great admirer of H.H. Richardson, salvaged the older architect's signature Romanesque arches from the Henry Adams House near the northwest corner of 16th and H Streets, N.W. The carved sandstone arches now define the facade of Stirling House. Arched windows on the second floor complement the curved main and garage entryways, while asymmetrically placed Tudor-inspired windows repeat the forms of the slate front gabled and main roofs. The effect is at once monumental and whimsical.

The arches originally sheltered the front entry and the kitchen window of Henry Adams' residence, which connected to the house of his great friend, John Hay. The Brookline, Massachusetts–based Henry Hobson Richardson, called by some the first great American architect, designed the Hay-Adams Houses in 1884 85. The Hay House, with its great Syrian arch above the main door on 16th Street, occupied 75 percent of the lot. The much smaller Adams House, located "behind" the Hay House, faced H Street and Lafayette Park.

When the Hay-Adams Houses were being demolished in 1927, Peaslee convinced prominent Washington real estate developer Harry Wardman to give him parts of the house, including the intricately carved sandstone arches. Peaslee moved them from H Street to 31st Street and greatly narrowed the one for the Stirlings' main entrance, and slightly narrowed the surround for the garage entry. Richardson's Assyrian-looking carved lion relief still stands on a Byzantine-inspired decorative capital, the columnar base of which defines the area where the two arches meet. Peaslee also commissioned a stone carver to add a thistle above the front door arch as an emblem of Dr. Stirling's Scottish heritage, and a rose over the other for Mrs. Stirling's Danish ancestry. The architect salvaged the handsome doorway of the John Hay

PART OF THE CARVED ENTRANCE ARCHES FROM THE HENRY ADAMS HOUSE

House and incorporated it into a house he was building for the Ruth family at 3014 Woodland Drive, N.W., two blocks from Stirling House.

The house's owner was Dr. William Calhoun Stirling Jr. (1894–1969), a native of Sulphur Springs, Texas (near Dallas), who received his medical degree from Vanderbilt University in 1917. He was the sixth-generation doctor in his family. While serving as a surgeon at Lawrence Hospital in Winston-Salem, North Carolina, Dr. Stirling married Margheritta Tillman in 1922 at St. Thomas Episcopal Church in Washington, D.C. Margheritta was a third-generation Washingtonian. Her maternal grandfather, Johan Cornelius Kondrup, was a career Danish diplomat, who had come to Washington in 1863 as assistant consul general. After the Civil War, he stayed on and became an American citizen. The Stirlings moved from Winston-Salem to Washington in 1925. Their children were Margheritta "Mickey"

LIBRARY, 1930s VIEW

Tillman, William, and Elizabeth. Mickey recalled the years the family lived there between 1927 and 1945. The first floor included a powder room near the front door and a small sitting room on the left front, where Mrs. Stirling kept her desk. Mickey remembers that the library had a number of curiosities, including an "elaborate spiked German helmet that Dad brought back from World War I that always scared and awed us a bit." The library was impressive because it was completely paneled in pecky cypress brought up from Florida while the house was under construction. The distinctive paneling had numerous deep grooves in the surface.

The dining room originally had French doors on three sides, two leading out to wrought-iron balconies overlooking the hillside, the third opening onto the terrace, which also connected to the library. Later, the terrace between the library and dining room was enclosed for a family room. Mickey remembers that the library had a large oriental rug over which a striking polar-bear-skin rug was placed in front of the fireplace. Her grandfather, a captain in the U.S. Navy, had brought it from Alaska. She and her sister and two brothers used to curl up on the bearskin rug in front of the fireplace to pop corn in wire baskets. A Hudson River School landscape painting hung over the fireplace. Also in the room were large portraits of her parents painted by Bjorn Egali, a Norwegian portraitist, who, during the Depression, paid her father for medical care with paintings. Egali also paid Dr. Stirling with a number of elegant watercolors of sailing ships, another of his specialties. He soon became quite successful and painted many prominent Washington figures.

The second floor included five bedrooms and two baths. The third floor was originally completely open and used for many purposes—including medical meetings by Dr. Stirling and a play area for the four children. A single window lights it in the front, and three dormer windows in the rear. Part of the third floor was partitioned during World War II for a guest bedroom. Since the house was built on a steep hill, the site could accommodate a full basement. In addition to the laundry and storage rooms, there were also servants' bedrooms and a small kitchen and bath used full-time by the black staff: Sarah, the family cook; Thomas, the butler-chauffeur; and part time by Effie, the nanny. The laundry room had an early form of clothes dryer—a large metal "closet" heated by lighted gas jets where clothes were hung to dry. Three terraces opened in the rear to gardens and a play area with a sandbox and a slide.

Dr. Stirling's practice kept him in Washington during the summer while his wife and three children stayed at the Tillman family's Shingle-style summer cottage on Jamestown Island across the bay from Newport, Rhode Island. The eldest child, Mickey, recalled in 2011 growing up at 2618 just before and during the early years of World War II. In summers the Oriental rugs were replaced with sisal rugs, and the heavy embroidered curtains were replaced with translucent "glass curtains." The family raised chickens and maintained a vegetable garden to help with the war effort—called at the time a victory garden. Entertainment for the children consisted of games such as hide-and-seek and kick-the-can, as well as favorite radio programs *The Shadow* and *Amos 'n' Andy*. Roller-skating and sitting in the tire-swing were great fun. All this made for a happy childhood on 31st Street.

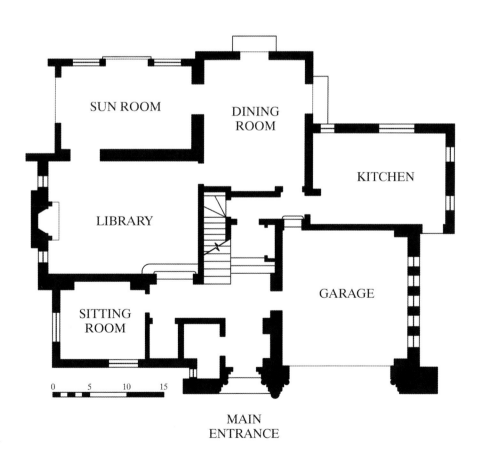

FIRST-FLOOR PLAN

ART DECO
HOUSES

Fealy House

Cafritz House

Mounsey House

FEALY HOUSE

2911 W STREET, S.E.
WASHINGTON, D.C.

1935

Architect: Harry Sternfeld
Designer: John Joseph Earley
Neighborhood: Anacostia
Status: Private Residence

FACADE

DETAIL OF PRECAST CONCRETE AGGREGATE PEBBLE PANELS OF THE FACADE

For a number of years Michael Carney, a communications consultant, and his wife, Aimee, owned a small row house on Capitol Hill. In 2004 they decided to buy a freestanding house with a front and rear lawn. Their search ended with the purchase of an unusual concrete mosaic paneled house built in 1935 in the Hillcrest section of Anacostia. The house was in good condition both inside and out. Little did they know at the time that their residence was of landmark importance: it was the first prefabricated house and one of the best residential examples of Art Deco in the District of Columbia. Its relatively remote location had kept it well concealed from public attention for more than 75 years.

Dr. Martin S. Fealy—who commissioned the house—was a prominent Capitol Hill pharmacist, who maintained a practice at 1024 Pennsylvania Avenue, S.E. Fealy's Pharmacy was in a large, turreted, red-brick Victorian on the northwest corner of Pennsylvania Avenue and 11th Street, S.E., known to

neighbors as Fealy's Corner. An 1897 graduate of the National College of Pharmacy, Fealy worked at this location for more than three decades. The pharmacy, the adjoining row houses, and adjacent streetcar tracks bordered by trees have long since disappeared. The proximity of Fealy's house in Anacostia to his business allowed him a 15-minute drive to work. Located on a steep hill on W Street, S.E., his was the first house on the block. Even the land in front of it was vacant. It had a striking, unobstructed view of the domes of the U.S. Capitol and the Library of Congress.

The one-story Fealy House is constructed of 9-foot-high panels of beige-colored concrete mosaic. The plan includes two bedrooms and a living room, dining room, study, bath, and kitchen. The front landscaping includes a sloping lawn covered with ivy, bordered by a stone retaining wall that abuts the sidewalk. A short driveway on the left terminates in the wrought-iron-gated garage set under the master bedroom. The front entrance on the right features a

ATTIC VENT

CHIMNEY DETAIL

door inset with three thin, square, concrete mosaic polychrome panels. Blue concrete mosaic panels flank the red-painted door. All the windows have steel casements, including the two prominent round front windows that light the living room. A low concrete ceramic-tile wall decorated with a striking red zigzag frieze with a thin blue border encloses the rectangular terrace adjacent to the entrance. Green ceramic tiles cover the low gabled roof; pierced circular concrete mosaic panels with chevron inserts decorate the gables. Even the top of the low chimney features alternating red and cream panels.

Decorative elements within the house are confined to the living and dining rooms. The focus of the living room is a beige concrete mosaic fireplace surround, where two rectangular concrete pilasters flank a central, multicolored geometric panel. The hearth is also a concrete mosaic panel with a dark blue-and-red border. The walls of the living room are paneled in walnut, as is the dining room, which also has a coved ceiling. Cedar closets are an unexpected amenity in this modest house.

Harry Sternfeld, the somewhat unorthodox Philadelphia architect who designed the Fealy House, trained at the University of Pennsylvania. He gave his drawings to John Joseph Earley to execute in concrete mosaic panels; it was the first such prefabricated house in Washington. Earley was born in Boston in 1881 to a fourth-generation Irish stone carver. In 1890 his family moved to Washington to take advantage of the building boom spurred by American millionaires.

In the early-20th century, Earley and his business partner, Basil Gordon Taylor, produced mainly architectural plaster work in the Earley Studio. A turning point came when the National Bureau of Standards hired Earley to investigate using concrete mosaic as a building material during World War I. In response he invented a process for constructing a field house with concrete mosaic panels. Success led him to take out a patent on his technique, which

Left: : FRONT DOOR WITH THREE
CONCRETE AGGREGATE PEBBLE PANELS

involved using the right size ratio of pebble (aggregate stone) to sand particle to prevent clumping; removing the wooden frames, or forms, before the concrete was fully set; and rubbing the concrete panels with steel wire brushes to reveal the stones.

Most of Earley's important work was produced between the two world wars. Calling himself an "architectural sculptor," Earley built five low-cost, lightweight, prefabricated houses on Colesville Road in Silver Spring, Maryland, in 1934. The five houses, designed by local architect J.R. Kennedy, were each built with 32 concrete mosaic panels. Most were beige and cast with square or round window openings. The concrete mosaic panels—9 feet tall and from 4 to 8 feet wide—were suspended from concrete columns so that they barely touched the floor. The 2-inch-thick panels were so light that a pair could be delivered by pickup truck, and erected using a single beam hoist. After these early Art Deco mosaic examples, including the Fealy House in Anacostia the following year, Earley produced panels for Colonial Revival houses, including two-story examples with dormer windows. He never intended to build houses himself, only to create the panels for builders.

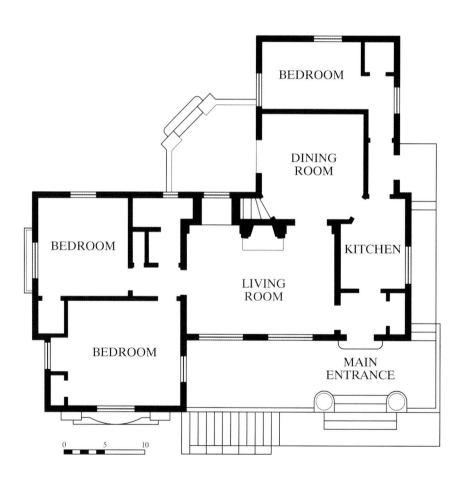

FIRST-FLOOR PLAN

CAFRITZ HOUSE

2301 FOXHALL ROAD, N.W.
WASHINGTON, D.C.

1936–38

Architects: Alvin L. Aubinoe & Harry L. Edwards
Neighborhood: Berkley
Status: Private School

SEMICIRCULAR MAIN ENTRANCE

ENTRANCE FACADE, 1930s VIEW

T HE MORRIS AND GWENDOLYN CAFRITZ
house on Foxhall Road is an unusual example
of streamline Art Deco executed on a grand scale.
Morris Cafritz (1888–1964) was one of the most successful real estate developers in the history of Washington, along with Harry Wardman and B.F. Saul.

Morris' grocer father, Nussen Kafitze, his wife,
and their five children left Russia for New York, where
they stayed briefly before moving to Washington in
1899. At the age of 17 Morris left school and went
into business—the same path taken by Wardman and
Saul. After first working in his father's grocery store,
Morris went into the wholesale coal business. With a
loan of $1,400 from his father, Morris expanded his
businesses by opening a saloon, an outdoor silent
movie theater, and a bowling alley. Endowed with a
keen business sense, he soon became the largest owner
of bowling alleys in the city. He used the profits from
that enterprise to move into real estate in 1921, when
he began buying and selling office buildings.

Cafritz's first major moneymaking project was
the development of Petworth. In 1922 Cafritz
bought the old Columbia Country Club golf course
adjacent to Georgia Avenue, when the club moved to
a new location on Connecticut Avenue and the present
East–West Highway. He carved 90 square city blocks
out of the property and built 3,000 brick row
houses—selling them for $9,000 each, with a $1,000
down payment. In the 1930s he directed his real estate empire from his office in the Ambassador Hotel
at 14th and K Streets, N.W., which he also built.
Cafritz anticipated the Depression and stopped construction well before the crash. But the Depression
did not last long in Washington due to a housing
shortage in the mid-1930s. The city's population
grew, thanks to the many New Deal government
agencies created in response to the crisis. Cafritz resumed construction with vigor, building a number of
distinguished Art Deco apartment houses on 16th
Street and downtown.

LOWER ENTRANCE

From the 1940s through the mid-1960s, Cafritz led the shift of the city's business center from F Street to the K Street corridor. He replaced the Victorian and Beaux-Arts mansions with office buildings along I, K, and L Streets. A significant percentage of the buildings he constructed are still extant and occupied.

Cafritz was 42 when he married Gwendolyn, the 19-year-old daughter of Dr. Laszlo Detre de Surany, a Hungarian physician who had recently moved from Budapest to Washington with his wife and two daughters. Six years later, Gwendolyn talked Morris into building a grand house. Cafritz purchased a 7-acre farm on Foxhall Road—then an area little developed. The couple gave their specifications to Alvin Aubinoe and Harry L. Edwards, two architects who worked for the Cafritz Company. The Cafritzes were inspired by a Modernist house built in 1934 for Richard Mandel near Bedford Falls, New York, which had been designed by Edward Durell Stone. The Mandel house

was low and horizontal, streamlined with both sharp-edged and rounded rooms. The Cafritzes' Foxhall Road house was of a dramatic type most people saw only in Hollywood movie sets of the period. It was designed in 1936 with two and three levels in a Y shape and built of common red brick painted white, overlooking spacious terraced lawns in the rear. The striking Art Deco rounded entrance reflected the contours of the front curved driveway. A two-story wing in the rear opened onto a panoramic view of the city and the Potomac River in the distance. The upper level was Gwendolyn's bedroom, and the lower floor contained a large dining room that could easily seat 22. Both rooms had unusual rounded corners.

The house was designed for grand entertaining. The large living room with a redwood floor opened onto a wide terrace with a wrought-iron balustrade set with swirls in rectangular panels. Steps led down to the spacious sloping lawn. The living room featured a stainless-steel mantel surmounted by a large mural

depicting seminude women in a Greco-Egyptian style. Andre Durenceau, who produced several murals for the 1939 New York World's Fair, painted the canvas for the Cafritzes in 1937. Eugene Schoen, a well-known designer and architect in New York, designed the furnishings here and in other rooms, as well as a number of interior architectural details. His modernist furniture incorporated bleached woods, sharp corners, and low-slung designs. Schoen also used indirect lighting and round mirrors, which were slightly colored to complement a woman's complexion.

The Cafritz House contained 15,000 square feet, including 58 rooms, 12 bathrooms, and an elevator. Modern art was on display even in the basement: the game room held a large linoleum mural of men in a stadium cheering their home team. The "nightclub" room on the same level featured a bar with benches of synthetic leather, a counter made of industrial plastic, and a dance floor laid in opaque glass and lighted from below.

FIREPLACE IN THE NIGHT CLUB

The most striking room, however, was the round foyer with a circular aluminum staircase and a spectacular Lucite-and-brass handrail. The marble floor was inlaid with eight brass figures, including a polo player, a conga drummer, a couple dancing the rumba, and the back of Einstein's head. The light in the gold-leaf ceiling could be set to shine white, gold, or silver.

Gwen held many large parties at the house from the time she and Morris moved in until he died in 1964, and even shortly thereafter. Her first rule for successful entertaining was to have enough pretty women and witty men at a party to compensate for the president's dour cabinet officers and their homely wives. Every year she gave two large cocktail parties for 300 guests, one in May and the other in October, and a dozen formal dinners in the dining room during the social season. Among her many distinguished guests were Hollywood celebrities and political and social figures on the order of Vice Presidents Alben Barkley, Richard Nixon, and Hubert H. Humphrey; Senator and Mrs. John F. Kennedy; and the Duke and Duchess of Windsor. Gwen's primary competitor in entertaining during that period was Perle Mesta, the heiress of Oklahoma oil wells and a Pennsylvania steel mill. Gwen was famous for her digs at Perle: "Darling, I just couldn't bother with Mrs. Mesta; I go with girls my own age." When someone asked her if Mrs. Mesta was invited to one of her big parties, Gwen replied, "Really, it won't be that big a party."

Social reporters for Washington's newspapers delighted in her frequent slipups, dubbed Gwenfritzisms, usually the result of her still rather broken English. One of her lady guests once looked bewildered when Gwen said to her, "My dear, you look positively strategic!" Another time she remarked to a reporter about an upcoming party: "Oh, there'll be

Following Pages: MURAL IN THE LIVING ROOM TODAY

millions of ambassadors, and some desultory food and caviar walking about." Another oft-quoted Gwenfritzism: "I know we are approaching the posterior of the afternoon."

When Gwen Cafritz died in 1988, the vast majority of her $140 million estate was left to the Cafritz Foundation. A stipulation was included that the Cafritz House be offered to the federal government as the residence of the U.S. secretary of state. When Congress refused to accept the house, it became part of the foundation's assets. For the next eight years her sons contested the will through litigation and won $7 million each, but the bulk of the estate went to the foundation.

Today the foundation manages a variety of assets, including numerous office buildings and apartment houses bequeathed by the Cafritz estate. But its board eventually sold Cafritz House to the Field School, a local preparatory school founded in 1972 by Elizabeth C. Ely, a lifelong educator who advocated a classical curriculum in an informal environment. After starting out with 44 students in a few cramped classrooms above Regina Cleaners near Dupont Circle, the school relocated in 1974 to larger quarters at 2126 Wyoming Avenue, N.W. Field continues to maintain small classes of 11 to 12 students, which allow for an intimate learning environment. Before moving to their new 7-acre campus in 2002, the Field School built two sizable buildings on the property—the main administration building to the right of the house and a gymnasium directly behind the house. The sweeping expanse of lawns became a large playing field. Today the Field School has more than 350 day students who glory in the hilltop setting.

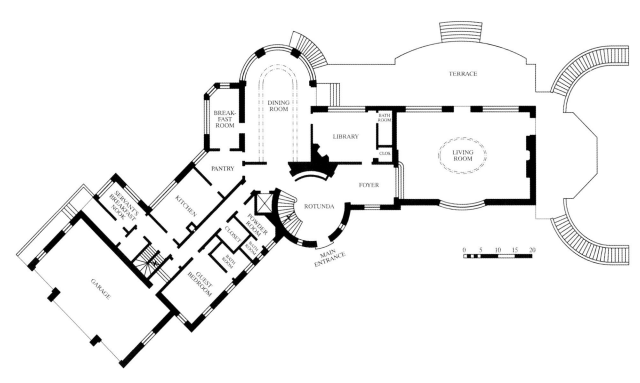

FIRST-FLOOR PLAN

MOUNSEY HOUSE

2915 UNIVERSITY TERRACE, N.W.
WASHINGTON, D.C.

1949–50

Designer: William D. Nixon
Neighborhood: Palisades
Status: Private Residence

FACADE

STAIR HALL

To come upon this house in the heart of the Palisades neighborhood is a surprise: a streamlined Art Deco structure of pale yellow brick, accented with glass blocks, semicircular entrance steps, and an aluminum banquette. Built on a steep hill, the striking house is two stories tall at street level and four stories in the rear, facing a heavily wooded area. The plan of the first floor consists of a spacious two-story foyer with a spiral staircase set in a curved wall, lighted by a zigzag ribbon of glass blocks. On the left are two rooms, the living room, featuring indirect lighting, and the kitchen in the rear. The second floor has five bedrooms, two baths, and an open porch, which has been enclosed.

The house's history is unusual as well. In 1949, an African American couple, Frank E. Mounsey and his wife, Dr. Ethel Nixon Mounsey, built it in the affluent white Palisades neighborhood of Washington. This area, encompassing Loughborough Road, MacArthur Boulevard, and Chain Bridge Road, was in fact home to five black families, descendants of freed slaves who had each purchased 3-to-5-acre lots for $80 per acre just after the Civil War.

The Mounseys, who were married in 1936, purchased a half-acre lot from one of the original owners on University Terrace in 1949. They had more than a comfortable income. Frank E. Mounsey worked his entire career for the federal government, first at the

Left: SOUTH ELEVATION

LIVING ROOM

Washington Navy Yard and then for the Post Office Department. Ethel Nixon Mounsey (1910–1953) earned an M.D. from Howard University. Unlike other nearby neighborhoods, the University Terrace area had no covenants prohibiting black ownership— African Americans had owned houses there since the end of the Civil War. Nevertheless, Washington banks would not provide a construction loan, and ultimately the Mounseys obtained funding from the Mosley Jewelry Store. William D. Nixon, Ethel's father, designed the house in 1949, and R.A. Morrison constructed it in 1950. The Mounsey family moved in in January 1951.

Tragically, Ethel Mounsey lived there only two years; she died of leukemia at the age of 42. She left three young daughters: Mera, Francine, and Delores. At the time of her death she held the position of assistant psychiatrist at the Johns Hopkins University Hospital. After her death, her father moved into the house to help raise the three girls.

William D. Nixon (1871–1962) was the son of former slaves Burrel and Maria Nixon. Burrel bought his freedom and that of his wife from their owner, Rebecca B. Scott, on October 19, 1860. His granddaughter, Delores Mounsey, now a medical technician retired from Howard University Hospital, has preserved the original manumission papers.

Following his graduation from Dunbar High School, a scholastically elite school for blacks, William Nixon earned his teacher's certificate from the Miner Normal School in Washington. After working in Detroit for a few years, in 1902 he returned to Washington, where he secured a position as an art teacher at Dunbar High School, which he held for

40 years, before retiring in 1942. While at Dunbar, Nixon and fellow art teacher Samuel Milton were enthusiastic designers of stage props for the pageants performed at annual graduations.

During the 1920s Nixon also became interested in architecture; he designed three buildings for friends—a small hotel at Truman's Point, Virginia; a beach house at Venice Beach, near Annapolis; and a bungalow in Herndon, Virginia.

As president of the Oldest Inhabitants (Colored) in Washington, Nixon began a concentrated effort to fight every aspect of segregation in the city by organizing pickets and boycotts of stores that did not hire black clerks even though half of their customers were black. In addition to attempting to desegregate the Washington Redskins, he also led the movement in 1953, along with local activist Mary Church Terrell, to integrate local movie theaters. He was instrumental in achieving desegregation in Washington restaurants in 1953 by initiating a case that went to the U.S. Supreme Court. Nixon also worked to integrate the police and fire departments and was active in other civil rights–related organizations, including the Urban League and the National Association for the Advancement of Colored People.

Following William's death in 1962, at the age of 91, Frank Mounsey continued to live at 2915 University Terrace with one of his daughters. The house was too large for them, and he sold it in 1973 and moved with his daughter to an apartment.

The second owners were Dan and Sharon Campbell, who lived there until they divorced in 1979. The third and present owners are two retired art professors from American University, Norma Broude and Mary D. Garrard. They are noteworthy themselves for pioneering and defining the new field of feminist art history. Four volumes of feminist art essays that they edited between 1982 and 2005 have become basic textbooks for art history and women's studies programs. Both have taken a passionate interest in preserving the architectural character of the Art Deco house for more than 31 years.

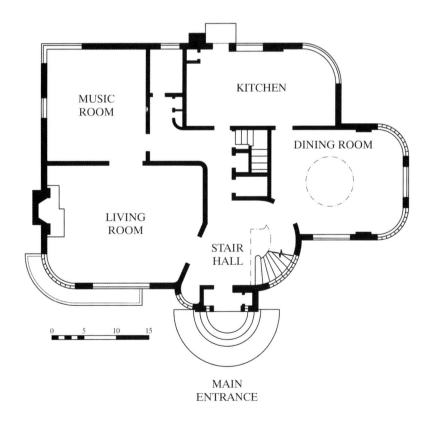

FIRST-FLOOR PLAN

MODERN
HOUSES

Marden House

Slayton House

Kreeger House

MARDEN HOUSE

600 CHAIN BRIDGE ROAD
MCLEAN, VIRGINIA

———————————

1952–59
Architect: Frank Lloyd Wright
Status: Private Residence

FRONT ENTRANCE

FRANK LLOYD WRIGHT AND HIS SUPERINTENDENT ROBERT BEHARKA
VISIT MRS MARDEN DURING CONSTRUCTION

ONE OF FRANK LLOYD WRIGHT'S MORE ELE-
gantly designed and beautifully sited Usonian
houses is the Marden House, perched on cliffs overlooking the Little Falls of the Potomac River. Beginning in 1936, Wright developed his Usonian houses
(the term perhaps derived from "United States of
North America") over a 15-year period, designing
more than a hundred of them across the country. They
were intended to be low-cost, one-story houses com-
bining beauty of materials and charm of living with
open and comfortable interior spaces. Their construction often included cinder-block walls, mahogany
paneling, colored concrete floors (with embedded

hot-water heating coils), built-in furniture, and large,
expansive windows.

Luis Marden (1913–2003), a photographer and
explorer employed by the National Geographic Society, and his wife, Ethel (1911–2012), commissioned
this distinctive house. Luis is credited for his pioneering work in underwater color photography with
Jacques Cousteau, and with the discovery of the
H.M.S. Bounty. Ethel was not only an early pioneer in
computer programming, but an aviatrix, race-car
enthusiast, and deep-sea diver. Both were avid sailors
known for retracing one of Columbus' routes to
America in their yacht.

Following Pages: RIVER FACADE

LIBRARY

In 1940 Luis Marden wrote to Frank Lloyd Wright and asked him to design a house. Wright replied that he would accommodate Marden when he and Ethel had selected a site. The Mardens found one by accident while fly-fishing in 1944; they spotted a 2-acre wooded tract on a cliff above Little Falls on the Potomac River. The Mardens were not satisfied with Wright's first design for the 2,500-square-foot house when it arrived eight years later, in 1952, having been delayed by a number of major commissions, including the Guggenheim Museum in New York. The Mardens asked Wright to change his traditional open carport design to a two-car enclosed garage; straighten the bowed-glass wall facing the river; alter the design of the three riverside terraces so that they would not block the view from the living room; move the maid's room from the main level to the basement; and add a wine cellar and darkroom there. Once the changes were made, construction began, in 1956. When Wright visited the site that year, he was so impressed with the river view that he attempted to get the Mardens to exchange their 2-acre site for a land-locked 4-acre one in Bethesda, Maryland, belonging to his son, Robert. Wright's apprentice, Robert Beharka, supervised construction of both the Marden House and the Robert Wright House.

The total cost of Marden House when it was finished in May 1959 was $76,000—much more than the Mardens had budgeted. Wright never saw the completed house; he died one month earlier, at the age of 91.

LIVING ROOM

Marden House is approached from Chain Bridge Road in McLean, Virginia, by a downhill gravel driveway that terminates in a small entrance court. The one-story, cinder-block house has an understated entranceway. On the right is a two-car garage, and on the left is a curved retaining wall designed with a series of slightly set-back horizontal tiers of concrete block, making what might otherwise have been a heavy wall a feature contributing to lightness and charm. Two stone boulders flank the entrance, and a Japanese maple tree at the left of the entrance adds a touch of color to the gray walls. Between the retaining wall and the house is a narrow walkway leading to the kitchen entrance. Space along this walkway provides storage for logs for the two fireplaces, a large one in the living room and a smaller one in the master bedroom.

Upon entering, one faces a small study on the right, where an ornamental cinder-block grille in a geometric pattern shields a large glass wall overlooking the Potomac River. To the left, one enters a remarkable 80-foot-long, low-ceilinged room that also faces the river. Through the vast expanse of glass set in eight panels is a breathtaking view of the Potomac rapids below. Opposite the glass is a curved, mahogany-paneled wall with cabinets and library shelves at the far end. Today, several of these shelves still contain dozens

Following Pages: LIVING ROOM DETAIL

WINDOWS AND CINDER-BLOCK GRILLE IN THE SMALL STUDY

MASTER BEDROOM

of issues of the *National Geographic Magazine* featuring Luis Marden's photographs. The master bedroom has a fireplace, a large clothes closet, and a large bathroom that retains the original tile walls and fixtures. Both this and the smaller guest bedroom have built-in beds, writing tables, and shelves.

The dining area occupies one end of the 80-foot-long room near the entrance. Adjacent to it are steps leading down to a glass door that opens to one of the three sunken terraces facing the river. The dining area has a long table with a concrete top, surrounded by a set of eight 1950s chairs by Danish designer Hans Wegner. Facing the river on one side, the room opens directly on the other side into a separate living room with a high ceiling and clerestory windows facing the land. The focus of the room is a 4-by-6-foot fireplace set in the cinder-block wall, with a tall, narrow window on the right containing wooden geometric panels designed by Wright's assistant, Robert Beharka. In addition to a large L-shaped sofa, the living room has a corner built-in banquette with bookcases above. The kitchen is off the living room, but separated from it by a tall wall. The original hot-water coils embedded in the concrete floors throughout the house provide radiant heating; the floors are scored and stained a "Cherokee red" color, which provides a pleasant contrast with the mahogany wall panels and light-gray concrete blocks.

The Mardens originally named the house *Fontinalis*, Latin for "Springs." The couple entertained friends here when Luis was not on assignment abroad for the National Geographic Society; however, they never showed the house to the public nor allowed it to be photographed.

By the time Luis Marden entered a nursing home in 1998, the house had deteriorated significantly. Eager to preserve this architectural gem, the executor of the Marden estate offered it to a new neighbor, James V. Kimsey, the founder of America Online, who was building a 21,000-square-foot house next door. Among the conditions of the $2.5 million sale were that the new owner allow Ethel Marden lifetime occupancy of the house, preserve the exterior, and spend at least $500,000 to correct the extensive water damage. Kimsey agreed to the terms and bought the house to protect both his privacy and his view of the river. When Luis Marden died in a nursing home in 2003, Ethel entered a retirement community, and the house came under Kimsey's control. The executor offered to sell Kimsey the house's original Wright furniture, but he declined. Soon afterward the Virginia Museum of Fine Arts in Richmond purchased most of it.

Immediately after Ethel Marden left the house, members of the Frank Lloyd Wright Building Conservancy met with Kimsey to discuss the importance of preserving both the house's interior and exterior. Kimsey agreed to preserve the house and hired contractor Bailey C. Adams of Chevy Chase, Maryland, and local architect Richard Williams, along with Robin Rose and Daniel Donnelly, to fully restore and furnish it. The project took 18 months between 2004 and 2006, and cost more than $1 million. Adams interviewed Wright's former assistant Robert Beharka and, through him, found one of the carpenters who had originally worked on the house. That craftsman returned to work—restoring and refinishing the extensive interior mahogany paneling and the garage doors. Ethel presented Kimsey with three original Wright furnishings still in her possession, as well as other of her and Luis' belongings, including books on

GUEST BATHROOM

nature, travel, and Frank Lloyd Wright. In the basement were other Marden items: Luis's fencing gear, fishing rods, oars, diving weights, and National Geographic photographs. Even though the adjacent wine cellar is empty, the original sign hangs above the entry: *Hic Habitat Felicitas* ("Here Resides Happiness").

Today, Kimsey uses Marden House for philanthropic fund-raising events. In addition, he comes here alone to read at the far end of the long room, enjoying a large, comfortable armchair and ottoman designed by Hans Wegner. Marden House also serves as a guesthouse and a place for intimate dinner parties overlooking the turbulent Potomac. At night floodlights illuminate the house.

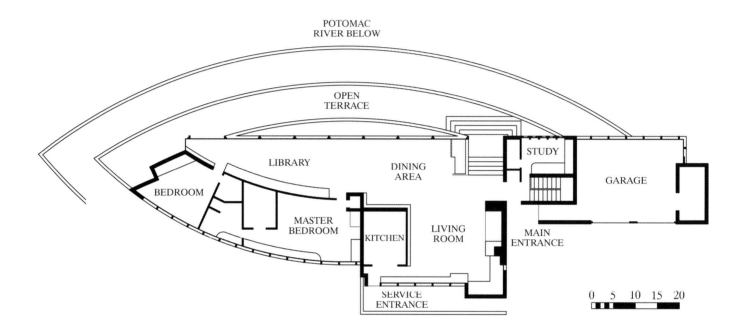

POTOMAC
RIVER BELOW

OPEN
TERRACE

LIBRARY

DINING
AREA

STUDY

GARAGE

BEDROOM

MASTER
BEDROOM

KITCHEN

LIVING
ROOM

MAIN
ENTRANCE

SERVICE
ENTRANCE

0   5   10   15   20

FIRST-FLOOR PLAN

SLAYTON HOUSE

3411 ORDWAY STREET, N.W.
WASHINGTON, D.C.

1958–60

Architect: I.M. Pei & Associates
Renovation Architect: Hugh Newell Jacobsen
Landscape Architect: Ray V. Murphy
Neighborhood: Cleveland Park
Status: Private Residence

REAR ELEVATION

ENTRY FACADE

ONE OF THE MOST STRIKING SMALL HOUSES IN Washington is the Slayton House, designed by renowned architect I.M. Pei. The split-level house sits on a quiet residential street in Cleveland Park. Pei designed this gem for his friend, William L. Slayton, in 1958; it was completed two years later.

Behind the 7-foot-high brick wall that surrounds the front lawn and pool is the most prominent feature—a triple-barrel-vault concrete roof. Both the front and rear elevations are glass walls. The rectangular house has solid, pale red brick side elevations to ensure privacy from its neighbors. Seven rooms cover 3,030 square feet on three levels, yet the lot is only 50 feet by 135 feet.

At the front of the house the long living room has three tall glass arches, two with sliding glass doors, which opens from the living room onto the pool area and surrounding terrace. From the 30-foot-wide living room there are two flights of stairs. One ascends to three bedrooms; the other descends to the lower level, which includes a dining room, den, and kitchen. The three arches in the facade facing Ordway Street are repeated in the rear elevation, which opens onto a spacious patio.

In 2002 the owners selected Washington architect Hugh Newell Jacobsen to direct a major renovation to upgrade the systems and replace worn materials. Improvements included replacing wall-to-wall carpeting with Jacobsen's signature travertine marble, opening up the living room, and installing a 5-foot-deep lap pool in the center of the front walled lawn.

The Slayton House is one of only three designed by world-famous Chinese American architect I. M. Pei. The two others are Pei's own house in Katonah, New York (1954), and the Tandy House in Ft. Worth, Texas (1969). Pei eschewed designing houses in order to concentrate on large municipal buildings and art museums.

Right: VIEW TO LIBRARY FROM LIVING ROOM

Following Pages: LIVING ROOM

Slayton (1916–1999) wanted to move from the Washington suburbs to Cleveland Park but could not afford the average $45,000 price for a house. He asked Pei to design a new house for a vacant site to be selected in that neighborhood. Pei chose one of three available lots and Slayton purchased it for $6,500. Then the architect designed the house, after consulting with the Slaytons about their preferences and needs. He received a $5,000 fee for the design, which situated the main entrance on the east side to save space and to preserve the classic lines of the three vaults of the one-and-a-half-story living room. The architect carefully selected the brick—red with silicone salts baked in, and light mortar applied with a grapevine joint. Although Pei called for travertine marble for the floor in the large living room, Mrs. Slayton selected carpeting to reduce the cost. The Slaytons moved into the house in 1960.

Ieoh Ming Pei (1917–) was born in Canton province, China, to a prominent business family. The Pei family garden, the Lion Forest in Suzhou, and his mother, a poet and musician, were strong influences on him. He spent his high school years in Shanghai, where his father served as manager of the Bank of China. He attended M.I.T. in the 1930s and was in the graduate school at Harvard for the duration of World War II.

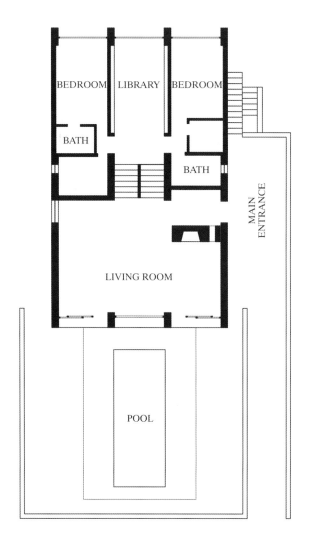

FIRST-FLOOR PLAN

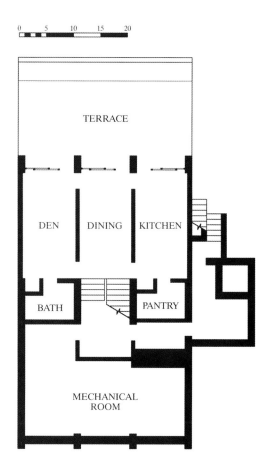

LOWER LEVEL-FLOOR PLAN

KREEGER HOUSE

2401 FOXHALL ROAD, N.W.
WASHINGTON, D.C.

───────────

1966

Architect: Philip Johnson and Richard Foster
Neighborhood: Berkley
Status: Historic House and Art Museum

FACADE

SCULPTURE TERRACE

T HE DAVID LLOYD KREEGER HOUSE IS ONE OF
Washington's premier modern houses. Renowned architect Philip Johnson designed the dramatic residence to display his client's outstanding
collection of 19th- and 20th-century paintings and
sculpture. Johnson created a refined and dignified
space by organizing the sprawling structure (200 by
100 feet) into eight domed modules, each 22 feet
square. The 6-acre site is shielded from the heavy
traffic on Foxhall Road by a high travertine wall.

A large circular driveway fronts Kreeger House.
The Kreegers enjoyed music as much as they did art,
so they built a recital hall into the building. The great
hall, comprising three modules, has 25-foot ceilings
and extends 66 feet from the front to the rear sculpture terrace. The walls of the house, inside and out,
are of travertine marble, while the floors, doors, and
paneling are finished in teakwood from Thailand.
The floor in the great hall is laid in a striking chevron
pattern. The rear of the house has a large open-air

Left: REAR ELEVATION SHOWING
THE OPEN-AIR SCULPTURE TERRACE

LIVING ROOM

terrace, also designed in 22-foot-square cubes, for the display of semiabstract modern sculpture, including works by Aristide Maillol, Jacques Lipchitz, Jean Arp, and Henry Moore. A domed roof with skylights covers each of these open-air cubes. On the ground level below is a walled terrace with a swimming pool.

David Lloyd Kreeger graduated from Rutgers University and Harvard Law School before coming to Washington in 1934 to work as a government lawyer in the departments of agriculture, interior, and justice. In 1947 he joined a small private firm with offices in the Investment Building on K Street. Kreeger's wealth, however, came from his position as general counsel, CEO, and president of the board of GEICO (Government Employees Insurance Company), founded in Fort Worth, Texas, in 1934 by an accountant and a banker who, two years later, relocated the headquarters to Washington. Kreeger was

Left: PRINCIPAL STAIRCASE

Following Pages: THE GREAT HALL

THE LOWER LEVEL SERVES AS AN ART MUSEUM

the major force in building GEICO into an auto in-surance giant during the 1950s and 1960s.

In 1948 Kreeger, his family, and friends bought 10 percent of GEICO stock when it became publicly traded. He joined GEICO full-time in 1957 as senior vice president and general counsel; he also supervised construction of the firm's new and then ultramodern headquarters on Western Avenue in Chevy Chase, Maryland. In 1964 he became president, CEO, and chairman of the company's board. The collapse of the stock market in 1972–73 crushed GEICO's stock, which between 1972 and 1976, fell from $61 a share to $2 a share. Kreeger helped shore up the company by supporting Jack Byrne for president and helping convince Warren Buffett to buy 48 percent of the stock in 1977. The company eventually rebounded and gained a solid footing.

In order to meet his personal obligations after the stock price fell, Kreeger was forced to sell a part of his extensive collection of 19th-century Impressionist and 20th-century abstract paintings. What remained, how-ever, was still significant. Kreeger had decided by 1988 to bequeath the house and art collection as a public museum to be administered by the Kreeger Foundation. On his death in 1989 the collection consisted of 50 sculptures and 150 paintings, including works by Picasso, Calder, Braque, Renoir, and Monet. It also holds more recent works by Thomas Downing, James Rosenquist, Milton Avery, and Larry Poons. The collection includes 33 pieces of African art as well, bought from the estate of Helena Rubinstein. These now make a spectacular display in a lower-level gallery.

Philip Johnson (1906–2005) was a pioneer in Modern architecture. While traveling in Germany in 1928, he met Ludwig Mies van der Rohe and admired his modern work. As a result Johnson and Henry Russell Hitchcock produced an exhibition at the new Museum of Modern Art in New York in 1932 called "The International Style," which was very influential in introducing Modern architecture to America.

Johnson designed a number of glass buildings, including his own Glass House on his Connecticut estate. He worked with Mies van der Rohe in designing the Seagram Building (1956) in New York, and he designed the New York State Theater and the central plaza fountain in Lincoln Center (1969). Johnson earned fame for his glass towers, among them PPG Place in Pittsburgh and the postmodern AT&T Building in New York.

This important house opened to the public as the Kreeger Museum in 1990, and director Judy A. Greenberg has coordinated the permanent exhibitions, special exhibitions, and research on the collection since that time. Kreeger's two children, Carol Kreeger Ingall and Peter L. Kreeger, serve as trustees of the Kreeger Museum, a great asset to the city.

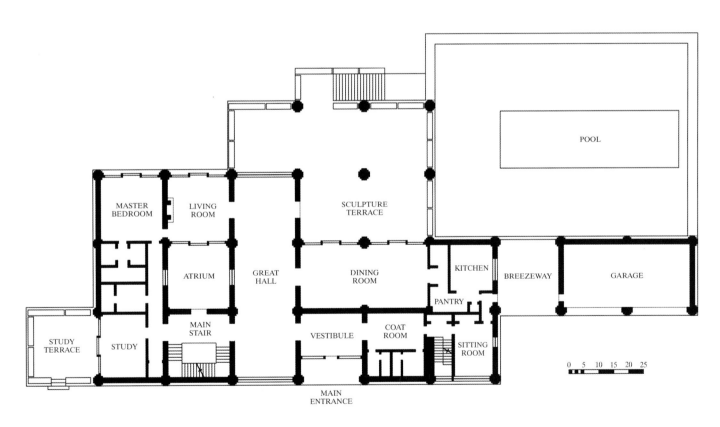

FIRST-FLOOR PLAN

BIBLIOGRAPHY

MOUNT VERNON

BOOKS

Dalzell, Robert F. Jr., and Lee Baldwin Dalzell.
George Washington's Mount Vernon, at Home in Revolutionary America. New York: Oxford University Press, 1998.

Greenberg, Allan. *George Washington, Architect.*
London: New Architects Group, 1999.

Griswold, Mac K. *Washington's Gardens at Mount Vernon.*
New York: Monacelli, 1999.

Johnson, Gerald W. *Mount Vernon, the Story of a Shrine.*
Mount Vernon, Virginia: The Mount Vernon Ladies' Association, 2002.

Lee, Jean B., ed. *Experiencing Mount Vernon: Eyewitness Accounts, 1784–1865.* Charlottesville: University of Virginia Press, 2006.

Manca, Joseph. *George Washington's Eye: Landscape, Architecture, and Design at Mount Vernon.* Baltimore: Johns Hopkins University Press, 2012.

McLeod, Steven, ed. *The Mount Vernon Ladies' Association: 150 Years of Restoring George Washington's Home.* Mount Vernon, Virginia: Mount Vernon Ladies' Association of the Union, 2010.

Pogue, Dennis J. "Giant in the Earth: George Washington, Landscape Architect," in Rebecca Yamin and Karen Bescherer Metheny, eds. *Landscape Archaeology: Reading and Interpreting the American Historical Landscape.* Knoxville: University of Tennessee Press, 1996.

———. "Mount Vernon: Transformation of an Eighteenth-Century Plantation System," in Paul A. Shackel and Barbara J. Little, eds. *Historical Archaeology of the Chesapeake.* Washington, D.C.: Smithsonian Institution Press, 1994.

Schwarz, Philip J., ed. *Slavery at the Home of George Washington.* Mount Vernon, Virginia: Mount Vernon Ladies' Association of the Union, 2001.

PERIODICALS

Pogue, Dennis J. "The Domestic Architecture of Slavery at George Washington's Mount Vernon." *Winterthur Portfolio* (Spring 2002).

DARNALL'S CHANCE

MANUSCRIPTS

"Darnall's Chance House Museum," Maryland–National Capital Park and Planning Commission, Silver Spring, Maryland.

BOOKS

Boucher, Jack, et al., *Landmarks of Prince George's County.* Baltimore: The Johns Hopkins University Press, 1993.

CARLYLE HOUSE

MANUSCRIPTS

National Register of Historic Places Inventory—Nomination Form: Carlyle House, Alexandria, Virginia. Washington, D. C.: National Park Service, 1969.

BOOKS AND PAMPHLETS

Crocker, Thomas E. *Braddock's March.* Yardley, Pennsylvania: Westhome Publishing, 2009.

"The John Carlyle House, Alexandria, Restoration Report for the Northern Virginia Regional Park Authority." Forest, Virginia: Fauber Garbee, Inc., Architects, July 1980.

The Green Family of Cabinetmakers: An Alexandria Institution, 1817–1887. Catalog of an Exhibition Held at the Alexandria Lyceum, ca. 1980.

Masson, Kathryn. *Historic Houses of Virginia.* New York: Rizzoli, 2006.

Mooney, Barbar Burlison. *Prodigy Houses of Virginia, Architecture and the Native Elite.* Charlottesville: University of Virginia Press, 2008.

Munson, James D. *Col. John Carlyle, Gent., 1720–1780, a True and Just Account of the Man and His House.* Fairfax, Virginia: Northern Virginia Regional Park Authority, 1986.

Smith, William Francis, and Michael Miller. *A Seaport Saga, Portrait of Old Alexandria, Virginia.* Virginia Beach, Virginia: Donning Company, 2001.

PERIODICALS

Bartlinski, Jim. "Carlyle House Celebrates 30 Years of Excellence." *Carlyle House Docent Dispatch.* Fairfax, Virginia: Northern Virginia Regional Park Authority, January 2006.

THE LINDENS

BOOKS

The Contents of The Lindens, The Collection of the Late Mrs. George Maurice Morris, January 23, 1983. New York: Christie, Manson & Woods International, 1983.

Kimball, Kiske. *Domestic Architecture of the American Colonies and Early Republic,* 1922. Reprinted, New York: Dover, 1966.

Lynn, Catherine. *Wallpaper in America, from the Seventeenth Century to World War I.* New York: W.W. Norton & Co., 1980.

Miles, Dorothy. *The Marblehead Hoopers, a Family of Merchant Kings and Their Marblehead Mansions.* Beverly, Massachusetts: Wilkscraft Creative Printing, 1999.

Morrison, Hugh. *Early American Architecture from the First Colonial Settlements to the National Period.* New York: Oxford University Press, 1952.

Parker, Franklin. *George Peabody, a Biography.* Nashville, Tennessee: Vanderbilt University Press, 1971.

PERIODICALS

Conroy, Sarah Booth. "Lindens Collection Auctioned." *Washington Post* (January 24, 1983).

_____. "Lovely Lindens." *Washington Post* (June 15, 1982).

Deitz, Paula. "Uncertain Future for 1754 Mansion." *New York Times* (September 2, 1982).

Essary, Helen. "The Lindens." *Washington Times* (March 5, 1938).

Fleishman, Sandra. "The Mansion That Found a 2nd Home." *Washington Post* (October 22, 2005).

"Historic House Will Be Brought Here." [Washington] *Evening Star* (September 11, 1934).

"The Lindens." *The Federal Architect* (April 1939).

"Rebuilding Historic House Called a Feat of Architecture." [Washington] *Evening Star* (November 18, 1935).

Seliger, Susan. "A House with History." *Washington Star* (November 9, 1980).

Wilfong, James C. Jr. "'Rusticated' Houses Here Abouts," *Washington Post* (March 23, 1974).

GUNSTON HALL

MANUSCRIPTS

Brown, Bennie Jr. "Gunston Hall," Historic American Buildings Survey. Washington, D.C.: National Park Service, 1982.

BOOKS

Beirne, Rosamond Randall, and John Henry Scarff. *William Buckland, 1734–1774, Architect of Virginia and Maryland.* Baltimore: Maryland Historical Society, 1958.

Copeland, Pamela C., and Richard K. McMaster. *The Five George Masons: Patriots and Planters of Virginia and Maryland.* Charlottesville: University Press of Virginia, 1975.

Dunn, Terry K. *The Recollections of John Mason: George Mason's Son Remembers His Father and Life at Gunston Hall.* Marshall, Virginia: EPM Publications, ca. 2000.

Mooney, Barbara B. *Prodigy Houses of Virginia: Architecture and the Native Elite.* Charlottesville: University of Virginia Press, 2008.

Taylor, Donald R. *Gunston Hall, Return to Splendor.* Mason Neck, Virginia: Gunston Hall Board of Regents, 1991.

PERIODICALS

Beirne, Rosamond Randall. "William Buckland, Architect of Virginia and Maryland." *Maryland Historical Magazine* 41 (September 1946): 199–218.

Beckerdite, Luke. "William Buckland, Reconsidered: Architectural Carving in Chesapeake Maryland, 1771–1774." *Journal of Early Southern Decorative Arts* (November 1982): 42–88.

_____. "William Buckland and William Bernard Sears: The Designers and Carvers." *Journal of Early Southern Decorative Arts* (November 1982): 6–40.

HAYES MANOR

MANUSCRIPTS

Dwyer, Michael F. Hayes Manor, Maryland Historic Trust Inventory Form, Maryland–National Capital Park and Planning Commission No. 35-10. Silver Spring, Maryland: n.d..

Leisenring, L. Morris. Hayes Manor, Historic American Buildings Survey, National Park Service, Washington, D.C., No. MD-202: 1961.

BOOKS

Echer, Grace Dunlap. *A Portrait of Old George Town.* Richmond, Virginia: Dietz Press, Inc., 1951.

Farquhar, Roger Brooke. *Historic Montgomery County, Maryland.* Silver Spring, Maryland: 1952.

PERIODICALS

Dunlop, G. Thomas, A. McCook Dunlop, and L. M. Leisenring. "Hayes, a Montgomery County House." *Maryland Historical Magazine* (June 1954): 88–115.

Walston, Mark. "Blueprint of the Past." *Bethesda Magazine* (November–December 2009).

ROSEDALE

BOOKS

Mann-Kenney, Louise. *Rosedale, the Eighteenth-Century Country Estate of General Uriah Forrest, Cleveland Park, Washington, D.C.* Washington, D.C.: privately printed, 1989.

PERIODICALS

Liebowitz, Denise. "Rosedale: Development When the
    Neighbors Take Charge." *Architecture D.C.* (Fall 2006):
    12–15.

Stanley, Kathleen. "A Happy Ending." *Builder*
    (September 2006).

WHITE HOUSE

BOOKS

Goldberg, Vicki. *The White House: The President's House in
    Photography and History*. New York: Little Brown, 2011.

McEwan, Barbara. *White House Landscapes*. New York: Walker
    and Company, 1992.

Monkman, Elizabeth. *The White House: Its Historic Furnishings
    and First Families*. New York: Abbeville Press, 2000.

Nelson, Lee H. *White House Stone Carving: Builders and Restorers*.
    Washington, D.C.: U.S. Government Printing Office,
    1992.

Seale, William. *The President's House, a History*. Washington,
    D.C.: White House Historical Association (2008). 2nd ed.

____. *The White House: The History of an American Idea*.
    Washington, D.C.: American Institute of Architects
    Press, 1991.

The White House, an Historic Guide. Washington, D.C.: White
    House Historical Association, 2011. 20th ed.

PERIODICALS

Bushong, William B. "Imagining James Hoban: Portraits
    of a Master Builder." *White House History* (Spring 2008).

Guinness, Desmond. "White House Irish Counterparts."
    White House History (Spring 2008).

Hoock, Holger. "The Second City in the British Dominions:
    Dublin in the Later Eighteenth Century." *White House
    History* (Spring 2008).

McDonald, Travis. "The East and West Wings of the
    White House: History in Architecture and Building."
    White House History (Summer 2011).

Seale, William. "Builder of the White House."
    White House History (Spring 2008).

"The Truman Restoration."
    White House History (Spring 1999).

White, Bruce. "Four Places in Hoban's Dublin: A Twenty-
    First-Century Photographer's View." *White House History*
    (Spring 2008).

THE OCTAGON

MANUSCRIPTS

*National Register of Historic Places Inventory—Nomination Form: The
    Octagon*. Washington, D.C.: National Park Service, 1983.

BOOKS AND PAMPHLETS

Kamoie, Laura G. *Irons in the Fire: The Business History of the Tayloe
    Family and Virginia's Gentry, 1700–1860*. Charlottesville:
    University of Virginia Press, 2007.

McCue, George. *The Octagon, Being an Account of a Famous
    Washington Residence: Its Great Years, Decline, and Restoration*.
    Washington, D.C.: A.I.A. Foundation, 1976.

Reinberger, Mark. *Utility and Beauty: Robert Wellford
    and Composition Ornament in America*. Newark: University
    of Delaware Press, 2003.

Ridout V, Orlando. *Building The Octagon*. Washington, D.C.:
    American Institute of Architects Press, 1989.

DUMBARTON HOUSE

MANUSCRIPTS

Andrews, Patrick. "Dumbarton House." National Register
    of Historic Places Registration Form. Washington, D.C.:
    National Park Service, 1991.

de Ferrari, John. "Dumbarton House, a Georgetown Gem."
    Unpublished manuscript, Washington, D.C., 2011.

BOOKS

Appleton, Marguerite. *A History of the National Society of the Colonial
    Dames of America*. Washington, D.C.: The National Society, 1974.

Buhler, Leslie. *Splendours of Georgetown: 25 Architectural Masterpieces*.
    Washington, D.C.: Tudor Place, 2001.

Davis, Deering, Stephen Dorsey, and Ralph Hall. *Georgetown
    Houses of the Federal Period, Washington, D.C., 1780–1830*.
    New York: Bonanza Books, 1944.

Fitzgerald, Oscar P. *In Search of Joseph Nourse, 1754–1841*.
    Washington, D.C.: The National Society of the Colonial
    Dames of America, 1994.

Miller, Hope Ridings. *Great Houses of Washington, D.C.*
    New York: Clarkson N. Potter Inc., 1969.

Richardson, Edgar P., Brooke Hindle, and Lillian B. Miller.
    Charles Willson Peale and His World. New York: Harry N.
    Abrams, 1982.

EVERMAY

INTERVIEWS

Interview with Harry Lammot Belin by James M. Goode,
    April 20, 2009.

Interview with Nina Gregg, curator of Evermay,
    by James M. Goode, May 8, 2009.

MANUSCRIPTS

Ganschinietz, Suzanne. *Evermay*. National Register of
    Historic Places Inventory—Nomination Form.
    Washington, D.C.: National Park Service, 1972.

White, John P. *Evermay.* Addendum, Historic American
Buildings Survey, No. DC-61, 1998.

BOOKS AND PAMPHLETS

"Evermay." *Splendours of Georgetown, 25 Architectural Masterpieces.*
Washington, D.C.: Commission of Fine Arts and the
Historic American Buildings Service, 2005.
Yesterday, Today and Tomorrow, Evermay Estate and Its Occupants,
1801–2007. Washington, D.C.: Evermay Society, 2007.

PERIODICALS

Ehrenberg, Ralph E. "Nicholas King, First Surveyor of the
City of Washington, 1803–1812." *Records of the Columbia
Historic Society 1969–1970* (1971): 31–65.

WOODLEY

BOOKS

Atwood, Albert W. *Francis C. Newlands, a Builder of the Nation.*
1969.
Beschloss, Michael. *Maret School, the First Hundred Years.*
TMG Custom Media, 2011.
Hodgson, Godfrey. *The Colonel: The Life and Wars of Henry
Stimson, 1867–1950.*
Kilborne, Al. *Woodley and Its Residents.* Charleston,
South Carolina: Arcadia, 2008.

PERIODICALS

Ridout, Orlando V., with Al Kilborne. "An Architectural
Exploration of Woodley." *Maret Magazine* (Fall 1998):
16–17.

TUDOR PLACE

MANUSCRIPTS

Tudor Place, Washington, D.C. National Register of Historic
Places Inventory—Nomination Form. Washington, D.C.:
National Park Service, 1962 and 1967.

BOOKS

Splendours of Georgetown: 25 Architectural Masterpieces. Washington,
D.C.: Tudor Place Historic House and Garden, 2001.
*Tudor Place Historic House and Garden, Georgetown, Washington,
D.C.* Washington, D.C.: Tudor Place Foundation, 2005.

PERIODICALS

Jackson, Cordelia. "Tudor Place." *Records of the Columbia
Historical Society 25* (1923): 68–87.

CALDWELL HOUSE

MANUSCRIPTS

Carmichael, William. "Monroe & MacFeely Houses."
Archives of the Arts Club (2010): 1–20.
"Timothy Caldwell House." National Register of Historic
Places Inventory—Nomination Form. Washington, D.C.:
National Park Service, 1963.

PERIODICALS

Montgomery, David. "Washington's Haven for Glad
Eccentrics." *Washington Post* (May 22, 2011).
Morris, Maud Burr. "An Old Washington Mansion
(2017 I Street Northwest)." *Records of the Columbia Historical
Society 21* (1918): 114–218.

RIVERSDALE

BOOKS

Callcott, Margaret Law, ed. *Mistress of Riversdale,
the Plantation Letters of Rosalie Stier Calvert, 1795–1821.*
Baltimore: The Johns Hopkins University Press, 1991.
The Calvert Mansion, Riversdale. Upper Marlboro, Maryland:
Maryland-National Capital Park and Planning
Commission, ca. 2000.
Lane, Mills. *Architecture of the Old South, Maryland.* New York:
Abbeville Press, 1991.
Olmsted, Frederick Law. *A Journey in the Seaboard Slave States.*
New York: Dix & Edwards, 1856.

PERIODICALS

Breningstall, Jeremy. "Governor Allocates Funds for Riversdale
Mansion Repairs." *Upper Marlboro Gazette* (April 20, 2000).
Goodman, Ellen. "Discovery Stalls Restoration Cash for
Historic Site." *Riverdale Journal* (May 19, 1986).
Hatcher, Renee. "Historic Riversdale Mansion to Be
Renovated." *The Prince George's Journal* (October 25, 1990).
"Plan of Farm Buildings for Animals." *The Country Gentleman.*
London, England (October 26, 1854).
"Riversdale, Seat of Chas. B. Calvert, Esq., Prince George's
County, Md." *The Country Gentleman.* London, England
(September 2, 1851).
Sweeney, Thomas W. "Riversdale Changes for the Better."
Historic Preservation News (December 1993–January 1994).

BLAIR HOUSE

BOOKS

Cornish, Dudley Taylor, and Virginia J. Lass. *Lincoln's Lee,
the Life of Samuel Phillips Lee, United States Navy, 1812–1897.*
Lawrence, Kansas: University of Kansas Press, 1986.

Gutheim, Frederick, and Antoinette J. Lee. *Worthy of the Nation: Washington, D.C., from L'Enfant to the National Capital Planning Commission.* 2nd ed. Baltimore: Johns Hopkins University Press, 2006.

Heck, Marlene E. *Blair House, the President's Guest House.* Washington, D.C.: The Blair House Restoration Fund, 1989.

Laas, Virginia Jeans. *Wartime Washington, the Civil War Letters of Elizabeth Blair Lee.* Urbana: University of Illinois Press, 1991.

Moroney, Rita Lloyd. *Montgomery Blair, Postmaster General, 1861–1864.* Washington, D.C.: Government Printing Office, 1963.

Shireman, Candace. *To Be Preserved for All Time, the Major and the President Save Blair House.* Washington, D.C.: White House Historical Association, 2009.

Smith, Elbert B. *Francis Preston Blair.* New York: The Free Press, 1980.

Smith, William Ernest. *The Francis Preston Blair Family in Politics.* New York: Macmillan Company, 1933.

Wilroy, Mary Edith, and Lucie Prinz. *Inside Blair House.* Garden City, New York: Doubleday & Co., 1982.

PERIODICALS

Blair, Gist. "Annals of Silver Spring." *Records of the Columbia Historical Society,* 21 (1918): 155–184.

Davis, Madison. "The Public Career of Montgomery Blair." *Records of the Columbia Historical Society* 13 (1910): 126–157.

Gibbs, Elaine M., and Candace S. Shireman. "Flights of Fancy at Blair House." *55th Washington Antiques Show.* Washington, D.C.: Washington Antiques Show (2010): 48–57.

Shireman, Candace S. "Good Neighbors: FDR, Major Gist, and Blair House." *White House History* (Spring 2010): 84–99.

ARLINGTON HOUSE

MANUSCRIPTS

Nelligan, Murray H. *Old Arlington, the Story of the Lee Mansion National Memorial.* Columbia University Ph.D. Dissertation, 1953.

BOOKS

Arlington House, the Robert E. Lee Memorial. Washington, D.C.: U.S. Department of the Interior, 2007.

King, Julia. *George Hadfield, Architect of the Federal City.* Farnham, Surry, England: Ashgate Publishing (2014).

Perry, John. *Mrs. Robert E. Lee, the Lady of Arlington.* Colorado Springs, Colorado: Multnomah Books, 2001.

Pryor, Elizabeth Brown. *Reading the Man, a Portrait of Robert E. Lee Through His Private Letters.* New York: Viking, 2007.

Thomas, Emory M. *Robert E. Lee.* New York: W.W. Norton, 1995.

Wilson, Richard Guy. *Buildings of Virginia, Tidewater, and Piedmont.* New York: Oxford University Press, 2002.

Zimmer, Anne Carter. *The Robert E. Lee Family Cooking and Housekeeping Book.* Chapel Hill: University of North Carolina Press, 1997.

MCCORMICK HOUSE

BOOKS

Miller, Kristie. *Ruth Hanna McCormick: A Life in Politics, 1880–1944.* Albuquerque: University of New Mexico Press, 1992.

Mitchell, Henry, and Derry Moore. *Washington, Houses of the Capital.* New York: Viking Press, 1982.

PERIODICALS

Alsop, Susan Mary. "Georgetown Doyenne." *Architectural Digest* (September 1994): 134–147.

Englefield, Carolyn. "Mane Traditions." *House & Garden* (August 1990): 128–133.

MACKALL SQUARE

MANUSCRIPTS

Oak Hill Cemetery Board minutes, Washington, D.C. (July 1, 1878).

BOOKS

Austrian, Geoffrey. *Herman Hollerith: Forgotten Giant of Information Processing.* New York: Columbia University Press, 1982.

Northrup, Mary. *American Computer Pioneers.* Berkeley Heights, New Jersey: Enslow Publishers, 1998.

PERIODICALS

Aul, William R. "Herman Hollerith: Data Processing Pioneer." *Think* (IBM's employee magazine) (November 1972): 22–24.

Gordon, William F. "Old Homes on Georgetown Heights." Washington, D.C., *Records of the Columbia Historical Society* 18 (1914).

Haffler, Sandra, Allison LaLand, Hugh Oates Jr., and Susan Safer. "Executive Offering, 1617–1633 29th Street, N.W., Washington, D.C." Washington, D.C.: Pardoe Real Estate Inc. (1994): 1–39.

Mackall, Sally Somervell. "Mackall Square." *Records of the Columbia Historical Society* 18 (1915): 92–94.

"Tour." *Washington Post* (November 11, 1967).

STEEDMAN HOUSE

MANUSCRIPTS

"Steedman-Ray House." National Register of Historic Places—Nomination Form. Washington, D.C.: National Park Service, 1990.

BOOKS

Gilmore, Matthew B., and Joshua Olsen. *Foggy Bottom and the West End*. Charleston, South Carolina: History Press, 2010.

Maury, William M. Alexander "Boss" Shepherd and the Board of Public Works. Washington, D.C.: George Washington University, 1975.

Miller, Francis T., ed., *The Photographic History of the Civil War*. New York: Thomas Yoseloff, 1865.

1925 F Street, a Rich History and Tradition in Washington, D.C. Washington, D.C.: George Washington University, 2009.

Small, Theresa. *The F Street Club*. Washington, D.C.: George Washington University, 1981.

PERIODICALS

McCardle, Dorothy. "New Landlord for F Street Club." *Washington Post* (August 3, 1974).

"Mrs. J.F. Curtis to Become Club Hostess in F Street House." *Washington Herald* (April 9, 1933).

"Mrs. Laura Curtis to Marry Official of Bethlehem Steel." *Washington Post* (27 July 1938).

OAK HILL CEMETERY GATEHOUSE

INTERVIEWS

Ella Pozell, superintendent of Oak Hill Cemetery, interviewed by James M. Goode, September 4 and 5, 2010.

MANUSCRIPTS

Reiff, Daniel D. *Oak Hill Cemetery Gatehouse*. Historic American Buildings Survey No. DC-249. Washington, D.C.: Commission of Fine Arts and National Park Service, 1969.

BOOKS

Scott, Pamela, and Antoine J. Lee. *Buildings of the District of Columbia*. New York: Oxford University Press, 1993.

CEDAR HILL

MANUSCRIPT

National Register of Historic Places Inventory—Nomination Form, *Frederick Douglass Memorial Home.* Washington, D.C.: National Park Service, 1969.

BOOKS

Hinds, James R. *Frederick Douglass Home, Cedar Hill, Historic Structures Report, Volume II (Historical Data)*. Washington, D.C.: National Park Service, 1968.

Foner, Russell S., and Harry Martin. *Frederick Douglass Home, Cedar Hill, Historic Structures Report, Volume I (Architectural Data)*. Washington, D.C.: National Park Service, 1970.

Muller, John. *Frederick Douglass in Washington, D.C.: The Lion of Anacostia*. Charleston, S.C.: History Press, 2012.

Quarles, Benjamin. *Frederick Douglass*. Washington, D.C.: The Associated Publisher, 1948.

HOUSE ONE

MANUSCRIPTS

Kowsky, Frank. "The Nineteenth-Century Buildings on the Campus of Gallaudet College, Washington, D.C." Ph.D. dissertation, New York State University College at Buffalo, 1970.

BOOKS

Atwood, Albert W. *Gallaudet College, Its First Hundred Years*. Washington, D.C.: Gallaudet College, 1964.

Boatner, Maxine Tull. *Voice of the Deaf, a Biography of Edward Miner Gallaudet*. Washington, D.C.: Public Affairs Press, 1959.

Carney, Margaret. *Lithophanes*. Atglen, Pennsylvania: Schiffer Publishing Ltd., 2008.

Gallaudet, Edward Miner. *History of the College for the Deaf, 1857–1907*. Washington, D.C.: Gallaudet College Press, 2002.

Gannon, Jack R., ed. *The Gallaudet Almanac*. Washington, D.C.: Gallaudet College Alumni Association, 1974.

Kowsky, Francis R. *The Architecture of Frederick Clarke Withers and the Progress of the Gothic Revival in America After 1850*. Middletown, Connecticut: Wesleyan University Press, 1980.

PERIODICALS

Bortner, Judy. *Gallaudet Today* (Spring 1972).

Flatley, Mary Margaret. "In Search of Gallaudet History." *Washington Star* (October 12, 1969).

Sinick, Heidi. "Finding Secret Drawers and Tapping on the Walls." *Washington Post* (November 23, 1969).

Sporkin, Elizabeth. "Victoriana Is Back." *The Washingtonian* (December 1981).

COOKE'S ROW

MANUSCRIPTS

Gibbs, Kenneth T. "The Architecture of Norris G. Starkweather." M.A. thesis in Architectural History, University of Virginia, 1970.

BOOKS

Mitchell, Mary. *Glimpses of Georgetown, Past and Present.*
    Washington, D.C.: The Road Street Press, 1983.
Pepper, Charles M. *Every-Day Life in Washington, With Pen
    and Camera.* New York: The Christian Herald, 1900.

PERIODICALS

"Cooke Mansion Sold." *Washington Post* (April 30, 1903).
"Cooke's Row Home Features Hidden Passageway."
    Northwest Real Estate, Washington, D.C.
    (February 18, 2004).
Holle, Peter. "Tale of Two Houses." *The Georgetowner* (1980).
Krucoff, Carl. "Georgetown Tenants Lose." *Washington Post*
    (August 31, 1978).
Mitchell, Henry. "Townhouses Grow in Georgetown."
    Washington Post (June 25, 1977).
Rogers, Patricia Dane. "Interiors: A Grand Gesture."
    Washington Home (November 30, 1989).

BREIDING HOUSE

BOOKS

Splendours of Georgetown: 25 Architectural Masterpieces.
    Washington, D.C.: Tudor Place Historic House
    and Garden, 2001.

DENMAN–WERLICH HOUSE

BOOKS

Brown, T. Robins. *Albany Architects: The Present Look at the Past.*
    Albany, New York: Historic Albany Foundation, 1978.
Kohler, Sue A., and Jeffrey R. Carson. *Sixteenth Street Architecture,
    Volume I.* Washington, D.C.: Commission of Fine Arts,
    1978.

PERIODICALS

"Among the Ateliers." *Washington Post* (June 19, 1898).
"Art and Architects." *Washington Post* (February 5, 1899).
"Died." *Washington Post* (October 12, 1895).
"Fight Denman Will." *Washington Post* (October 17, 1902).
Forgey, Benjamin. "Old House, New Lives."
    Washington Post (February 23, 1991).
Gorney, Cynthia. "Grande Dame's Date with Death."
    Washington Post (January 21, 1976).
"In an Artist Studio." *Washington Post* (December 31, 1893).
Milloy, Courtland. "Opening Doors for the Mentally Ill."
    Washington Post (September 19, 1989).
"Two Convicted in Fatal Attack on Woman, 85."
    Washington Post (February 8, 1977).
Williams, Juan. "Gladys Werlich's Private, Genteel World
    Is Revealed." *Washington Post* (January 21, 1976).

BROWN–TOUTORSKY HOUSE

BOOKS

Carson, Jeffrey R., and Sue A. Kohler. *Sixteenth Street Architecture.*
    Washington, D.C.: Commission of Fine Arts, 1978. Vol. I.

PERIODICALS

Emery, Theo. "Fixing Up Embassy, Congo Republic Raises
    Hackles in Capital." *New York Times* (December 22, 2011).

CLARA BARTON HOUSE

BOOKS

Pryor, Elizabeth Brown. *Clara Barton, Professional Angel.*
    Philadelphia: University of Pennsylvania Press, 1990.

PERIODICALS

"Clara Barton, a Lifetime of Service." Washington, D.C.:
    National Park Service, ca. 2010.
Lampl, Elizabeth Jo. "A Quiet Partnership: Clara Barton,
    Julian Hubbell, and the Forging of the American Red
    Cross." *Maryland Historical Magazine* (Winter 2002):
    445–475.
"The Life of Clara Barton, a Chronology, 1821–1912."
    Washington, D.C.: National Park Service.

HEURICH HOUSE

MANUSCRIPTS

Taylor, Nancy C. "Christian Heurich House." National
    Register of Historic Places Inventory—Nomination
    Form, National Park Service, 1969.

PERIODICALS

Colket, Meredith B. Jr. "General Grant and the Christian
    Heurich Memorial Mansion." *Records of the Columbia
    Historical Society* (1966–69): 365–368.
Evans, Richard F. "The 19th-Century High-Tech Systems
    of Christian Heinrich's Mansion." *Washington History*
    (Spring/Summer 1996): 38–53.
Heurich, Gary F. "The Christian Heurich Brewing
    Company, 1872–1956." *Records of the Columbia Historical
    Society* (1973–74): 604–615.
Hoagland, Alison K. "Nineteenth-Century Building
    Regulations in Washington, D.C." *Records of the Historical
    Society* 52 (1989): 57–77.
Rubincam, Milton. "Major General U.S. Grant 3rd, 1881–
    1968." *Records of the Columbia Historical Society* (1966–68):
    369–398.
_____. "Mr. Christian Heurich and His Mansion."
    Records of the Columbia Historical Society (1969–70): 167–205.

Shireman, Candace. "The Rise of Christian Heurich and His Mansion." *Washington History* (Spring/Summer 1993).

THE OWL'S NEST

MANUSCRIPTS

National Register of Historic Places—Registration Form: Crouse House. Washington, D.C.: National Park Service, 2001.

Elfin, Margery L., and Paul K. Williams. *Forest Hills.* Charleston, South Carolina: Arcadia, 2006.

PERIODICALS

Sergent, Jennifer. "The Owl's Nest Reborn, Chris and Karen Donatelli Bring Historic D.C. Estate Back to Splendor." *Washington Spaces* (Summer 2009): 137–143.

BARNEY STUDIO HOUSE

MANUSCRIPTS

Memorandum, Tom Freudenheim to Robert McC. Adams, November 27, 1987, Smithsonian Institution Archives.

National Register of Historic Places—Registration Form: Barney Studio House. Washington, D.C.: National Park Service, 1995.

BOOKS

Kling, Jean L., and Wanda M. Korn. *Alice Pike Barney: Her Life and Art.* Washington, D.C.: Smithsonian Institution Press, 1994.

PERIODICALS

Conroy, Sarah Booth. "A Landmark in Danger, Smithsonian Considers Sale of Elegant Studio House." *Washington Post* (May 17, 1993).

_____. "The Salon Days of Studio House." *Washington Post* (February 25, 1990).

Forgey, Benjamin. "A Real Fixer-Upper. Smithsonian Ponders Sale of Historic House." *Washington Post* (March 18, 1995).

Kling, Jean. "Alice Pike Barney, "Bringing Culture to the Capital." *Washington History* (Spring 1990): 69–89.

May, Stephen. "The House That Alice Built." *Historic Preservation* (September–October 1994): 61–66, 95–102.

"Nude Beauty Covered." *Washington Post* (October 11, 1910).

"Studio House Given to Smithsonian." *Washington Post* (December 20, 1961).

MORSE STUDIO HOUSE

BOOKS

Peterson, Anne E. *Hornblower & Marshall, Architects.* Washington, D.C.: Preservation Press, 1978.

PERIODICALS

"Maury-Mohler Presents Home at 2133 R Street." *Washington Post* (April 5, 1936).

McClain, Buzz. "Light-filled Interior Is a Surprise in Kalorama Heights Home." *Washington Times* (June 12, 1992).

Smith, Delos. "Obituary, James Rush Marshall." *Journal of the American Institute of Architects* (August 1927): 266.

"Steeped in History." *Washington Times* (June 12, 1992).

Wagner, Ruth. "Old Morse Studio Is Now a Modern Dream House." *Washington Post* (September 1, 1968).

GRANGER COTTAGE

INTERVIEWS

Eleanor Granger, interviewed by James M. Goode, February 3, 2009.

Mathew Evans, interviewed by James M. Goode, February 3, 2009.

DUMBLANE

MANUSCRIPTS

Bird, Betty. "Dumblane." Washington, D.C., National Register of Historic Places—Nomination Form, 2004.

INTERVIEWS

With Mrs. R Kendall Nottingham by James M. Goode, Washington, D.C., May 16, 2009.

BOOKS

Cathers, David. *Gustav Stickley.* London: Phaidon, 2003.

Stubblebine, Ray. *Stickley's Craftsman Homes: Plans, Drawings, Photographs.* Salt Lake City: Gibbs Smith, 2006.

Tucker, Kevin W., et al. *Gustav Stickley and the American Arts and Crafts Movement.* Dallas, Texas: Dallas Museum of Art and New Haven: Yale University Press, 2011.

PERIODICALS

Bond, S. Hazen. "Dumblane." *The Craftsman* (February 1913).

Stubblebine, Ray. "A House in Washington." *The Craftsman* (February 1913).

PATTERSON HOUSE

MANUSCRIPTS

Ganschinietz, Suzanne. "Patterson House, Washington, D.C." National Register of Historic Places Inventory—Nomination Form, National Park Service, 1971.

INTERVIEWS

Amy Ballard, Chairperson of the Patterson House
Restoration Committee, interviewed by James M. Goode,
September 14, 2009.

Maribelle Moore, President of the Patterson House
Preservation Foundation, the Washington Club,
interviewed by James M. Goode, October 12, 2008.

BOOKS

Atherton, Charles H., et al. *Massachusetts Avenue Architecture,
Volume I, Northwest Washington, District of Columbia.*
Washington, D.C.: Commission of Fine Arts, 1973.

Roth, Leland. *McKim, Mead & White, Architects.* New York:
Harper & Row, 1983.

White, Samuel G. *The Houses of McKim, Mead & White.*
New York: Rizzoli, 1998.

TOWNSEND HOUSE

MANUSCRIPTS

Alter, Harvey, ed. *Notes for Tours of the Townsend Mansion,
Home of the Cosmos Club.* September 2010.
Cosmos Club Archives.

Myers, Denys Peter. *The Townsend House, 2121 Massachusetts
Avenue, N.W.* August 1990. Cosmos Club Archives.

Weimer, Douglas. *"At Home" With Mrs. Townsend and
Undersecretary and Mrs. Welles, an Informal History of 2121
Massachusetts Avenue, N.W., Washington, D.C.,* 2001.
Library of Douglas Weimer.

BOOKS

Atherton, Charles H., et al. *Massachusetts Avenue Architecture,
Volume I, Northwest Washington, District of Columbia.*
Washington, D.C.: Commission of Fine Arts, 1973.

Hewitt, Mark Alan, et al. *Carrère & Hastings, Architects.*
New York: Acanthus Press, 2006.

Ossman, Laurie, and Heather Ewing. *Carrère & Hastings:
The Masterworks.* New York: Rizzoli, 2011.

Placzek, Adolf K., ed., *Macmillan Encyclopedia of Architects.*
New York: The Free Press, 1982.

Seale, William. *The Imperial Season: America's Capital in the Age of
the First Ambassadors.* Washington, D.C.: Smithsonian Books,
2013.

Welles, Benjamin. *Sumner Welles, FDR's Global Strategist.*
New York: St. Martin's Press, 1997.

PERIODICALS

Krinsley, Daniel. "The Evolution of Mrs. Townsend's
Ballroom." *Cosmos Club Bulletin* (July–August 1992).

ANDERSON HOUSE

MANUSCRIPTS

Jensen, Carole A., Letter. Hingham, Massachusetts,
to the Society of the Cincinnati, April 1, 1986.
Archives, Society of the Cincinnati, Anderson House,
Washington, D.C.

National Register of Historic Places: Anderson House.
Washington, D.C.: Department of the Interior, National
Park Service, 1968.

BOOKS

Anderson, Isabel, ed. *Larz Anderson, Letters and Journals of a
Diplomat.* New York

_____. *Presidents and Pies, Life in Washington 1897–1919.* Boston:
Houghton Mifflin Co., 1920.

_____. *Under the Black Horse Flag.* Boston: Houghton Mifflin
Co., 1926.

Atherton, Charles H., et al. *Massachusetts Avenue Architecture,
Volume I: Northwest Washington, District of Columbia.*
Washington, D.C.: U.S. Commission of Fine Arts, 1973.

Friend, Amy. *Rediscover Weld at Larz Anderson Park: A Self-Guided
Walking Tour.* Brookline: Massachusetts Museum of
Transportation, 1999.

PERIODICALS

Forgey, Benjamin. "History Repeats Itself."
Washington Post (February 28, 1998).

Lambert, Craig. "The Welds of Harvard Yard."
Harvard Magazine (November–December 1998).

"Lars Anderson, 1866–1937." *Phillips Exeter Bulletin*
(July 1937).

"Two Noted Families Linked." *Boston Daily* (June 11, 1897).

BEALE HOUSE

BOOKS

Atherton, Charles H., et al. *Massachusetts Avenue Architecture,
Volume I, Northwest Washington, District of Columbia.*
Washington, D.C.: Government Printing Office for the
Commission of Fine Arts, 1973.

Highsmith, Carol M., and Ted Landphair. *Embassies of
Washington.* Washington, D.C.: National Trust for Historic
Preservation, 1992.

EVERETT HOUSE

BOOKS

Atherton, Charles H., et al. *Massachusetts Avenue Architecture,
Volume I, Northwest Washington, District of Columbia.*
Washington, D.C.: Commission of Fine Arts, 1973.

Chessman, G. Wallace, and Curtis W. Abbott. *Edward Hamlin Everett, the Bottle King.* Granville, Ohio: Robbins Hunter Museum, ca. 1990.

Hasse, John Edward. "The Swinging Scions: How the Ambassador's Sons Jazzed Washington and the Nation." *The Turkish Ambassador's Residence and the Cultural History of Washington, D.C.* Istanbul: Istanbul Kultur University Press, 2013.

Hickman, Caroline Mesrobian. "A Century of Architecture, Art, and Diplomatic History." *The Turkish Ambassador's Residence and the Cultural History of Washington, D.C.* Istanbul: Istanbul Kultur University Press, 2013.

Moskey, Skip. "The Bottle King Comes to Washington." *The Turkish Ambassador's Residence and the Cultural History of Washington, D.C.* Istanbul: Istanbul Kultur University Press, 2013.

Riley, J. J. *A History of the American Soft Drink Industry: Bottled Carbonated Beverages, 1807–1957.* New York: Arno Press, 1972.

MARLY

BOOKS

Belgium Embassy, Washington. Brussels: Belgian Ministry of Foreign Affairs, 2010.

Kathrens, Michael C. *American Splendor: The Residential Architecture of Horace Trumbauer.* New York: Acanthus Press, 2002.

Residence of the Ambassadors of Belgium in Washington, D.C. Brussels: Belgian Ministry of Foreign Affairs, 2010.

MARWOOD

MANUSCRIPTS

Marwood. Maryland Historical Trust State Historic Sites Inventory Form, Montgomery County Courthouse, Rockville, Maryland, 1976.

BOOKS

Harris, Ann Paterson. *The Potomac Adventure, Pre-History to 1976.* Potomac, Maryland: A Bicentennial America in Potomac Publication, 1976.

Kelly, Clare Lise. *Places from the Past: The Tradition of Gardez Bien in Montgomery County, Maryland.* Rockville: Maryland-National Capital Park and Planning Commission, 2001.

PERIODICALS

Berry, Nancy E. "Marwood, Potomac, Maryland." *Period Homes* (November 2010).

Patner, Myra. "Gores Save Marwood by Filing Chapter 11." *Bethesda Gazette* (July 1, 1992).

Walston, Mark. "River Palace, Potomac's Marwood Estate." *Bethesda Magazine* (March–April 2009).

WEBSITES

Monumental Sports Entertainment. Owners: Ted Leonis. www.monumentalsports.com/owners/ted-leonis (accessed 25 July 2012).

DUDLEA

BOOKS

Abell, William S. *Arunah Shepherdson Abell (1806–1888), Founder of the Sun of Baltimore.* Baltimore: privately printed, 1989.

Bowie, Effie Gwynn. *Across the Years in Prince George's County.* Richmond, Virginia: Garrett & Massie, 1947.

Bowling, Kenneth R. *Peter Charles L'Enfant, Vision, Honor, and Male Friendship in the Early American Republic.* Washington, D.C.: Friends of the G.W. Libraries, 2002.

Goode, James M. *The B.F. Saul Company, Real Estate and Finance in the Nation's Capital Since 1892.* Washington, D.C.: privately printed, 2011.

_____. *Capital Losses, a Cultural History of Washington's Destroyed Buildings.* Second Edition. Washington, D.C.: Smithsonian Books, 2003.

Hienton, Louise Joyner. *Prince George's Heritage.* Baltimore: Maryland Historical Society, 1972.

PERIODICALS

Clinton, Amy Cheney. "Historic Fort Washington." *Maryland Historical Magazine* 32 (1937): 228–247.

Morgan, James Dudley. "Historic Fort Washington on the Potomac." *Records of the Columbia Historical Society* 7 (1904): 1–19.

Ramsburgh, Edith Roberts. "Sir Dudley Digges, His English Ancestry and the Digges Line in America." *Daughters of the American Revolution Magazine* (March 1923): 125–139.

WOODROW WILSON HOUSE

MANUSCRIPTS

Eig, Emily H. "Woodrow Wilson House Historic Structures Report." Manuscript, 1988.

O'Hagan, James F. "The Woodrow Wilson House." National Trust for Historic Preservation, 1997.

BOOKS

Grayson, Rear Admiral Cary. *Woodrow Wilson: An Intimate Portrait.* Washington, D.C.: Potomac Books, 1977.

McAdoo, Eleanor Wilson. *The Woodrow Wilsons.* New York: Macmillan Company, 1937.

Smith, Gene, and Allen Nevins. *When the Cheering Stopped: The Last Years of Woodrow Wilson.* New York: 1964.

Wilson, Edith Bolling. *My Memoirs.* Indianapolis: The Bobbs-Merrill Co., 1938.

Smith, J.W. Rixey. "My Neighbor Woodrow Wilson." *Collier's, The National Weekly* (October 21, 1922).

DUMBARTON OAKS

BOOKS
Brown, Jane. *Beatrix: The Gardening Life of Beatrix Jones Farrand, 1872–1959.* New York: Viking, 1995.

Carder, James N., ed. *A Home of the Humanities, the Collecting and Patronage of Mildred and Robert Woods Bliss.* Washington, D.C.: Dumbarton Oaks Research Library, 2010.

Goode, James M. *Capital Losses, a Cultural History of Washington's Destroyed Buildings.* Washington, D.C.: Smithsonian Books, 2003. 2nd ed.

Mould, David, and Missy Loewe. *Remembering Georgetown, a History of the Lost Port City.* Charleston, South Carolina: History Press, 2009.

Tamulevich, Susan. *Dumbarton Oaks: Garden into Art.* New York: Monacelli Press, 2001.

Tankard, Judith. *Beatrix Farrand: Private Gardens, Public Landscapes.* New York: Monacelli Press, 2009.

Whitehead, Walter Muir. *Dumbarton Oaks: The History of a Georgetown House and Garden, 1800–1966.* Cambridge, Massachusetts: Harvard University Press, 1967.

BRITISH AMBASSADOR'S RESIDENCE

MANUSCRIPTS
Blakely, Julia. "History of the British Embassy in Washington, D.C." Unpublished manuscript, British Embassy Archives, Washington, D.C., 2011.

BOOKS
Bertram, Mark. *Room for Diplomacy, Britain's Diplomatic Buildings Overseas, 1800–2000.* Reading, England: Spire Books Ltd., 2012.

Hopkins, Andrew, and Gavin Stamp, eds. *Lutyens Abroad: The Work of Sir Edwin Lutyens Outside the British Isles.* London: British School at Rome, 2002.

PERIODICALS
Argetsinger, Amy. "The Reliable Source: Embassy's Artful Change." *Washington Post* (May 2, 2012).

WOODEND

MANUSCRIPTS
Audubon Naturalist Society of the Central Atlantic States, Chevy Chase, Maryland, miscellaneous papers.

Maryland National Capital Parks and Planning Commission, Historic Preservation Office, Silver Spring, Maryland, Woodend folder.

Woodend, Maryland Historical Trust Inventory of Historic Properties, Silver Spring, Maryland. Site No. M-35-12.

Smithsonian Institution Archives. Record Unit 7294 and Accession 02-183 and 06-110, Audubon Naturalist Society of the Central Atlantic States. Record Unit 7417, Florence Marian Bailey. Record Unit 7006, Alexander Wetmore.

BOOKS
Bedford, Stephen McLeod. *John Russell Pope, Architect of Empire.* New York: Rizzoli, 1998.

Garrison, James B. *Mastering Tradition: The Residential Architecture of John Russell Pope.* New York: Acanthus, 2004.

HILLWOOD

BOOKS
Chung, Estella M. *Living Artfully: At Home with Marjorie Merriweather Post.* Washington, D.C.: Post Foundation, 2013.

Odom, Anne, and Liana Paredes Arend. *A Taste for Splendor: Russian Imperial and European Treasures from the Hillwood Collection.* Alexandria, Virginia: Art Services International, 1998.

Rubin, Nancy. *American Empress: The Life and Times of Marjorie Merriweather Post.* London: Universe, Inc., 2004.

STIRLING HOUSE

MANUSCRIPTS
Allardice, Margheritta Stirling. "Snapshots, Some Family History." Unpublished memoir, 14 pages. February 2010.

INTERVIEWS
Margheritta Stirling Allardice, interviewed by James M. Goode, January 4, 2010.

BOOKS
Goode, James M. *Capital Losses, a Cultural History of Washington's Destroyed Buildings.* Washington, D.C.: Smithsonian Books, 2003, 2nd ed.

Ochsner, Jeffrey Karl. *H.H. Richardson: Complete Architectural Works.* Cambridge, Massachusetts: MIT Press, 1982.

FIRENZE HOUSE

BOOKS
Highsmith, Carol M., and Ted Landphair. *Embassies of Washington.* Washington, D.C.: Preservation Press, 1992.

PERIODICALS

Beale, Betty, and Susan Axelrod. "Italy Buys Firenze House
 as Embassy." [Washington] *Evening Star* (December 19,
 1976).
Dan, Sharon Jaffe. "Private Tour: Villa Firenze."
 Home & Design Magazine (May–June 2010): 44–49.
"Guggenheims Give Gala Party, Singers Honored."
 Washington Post (December 7, 1945).
"Karl G. Roebling Dies at Spring Lake Home."
 New York Times (May 30, 1921).
"Valuable Art Objects Damaged in Blaze at Guggenheim
 Mansion." *Evening Star* (January 31 1946).

LAWRENCE HOUSE

BOOKS

Jordan, John W. *Encyclopedia of Pennsylvania Biography*. New York:
 Lewis Historical Publishing Co., 1914.
Fouace, Jean, and Pam Scott. *La résidence de Kalorama/The French
 Residence in Kalorama*. Paris: Artistic Printing for the French
 Government, 2009.
Who's Who in New York City and State. New York: L.R. Hamersly
 & Company, 1909.

PERIODICALS

Barnes, Tom. "2 Lawrence Buildings Start Falling."
 Pittsburgh Post–Gazette (June 12, 2001).
"John Hays Hammond House." *Evening Star*
 (January 8, 1944).
Kennedy, George. "Kalorama, Show Place of 1800s,
 Still Boasts Some of the City's Finest Mansions."
 Evening Star (October 2, 1950).
"New $400,000 Home of French Ambassador."
 Washington Times (January 16, 1936).

FEALY HOUSE

INTERVIEWS

Michael and Aimee Carney,
 interview by James M. Goode, May 3, 2009.

BOOKS

Cron, Frederick W. *The Man Who Made Concrete Beautiful:
 A Biography of John Joseph Earley*. Fort Collins,
 Colorado: Centennial, 1972.
Jandl, H. Ward, John A. Burns, and Michael J. Auer.
 *Yesterday's Houses of Tomorrow: Innovative American Homes
 1850 to 1950*. New York: Preservation Press, 1991.
Wirz, Hans, and Richard Striner. *Washington Deco: Art Deco
 in the Nation's Capital*. Washington, D.C.: Smithsonian
 Institution Press, 1984.

CAFRITZ HOUSE

BOOKS

Solomon, Burt. *The Washington Century: Three Families and the
 Shaping of the Nation's Capital*. New York: Harper Collins,
 2004.
Eugene Schoen: Furniture from the Morris & Gwendolyn Cafritz Estate.
 New York: Donzella, 2000.
Wirz, Hans, and Richard Striner. *Washington Deco, Art Deco
 Design in the Nation's Capital*. Washington, D.C.: Smithsonian
 Institution Press, 1984.

PERIODICALS

Barnes, Bart. "D.C. Hostess Gwendolyn Cafritz Dies."
 Washington Post (November 30, 1988).
"Cafritz Shaped City's Skyline." *Washington Post*
 (June 12, 1964).
Conroy, Sarah Booth. "Appreciation: The Cafritz Largesse."
 Washington Post (November 30, 1988).
"Gwen Cafritz Bound, Robbed; Home Looted."
 Washington Post (January 16, 1969).
Haggerty, Maryann. "Cafritz's New President Wants
 to Build a Strong Foundation." *Washington Post*
 (November 8, 1993).
Lewis, Alfred E. "Four Thugs Raid Cafritz Mansion."
 Washington Post (January 17, 1969).
Lyons, Richard L. "$1,400 Loan Helped Cafritz to Start
 Climb as Builder." *Washington Post* (September 18, 1955).
McNair, Marie. "Elegant Era Revival Seen at Cafritz Fete."
 Washington Post (November 17, 1947).
_____. "Guests Throng Cafritz Easter 'At Home'."
 Washington Post (April 11, 1955).
"Morris Cafritz Dies; Civic Leader, Builder." *Evening Star*
 (June 12, 1964).
Pack, Robert. "The Streets Were Paved in Gold."
 The Washingtonian (April 1984): 114–117, 166–174.
Tully, Andrew. "The Story of Gwen Cafritz."
 Washington Daily News (December 9, 1959).
Williams, Marjorie. "Cafritz v. Cafritz."
 Washington Post Magazine (February 25. 1990): 16–21.

MOUNSEY HOUSE

INTERVIEWS

Mera M. Archambeau,
 interviewed by James M. Goode, October 5, 2011.
Norma Broude,
 interviewed by James M. Goode, October 1, 2011.
Mary Garrard,
 interviewed by James M. Goode, October 1, 2011.
Delores Mounsey,
 interviewed by James M. Goode, September 4, 2011.

MANUSCRIPTS

Mayhew, J.A. Chief Engineer, D.C. Fire Department, to
William D. Nixon, 12 October 1951.

Nixon, William D. President of the Oldest Inhabitants
(Colored), Inc., to the Editor of *Washington Post*, 1951.

Nixon, William D. President of the Association of Oldest
Inhabitants (Colored), Inc., to Commissioners of the
District of Columbia, October 9, 1947.

BOOKS

McMahan, Virgil E. *The Artists of Washington, D.C., 1796–1996*.
Washington, D.C.: The Artists of Washington, D.C.,
1995.

PERIODICALS

Davis, Charles E. Jr. "Land Titles Tell a Story of Freedom."
[Washington, D.C.] *Times-Herald* (December 3, 1952).

"Dr. Ethel Louise Nixon Mounsey."
Journal of the National Medical Association (November 1953).

"Fire Department Hiring Policies Are Protested."
Washington Post (December 13, 1944).

"He Was the Gentlest of Men." [Washington, D.C.]
The Spotlight (March 9, 1962).

"Oldest Inhabitants (Colored), Inc., Won't Let Nixon Quit."
Washington Afro-American (August 15, 1951).

Oman, Anne H. "Deco Echoes."
Washington Post (March 20, 1981).

MARDEN HOUSE

BOOKS

Pfeiffer, Bruce Brooks. *Frank Lloyd Wright, 1943–1959,
The Complete Works*. Cologne, Germany: Taschen, 2009.

PERIODICALS

Able, Aaron. "The Marden House by Frank Lloyd Wright."
New York Times (November 2, 2008).

Groer, Annie. "Falling for Mr. Wright." *Washington Post*
(February 8, 2007).

McKeon, Nancy. "A Family Home, a Family Legacy,
Frank Lloyd Wright's Grandson Lives in One of
His Famed Houses." *Washington Post* (August 21, 2010).

Newman, Cathy. "The Art of Being Luis Marden."
National Geographic Magazine (November 2000): 66–83.

Stafford, Susan H. "The Luis and Ethel Marden House:
Adventure in Restoration." *The Frank Lloyd Wright Building
Conservancy Bulletin* 18 (Issue 3, Summer 2008): 1, 4–7.

Viladas, Pilar. "Rear Window." *New York Times Magazine*
(November 2, 2008): 50–55.

SLAYTON HOUSE

MANUSCRIPTS

Berk, Sally. *William L. Slayton House, Washington, D.C.* National
Register of Historic Places—Nomination Form, 2009.

Slayton, William L. *Vignettes*, unpublished manuscript, 1990.

BOOKS

Cleveland Park—Slayton House. Washington, D.C.: Washington
Fine Properties, 2009.

Smith, Herbert L. Jr., ed. *25 Years of Record Houses*. New York:
Architectural Record Books, 1981.

PERIODICALS

McCann, Hannah. "A Masterpiece of a Home, Cleveland
Park Residence Has Powerful Draw." *AIA D.C. Magazine*
(Summer 2003).

KREEGER HOUSE

MANUSCRIPTS

Pelton, Eloise. *GEICO and David Lloyd Kreeger*.
Washington, D.C.: Kreeger Museum.

BOOKS

Jenkins, Stover, and David Mohney. *The Houses of Philip Johnson*.
New York: Abbeville Press Publishers, 2001.

Pelton, Eloise, ed. *From Our Archives, Columns in The Kreeger
Update, July 2005–July 2008*. Washington, D.C.: Kreeger
Museum, 2008.

_____. *From Our Archives, Vol. II, Columns in The Kreeger Update,
August 2008–August 2010*. Washington, D.C.: Kreeger
Museum, 2010.

PERIODICALS

Conroy, Sarah Booth. "Art Museum Is Planned by Kreegers."
Washington Post (November 23, 1988).

Henry, Helen. "Mansion Houses a Museum: Everything
Is Subservient to Art—Elegant Kreeger Home."
The Sun Magazine, Baltimore Sun (September 13, 1970): 1–4.

Percey, Henry. "At Home in a Museum." *Saturday Review*
(April 1981): 32–33.

IMAGE CREDITS

———

All floor plans and maps are by Paul Davidson.
All photographs are by Bruce M. White except for those listed below.

INTRODUCTION

MOUNT VERNON

THE LINDENS

ROSEDALE

WHITE HOUSE

EVERMAY

BLAIR HOUSE

ARLINGTON HOUSE

STEEDMAN HOUSE

CEDAR HILL

Page 186. Photo, portrait of Frederick Douglass and second wife. Courtesy National Park Service

HOUSE ONE

Page 195. Drawing, original
site plan. by Calvert Vaux, 1866
Courtesy Gallaudet
University
Page 196. Photo, Edward
Gallaudet & family on porch & lawn
Courtesy Gallaudet University.

DENMAN–WERLICH HOUSE

Page 213. Photo, roof, by Ken Rahraim
Courtesy Ken Rahaim

GRANGER COTTAGE

Page 266. Facade, by Ken Rahaim
Courtesy Ken Rahaim
Page 268. Living room, by Ken Rahaim
Courtesy Ken Rahaim
Page 268. Photo, staircase, by Ken Rahaim
Courtesy Ken Rahaim

DUMBLANE

Page 271. Photo, facade, by Ken Rahaim
Courtesy Ken Rahaim

DUMBARTON OAKS

Page 368. Photo, music room, by Joseph Mills
Courtesy Dumbarton Oaks

STIRLING HOUSE

Page 420. Photo, library in 1939
Courtesy Marheritta Stirling Allardice

CAFRITZ HOUSE

Page 430. Photo, south wing in 1940
Courtesy Cafritz Foundation
Page 432. Photo, Mrs. Cafritz,
Cafritz Foundation

MARDEN HOUSE

Page 445. Photo, Frank Lloyd Wright and Mrs. Marden
Courtesy of James V. Kimsey

SLAYTON HOUSE

Page 457. Photo, front facade, by Ken Rahraim
Courtesy of Ken Rahaim
Page 458. Photo, rear elevation, by Ken Rahraim
Courtesy Ken Rahaim
Page 459. Photo, living room, by Ken Rahraim
Courtesy of Ken Rahaim.

ACKNOWLEDGEMENTS

The photographer for this book, Bruce M. White, and I both thank the more than 100 people who have assisted us in entering and photographing the 56 historic houses covered here over the past seven years. These have included the private owners of houses, the staffs of eight embassies, the directors and curators of private historic house museums, the National Park Service which maintain four of the houses used in the book, the White House Historical Association, and even private clubs who now reside in a number of these historic houses.

For the Georgian houses, thanks go to the staffs at Mount Vernon—Jim Rees, Stephen McLeod, Susan Schoelwer, Mary V. Thompson, Michele Lee, Dawn Bonner, Esther White, Tom Rinehart, Joan Stahl, Elizabeth Chambers, and Carol Borchert Cadou; Darnall's Chance—Susan Reidy and Marsha Miller; Carlyle House—Susan Coster and Helen Wirka; The Lindens—Kenneth D. Brody and Margi Conrids; Gunston Hall—Caroline M. Riley, Susan Blankenship, Frank N. Barker, Mark Whatford, and David Reese; and Hayes Manor—Ellen Charles, Jennifer L. Farris and Robert Obrist.

Many people helped with the ten Federal houses: The White House—Marcia Anderson, Betty Monkman, and William Allman; Tudor Place—Leslie Buhler, Heather Bartlow, Erica Prikle, Erin Kuykendall, and William Allen; The Octagon—Erica Rioux Gees, Rhonda Bernstein, and Don Myer; Dumbarton House—Scott Scholz and Hannah Cox; Evermay—Harry Belin and Nina Gregg; Riversdale—Edward Day, Ann Wass, Jennifer Flood, and Heather Haggstrom; Woodley—Al Kilborn and John Young; Blair House—Candace Shireman.

The three Greek Revival houses were opened to us by: Arlington House—Maria Capozzi, Brendon Bies, and Kimberly Robinson; Mackall Square—Ben I. Johns, Jr.; Steedman House—Mrs. Steven Knapp, Barbara A. Porter, and Dawnita Altieri.

The scheduling to photograph the nine Victorian houses took a good deal of time. The photography was assisted by: Oak Hill Cemetery Gatehouse—Ella Pozell; Cedar Hill—Braden Paynter and Julie Kutruff; Cooke's Row—Greg Mulkner, Jim Bell, and Betsy Cooley; House One—Paul Blakely, Catherine Murphy, Mrs. Alan Hurwitz, Ulf W. Hedberg, Jeffrey K. Peterson, and Michael J. Olson; Breiding House—Bernice and David Blair; Denman-Werlich House—Guy d'Amecourt; Nancy Woodward, Mary Kay Menard; Brown-Toutorsky House—Anne Selene, Charles Robertson, Bruce Johnson, Ambassador Serge Mombouli of the Republic of The Congo; Heurich House—Scott Nelson, Jan Evans Houser and Kim Bender; Clara Barton House—Kim Robinson and Robbin M. Owen.

Most of the six Arts and Crafts houses are unknown to the public. Assistance came from: The Owl's Nest—Christopher and Karen Donatelli and Leslie Buhler; Barney Studio Hosue— Liana Eglite, Charles Robertson, and Anne Selline; Dudlea—Tricia and Frank Saul, Cecilia Morgan, Carolyn Morgan, and Diana Morgan; Morse House—Richard Squires; Dumblane—Betty Nottingham; Granger Cottage—Eleanor Granger, Nell Stewart, and R. van Bismarck.

Beaux Arts houses include Patterson House—Maribelle Moore, Amy Ballard, and Jann Henrotte; Townsend House—Bill Caldwell and Doug Weimer; Anderson House—Ellen Clark, Elizabeth Frengel, Emily Schultz, Carolyn C. Pauley, Hannah Cox and Skip Moskey; Everett House—Ambassador and Mrs. Namik Tan, Can Oguz, Caroline Hickman and Skip Moskey; Marley—Belgium Ambassador and Mrs. Jan Jozef Matthysen and Andrea Murphy; Marwood—Ted and Lynn Leonsis, Jane Battle, and Kurt Kehl.

Access to interior spaces of Georgian Revival houses were facilitated by: Woodrow Wilson House—Frank Aucella and John Powell; Dumbarton Oaks—James Carder and Gail Griffin; British Ambassador's Residence—Amanda Downes, Ken Doggett, and Jane Loeffler; Hillwood—Ellen Charles, Kristen Regina, Liana Paredes, Estella Chung, and Maria DiVietro; Woodend—Ned Kitzpatrick, Pam Owen, Lisa K. Alexander, and Jeff Stann.

For the Tudor Revival houses the following helped: Lawrence House—French Ambassador and Mrs. Francois Marie Delattre, Celette Roland, and Anne Burley; Firienze House—Donatella Verrone and Richard Graham; Stirling House—Margheritta Stirling Allardice, Jan Evans Houser, and Mr. and Mrs. Peter Kovler;

Although Washington does not have many Art Deco houses the occupants of these three opened their doors: Fealy House—Aimee and Mike Carney; Cafritz House—Eric Kohler and the staff of the Field School; Mounsey House—Mary Garrard, Norma Broude, and Delores Mounsey.

International Style houses include: Marden House—James V. Kimsey, Knight Kiplinger, and Nancy S. Merritt; Slayton House — Dan Snyder; Kreeger House—Judy Greenberg, Eric Keel, and Eloise Pelton.

Editing of the manuscript over a six year period was graciously undertaken by Mary Huntington. She also worked on editing my last book, *Capital Views*. The entire manuscript was also edited by Caroline Hickman, William Allen, Richard W. Longstreth, Charles Robertson, Anne Sellin, Peter Maxson, and William Seale when it was completed in January 2-15. Others who offered suggestions for improvement of parts of the text include Knight Kiplinger, Woodey Reagan, Douglas Weimer, Skip Moskey, John de Farrari, Robert Vogel, Peter Penczer, Kim Williams, Robert Wiser, Ken Bowling, and Ross Heasley. Steven Troxel provided research assistance and also edited the manuscripts.

In the D.C. Public Library both Jerry McCoy and Mark Greek helped me for seven long years finding information on the houses through their extensive vertical files of newspaper clippings. Marcia Anderson and Fiona Griffin in the White House Historical Association did a great favor by introducing me to Bruce M. White who became the photographer for this book. Paul Davidson produced outstanding work in drawing the floor plans for all 56 houses.

The cost of floor plans, printing of color photographs, and Xeroxing was unusually high. Mrs. Charles Wrightsman of New York City was generous in a grant to defray travel expenses for photography. A number of grants were made to the Goode-White Photography Research Fund set up at the National Gallery of Art where all of the original images will be donated. It was a pleasure working with Greg Most and Andrea Gibbs in the Images Division there. Donations for research costs were generously made by B. Francis Saul II, the late Robert Alvord, Knight Kiplinger, Mark G. Griffin, and Albert H. Small. Both B. Francis Saul II and Ellen Charles made last minute grants to keep the large size of the book intact.

INDEX